Is pleased to present you with
this complimentary copy of
Return on Impact.

A Clear Commitment to America's Waters

Network with your
clean water colleagues at
www.NACWAengage.org **or**
visit us at *www.NACWA.org*

THE NACWA NETWORK

What business and association leaders have to say about *Return on Impact* and working with David Nour:

"Whether you call them members or customers, if you want to engage them more effectively, impact them more intently, and transform them more consistently, you need to read *Return on Impact* now!"

— Daniel Burrus, CEO—Burrus Research Associates, and author of the New York Times best seller *Flash Foresight*

"David Nour spoke to our leadership and board and without question, they chose to think and lead differently than our industry counterparts shortly after his session. If you're trying to help your organization get beyond reactive social media, *Return on Impact* is your roadmap to a more strategic approach to social."

— Barbara Springer, General Counsel & Vice President Administration—Delta Dental of Colorado

"I've had the pleasure of hearing many great speakers during my 27 years with PMA. So it takes someone exceptional to cut through the clutter and make a unique impression. You did that and then some. Your presentation and the subsequent Q&A with attendees at our Leadership Symposium were really outstanding."

— Bryan Silbermann, President & CEO—Produce Marketing Association

"Your presentation on the new media and how it can work effectively for all our operating companies was very well received…many have said that it's the best Advisory Committee meeting we've had in a long time."

— Gerald Sullivan, Chairman—The Sullivan Group

"What an honor it was to have you speak at our National Cornerstone meeting. Your enthusiasm, expertise, and stage presence had the entire audience on the edge of their seats for the entire program. I received rave reviews from our clients and senior managers. Additionally, the webinars post the meeting allow our clients to continue their learning on social media. Thank you for being personally engaged with our company and our clients."

— Nick Alexander, Vice President—Chubb Personal Insurance

"Our firm relies on David Nour's unique perspective and diverse expertise to guide us in developing strategic business partnerships, marketing, and most recently social media. Additionally, David is a well respected and highly sought-after speaker within the nonprofit industry Fernley & Fernley serves. Many of our association clients have had the opportunity to feature David at their annual conventions where he always delivers a professional, entertaining, and informative presentation. I highly recommend David Nour."

— Taylor Fernley, President and CEO—Fernley & Fernley

"Thank you so much for presenting at the 2011 Amerinet Member Conference. The session was a huge hit and so well received. As you know, social networking is relatively new to the healthcare field and most of our attendees came into the session knowing very little about how it can apply to them. At the end of your session and in follow up emails, I received more requests for your information than any other speaker—you also received the highest marks on the evaluations."

– Kerry Price, Vice President of Strategic Customer Engagements—Amerinet

"Your presentation at the North American Pedorthic Congress was a huge hit. Immediately following your presentation, I had several delegates ask me: where did you find him, how do we get him to speak at our office, and can he consult for our company? I think these questions outline how well your presentation was received. Our firm will continue to recommend you highly."

– Jonathan Strauss, President—Strauss Event and Association Management

"As a corporate meeting planner with over 20 years of experience, I pride myself in knowing a fantastic speaker. You proved me right by receiving glowing reviews from the attendees at the Sun Microsystems Annual Partner Summit. The most important factor was not how well you did on stage but how prepared you were when you engaged the executive owner of the event. Your presentation is not prefabricated; it is created up until you step on stage. Several clients, including the HP Managers, ranked you as the top speaker from the event and insisted that you come back."

– Brooke Sommers, CMP, CMM, President—Strategic Conferences and Events

"Your presentation was not only exceptional, but also relayed the type of interpersonal and business skills it takes to succeed in today's workplace. I believe that engaging, relevant presentations such as yours helped make this year's conference one of our strongest shows in recent years, with nearly 5,000 people in attendance."

– Tony Keane, CAE, President & CEO - International Facility Management Association

"David Nour is the foremost expert on business connectivity and use of social networking, and he had our audience of 150 CEOs, presidents and top managers enthralled with the power of his message."

– Steve King, President—Pet Industry Distributors Association

"David Nour was the keynote speaker at our Annual Convention & Exposition. What a treat! David's professionalism started the moment we began working with him on this event. He researched our industry and learned what information would be most useful to our attendees. His high energy and engaging style were very well received by our group and the information he provided on business relationships and social media was right on target. There were a lot of practical takeaways, which the audience appreciated. We had nothing but positive feedback on this session and hope to work with David again in the future."

– Heidi Zimmerman, CAE, Executive Director—Association of Water Technologies

return
onimpact

Leadership Strategies For
The Age of Connected Relationships

DAVID NOUR

The Center for Association Leadership

WASHINGTON, DC

Information in this book is accurate and consistent with industry standards at the time of publication. As research and practice advance, however, standards and best practices may change. For this reason, it is recommended that readers evaluate the applicability of any recommendations in light of particular situations and changing standards.

ASAE: The Center for Association Leadership
1575 I Street, NW
Washington, DC 20005-1103
Phone: (202) 626-2723; (888) 950-2723 outside the metropolitan Washington, DC area
Fax: (202) 220-6439 Email: books@asaecenter.org

We connect great ideas and great people to inspire leadership and achievement in the association community.

Keith C. Skillman, CAE, Vice President, Publications, ASAE: The Center for Association Leadership
Baron Williams, CAE, Director of Book Publishing, ASAE: The Center for Association Leadership

This book is available at a special discount when ordered in bulk quantities. For information, contact the ASAE Member Service Center at (202) 371-0940.

A complete catalog of titles is available on the ASAE website at asaecenter.org.

Published by Association Management Press, an imprint of ASAE: The Center for Association Leadership

ISBN-13: 978-0-88034-336-7
ISBN-10: 0-88034-336-2

Cover design by Beth Lower
Interior design by Troy Scott Parker, Cimarron Design, cimarrondesign.com

Printed in the United States of America.

10 9 8 7 6 5 4 3 2 1

Contents

Integrated QR Codes   **vii**

Welcome to the Age of Empowered Customers!   **ix**

CHAPTER 1
Do You Still Matter?   **1**

CHAPTER 2
Develop a Robust Social Strategy, an Imperative First Step   **25**

CHAPTER 3
Embrace World-Class Engagement   **49**

CHAPTER 4
Build a Different Kind of Organization   **67**

CHAPTER 5
"iTunify" Your Capabilities   **93**

CHAPTER 6
Attract and Develop Unparalleled Social Talent   **121**

CHAPTER 7
Socially Enable Your Execution   **151**

CHAPTER 8
Deploy Social Analytics to Listen Louder and Tell a Compelling Story   **173**

CHAPTER 9
Fail Intentionally and Learn From It   **195**

CHAPTER 10
Reinvent ROI   **215**

Acknowledgements   **231**

About the ASAE Foundation   **233**

About the Author   **235**

Other Books by the Author   **237**

David Nour Speaking Topics   **239**

Integrated QR Codes

With *Return on Impact*, I wanted to integrate the fundamental values of collaboration—not just in the interviews of the association executives, the gathering of the influentials at the 2011 ASAE Annual Meeting, best practices from the corporate world, or the use of social media in capturing ideas and perspectives in writing this book—but in how the readers could interact with additional multi-modality content, as well as to engage other like-minded individuals in an open community. I hope this effort will enhance your experience with this book and more importantly the ideas captured within.

QR Codes

A QR code—Quick Response code—is a two-dimensional code which consists of modules in a square pattern. The user needs a QR reader application on their smartphone to scan the code through the phone's camera. QR codes contain information encoded in text, URL, or other data formats.

These codes provide immediate and multimodal communication channels between producer and consumer of information and thus are ever-increasingly utilized among broader industries and their respective constituents. They may be used to display text, video, vCard in magazines, on signs, buses, business cards, or almost any object about which users might need complementary information.

Below is a list of software vendors where you can select and download a QR code reader:

- KAYWA Reader
- Nokia Reader
- i-nigma Reader
- Lynkee Reader

- UpCode
- QuickMark
- SnapMaze
- BeeTagg
- NeoReader
- ScanLife
- MobileTag

After you install the app, please read the QR code below to get started.

Welcome to the Age of Empowered Customers!

Visionary organizations are constantly scanning the horizon of our rapidly evolving digital world in search of unique approaches that generate value for members, customers, partners, and shareholders. The choicest approach engages a broad base of constituents, better integrates and more effectively manages the value chain, and puts the member or customer at the center of decisions and actions. The resulting loyalty, revenue and margin growth, and agility can uniquely advance an industry, member organizations, and customers' *perceived value*.

Visionary organizations are redefining the value chain in the age of connected relationships, and visionary leaders are embracing this perspective of the market and capitalizing on these changes to *lead differently*.

Today's customers are a new breed, dictating universal terms in the dynamic between buyers and sellers not only for products and services but also for ideas, perspectives, and advocacy, and they are empowering themselves in an explosion of mobile and social interaction:

- There are an estimated 6 billion mobile phone connections globally.
- More than 600 million people are Facebook users.
- About 45 percent of consumers ask friends for advice before making purchases.
- It's estimated that 64 percent of consumers make a first purchase as a result of a digital experience.

According to recent McKinsey research, almost 50 percent of online U.S. consumers are advanced users of smartphones, social networks, and other emerging tools, up from 32 percent in 2008. Almost everything we use and everyone we interact with is becoming increasingly connected; digital links and connected relationships are being built among people, groups with similar interests, data from multiple sources, objects, machines, and computers.

Digital technology continues to get smaller and less expensive while becoming more powerful and prevalent. Technology and transparency are enabling decision-making processes for consumers, members, employees, partners, and shareholders, who expect and often demand to connect with organizations whenever they want and on the device of their choosing. They are wireless, mobile, sensor-equipped, plugged-in, and far more intelligent and *empowered* than ever before. As customers, they want a consistent experience in all channels—physical, digital, and mobile. They read and believe others' comments about organizations, products, services, and experiences more than they believe marketing or advertising. They compare notes and instantly share personal experiences. They champion a brand or sully a reputation with one click. The intelligence and connections available to customers are forever changing the business of designing, creating, selling, and delivering information, products, and services. Whether as members or customers, consumers have soaring expectations.

The disruptive forces of social-media–savvy consumers are rippling through to organizations and across entire industries, affecting the fundamental need for credible content and interaction within a community of like-minded individuals working toward a common mission and vision or against an enemy, such as legislation. At the individual member or customer level, it's not just about the connected consumers' driving the "iTunification" of business; the networked workforce is collaborating in new ways both inside and outside organizations. Empowered citizens are digitally engaged and networked, making their voices and votes count on Wall Street, in ballots, with proxies, and on Twitter.

At the organizational level, business and revenue models must evolve to capture value across multiple channels, products, services, members, and customers. Optimized digital operations transform how products and services are created, marketed, sold, delivered, and maintained after initial acquisition. A connected organization must evolve in its operating structure and people dynamics.

At the industry level, value is migrating along the value chain, often moving closer to the end consumer of the information, product, or service. Changing roles and relationships of industry players are redefining value chains, and new industry entrants are disrupting broader systems as they capture significant value with far greater agility than historically dominant players.

For member-based organizations, the breakneck, mind-numbing velocity that has driven Facebook to more than 600 million users in less than seven years and Apple's iPhone to 140 million in less than three has outpaced the speed with which many leadership teams have reacted. Membership organizations are by definition, *social networks,* principal purveyors of networking among professionals, organizations, and industries. However, that franchise is eroded when individual members and their organizations can gather information, get education, and activate their own armies of stakeholders for advocacy purposes at local, state, and even national levels. As such, social interactions both threaten associations and association-like organizations and create opportunities for them to listen louder and to proactively engage and influence the thinking, perspective, and action of members.

"There are no shortcuts!"

An omnipresent sign at the gym where I train displays those words. Incremental neglect seldom highlights the greater impact; in other words, you don't feel worse by skipping a workout or dramatically different after one. But should you skip exercising for a whole year, you are sure to feel accelerated breathing up a flight of stairs, loss of muscle mass, or a tighter fit around your waistline. Responding to the evolutionary digital landscape isn't a switch; it's a dial. You have to *lead differently!* Leadership strategy for the age of connected relationships isn't about putting up a Facebook fan page or the CEO's tweeting three times a day! It's about the unequivocal need to *think and act differently* as a leading organization *because* of social: to harness its power and promise while avoiding its inevitable pitfalls, to embrace it as an enabler of your value-add, not block access to it out of fear of malice.

This is perhaps an opportune time to clarify my use of *social,* particularly as a noun. In English, the use of social refers to an informal gathering, as in a "neighborhood social." I'm taking liberty of using the same reference to informal gatherings via digital interactions, within and external to an organization. As described in the forthcoming chapters, my reference to social is more than social networking such as LinkedIn, Twitter, or YouTube. My reference to social is more than social media such as forum, blogs, or discussion groups. As such, we need a new definition for social as a fundamental shift in mindset, toolset, and roadmap for an individual, a team, and the organization to:

- Put its customers/members at the center of its structure, suite of offerings, job descriptions, and value creation efforts;
- Creatively collaborate in real time, while becoming more agile, responsive, streamlined, and direct;
- More open in its communication and transparent in its governance, encouraging, authentic, and trusted;
- More caring, accessible, agile, and innovative; and
- Proactive, engaged, connected, and self-directed.

None of the above attributes happen overnight. It's a work in progress led by a vision to think and act, and maybe even, lead differently. You see, leadership strategy isn't about Twitter; it's how microblogging 140 characters at a time empowers ambient-aware individuals and organizations, because the more information you glean about key individuals engaged online or offline, the more proactively you can manage those relationships.

If the power has shifted to the consumer and is compressing margins and changing paradigms, it makes sense for every organization to understand and anticipate buyer behavior by listening to members and customers and turning insight into immediate action. It's not just about reacting, but predicting and adapting your value-add based on member demands and then seamlessly orchestrating that value among your trading partners and suppliers. It's about marketing to a much broader audience, selling and fulfilling the right product and service at the right price, right time, and right place. It's about serving your customers flawlessly and learning from their behavior so you can predict and take action for the next interaction.

Social is more than a communication channel. Social is a wake-up call to engage members and customers alike, *differently*. It requires commitment from the entire organization and a redefined value proposition. Social customer relationship management (CRM) is about truly understanding the impact you're having in the market, one engagement at a time. Social analytics will force you to examine more intently what your members or customers are saying about your industry or brand and what matters most to them. What does your industry or brand do to improve their condition? Are they better off because of your value-add? Do you delight or annoy them? Is your value-add simply talk or does it act to become *value-perceived* by those most critical to your future prosperity?

The investments you make in leading differently because of social must be measured and justified. ROI will be reinvented because of social—from investment to impact; from income to influence; from incremental to innovative. *Return on Impact* is about leadership strategies for the age of connected relationships, employing both a strategy and a repeatable and predictable execution process as well as employing social media and social influencers to achieve the business needs of the organization. What you'll read in the following pages are ideas that will help you recognize, account for, and tap into the fact that your potential members, customers, employees, partners, and shareholders are making decisions while being influenced by different circles of connected relationships. Their perceptions of you are being shaped by others: whether or not they should work for you, engage you, buy from you, invest in you, advocate your differentiation, and defend you and your brand in times of need.

Keep in mind that with any leadership strategy, version one is better than version none! As a friend often reminds me, the goal is progress, not perfection. And finally, keep in mind the differences between conversation types: email is one-dimensional; audio/video and some social conversations are two-dimensional, because tone can be gauged; face-to-face/in person conversation is three-dimensional and has a unique value that will never be replaced within the organization, with prospective and current members and customers, or within any industry.

Read on and then let's do something worth talking about.

– David Nour
  @davidnour

P.S.
Scan the QR code at the end of each section to get practical, pragmatic application and implementation ideas.

## CHAPTER 1

Do You Still Matter?

"**H**OW ARE YOUR members better off because of your organization?" That's a question I asked more than 100 association executives this year. Similarly, I asked corporate leaders, "How are customer situations dramatically improved because of your value-add?" Many automatically referred to their portfolio of products and services. One confident executive replied, "We have a monthly magazine, an annual convention, and educational resources we sell them." Unfortunately, that didn't answer the question I asked. How are *they* better off because of the organization you've built, the products and services you market, the network of niche constituents you gather, and the educational sessions you provide? If you've ever analyzed the total addressable market, what percentage are members? What's your market share? Unless you have garnered an overwhelming percentage of the total market or serve a very unique niche market with limited players, what are all the other members or customers doing in lieu of your value-add? How else are they getting the same information, education, and networking opportunities? All too often the answer was, "They're not," an uninformed—if not intellectually lazy—response.

When I inquired further about the competitive landscape, the resounding response was, "No one else does what we do!" *Really?* Your members are skipping your annual meeting and your magazine is one of 50 on their desks. Okay, so they're talking about you on Twitter, chatting with you on Facebook, and searching for you on Google. In a world that is increasingly empowered by social media and connected screens, out of your control, and enthralled by innovation, how can you be sure you are still relevant? I respectfully suggest that all that matters is the story your members or customers tell about your brand or your brand's value, in 140 characters or less. Is it a compelling story, a disappointing story, or no story at all?

Storytelling as a Core Competency

Corporations are pouring an enormous amount of resources into understanding and implementing relevant social media. Nonprofit boards are (or should be) more or less still at the inquiry phase, asking whether or not this seemingly revolutionary platform will dramatically affect every aspect of the organization, from membership models to product and service development and digital delivery, or whether it's just another marketing fad propagated by vendors with self-serving purposes.

Associations and member-based organizations have an enormously untapped resource of amazing stories, as do companies. The stories are not about themselves, but of members and customers, employees and suppliers, all who dramatically altered their paths because of the impact of the organization. Our lives revolve around stories. We think narratively and record our history through narrative; where were you on 9/11? Our culture is, in essence, a story; stories teach us values, and we create and share bonds through them. Stories are especially effective in communicating ideas, and very often there are people who "get it" through stories.

They're Happy Because They're Eating Lard

Have you seen the image of a happy family walking on the beach with the title "They're Happy Because they eat LARD?" Unfortunately I couldn't reach the executive director at the Lard Information Council for an interview, largely because both the image and the organization are a spoof. But the image did make me wonder: What organizations are no longer around because they missed key market trends, didn't listen to various constituents, couldn't innovate, or outright ignored insights right in front of them?

An interesting *Wall Street Journal* article in 2008 highlighted how after 60 years, the Men's Dress Furnishings Association (MDFA), the trade group that represented American tie makers, shut down. Membership declined yearly following the 1980s power-tie era, as U.S. neckwear companies consolidated or closed because of overseas competition. Members lost interest, but more importantly, the market stopped wearing ties, as highlighted by a Gallup Poll. Several members of the association sensed the trend years earlier, when a number of people showed up tieless at the group's annual luncheon in New York.

Marty Staff, chief executive of the men's clothing company JA Apparel Corp., which had a vested interest in the organization, was one of the men who left his tie at home in a deliberate attempt to make a statement to his colleagues. While they had been focused on designing and producing ties, a new generation of menswear manufacturers and fashion designers had grown up viewing ties as optional and were agnostic about wearing them.

Does this story sound familiar? Let's consider the trend in the medical community. More than one million doctors are licensed to practice in the United States, but only a fraction—an estimated 270,000—belong to the American Medical Association (AMA). So many practitioners are becoming specialists and gravitating toward niche communities that many medically related organizations have spun off and created their own associations (see Figure 1.1).

Organization Names

Academy of Medical-Surgical Nurses	American Medical Massage Association
Alliance for Continuing Medical Education	American Medical Technologists
American Academy of Medical Acupuncture	American Medical Writers Association
American Academy of Medical Management	American Registry for Diagnostic Medical Sonography
American Association of Medical Assistants	American Registry of American Assistants
American Board of Medical Specialties	Association for Medical Imaging Management
American College of Medical Practice Executives	Association for the Advancement of Medical Instruments
American College of Medical Quality	Association of Air Medical Services
American Medical Directors Association	Association of American Medical Colleges
American Medical Informatics Association	International Society for Medical Publication Professionals

Figure 1.1—Sampling of Hundreds of Medical Associations

My perspective isn't an attack on Dr. Michael Maves, executive vice president and CEO of the AMA. What is important in both examples is the dramatic impact on an organization if it disenfranchises a certain constituent category. No one organization can effectively cater to a broad spectrum of constituents, despite the many that try, and I will address this in later chapters. Social dramatically elevates dialogue, especially dissent or less than stellar experiences, and accelerates the formation of alternatives. Social heightens the awareness around experiences and the perceived value and relevancy of associations—and their corporate members alike.

Meet Sermo

Here is a glaring example of competition for mindshare and wallet share. Founded in 2006, Sermo.com (Figure 1.2) has amassed the largest online physician community in the United States—more than 120,000 members spanning 68 specialties in all 50 states who collaborate on difficult cases and exchange observations about drugs, devices, and clinical issues. Sermo is the "Facebook for Doctors," where physicians get help with everything from patient care to practice management. Members of this community have described it as "therapeutic," a "virtual water cooler," and "vital to my everyday practice."

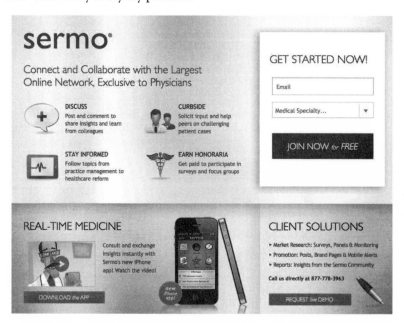

Figure 1.2—Sermo.com

Sermo has built a viable community of like-minded individuals who understand that no one physician is as knowledgeable as physicians working together. Sermo operates as a research medium, harnessing the collective power of physicians' observations. It allows physicians to improve patient care through the rapid exchange of observations. In turn, Sermo clients benefit from instant insight into clinical events and medical trends.

"Yeah, but associations are *the* source of credibility," commented one association executive at a recent roundtable discussion. Respectfully, I ask, when did you corner the market on credibility? Sermo uses a proprietary technology to verify physicians' credentials in real time to create an environment of trust and collaboration. They also leverage aspects of social network theory, game theory, prediction markets, and information arbitrage. It's completely scalable and sustainable as a social media platform and communication tool. Peer reviews and user-reviewed rating systems ensure that medical reporting is accurate and supported by the physician community.

Sermo is free to practicing physicians, so how do they monetize this community? What's their business model? Revenue is generated as healthcare institutions, financial services firms, and government agencies purchase Sermo products to access this elite group of practitioners. They've raised an estimated $70 million in venture capital and were named one of 2010's Top 10 Most Innovative Healthcare Companies by *Fast Company* magazine. Where is AMA in all of this? They signed a partnership agreement in 2007, whereby "teaming with Sermo, the AMA will be able to address important professional and public health issues in a multiphase, multiyear alliance aimed at improving medical practice, physician advocacy, and patient care."

The Sermo community represents an innovative forum for physicians to share their voice with the AMA and discuss emerging issues on the front lines of medicine," said Cecil B. Wilson, M.D., chair of the AMA Board. "Engaging with Sermo's virtual community adds to the resources the AMA can call upon to rapidly assess and respond to the issues and concerns of physicians across the United States.
– Sermo.com press release, May 30, 2007

In September 2010, Sermo became a political force when members amassed 10,000 signatures for a petition opposing the AMA's acceptance of the House healthcare reform bill. My bigger question to Dr. Michael Maves would be: Why isn't Sermo an entity *within* AMA, a 190-year-old organization? The lesson for every other organization, member-based or customer-centric, is that new, for-profit competitors will surface, look, walk, and talk like associations, yet won't charge membership fees. And they will be very real potential threats to your perceived market dominance.

The Rest of the Story...

The founders of Sermo are clearly strong storytellers to a broad base of constituents. Time will tell whether their business model will survive or whether the organization will continue to prosper. What's important to take away is that good stories have three primary components:

- Knock-the-cover-off-the-ball beginnings—to grab the intended audience;
- An equally strong message—to be remembered and repeated; and
- A point of impact—the "so what?" and "now what?"

Unfortunately, many organizations confuse stories with situations—first this happened, then that happened, and here is how it turned out—almost as a matter of fact. A great story takes the middle part and creates tension and conflict, which draws all of us in to learn what happens next.

Stories are so much more memorable than statistics or simple anecdotes and are the fuel that allows social communities to grow. Strong stories become infectious and, when told well, become interwoven into the fabric of an organization. *With stories, the culture becomes the vision delivered.*

According to Jennifer Aaker and Andy Smith, the authors of *The Dragonfly Effect* (Jossey-Bass, 2010), there are four important stories that all organizations should have readily available in their portfolio:

1. "Who Are We?"—How we got started;
2. "Vision"—Where we're going in the future;
3. "Apology and Recovery"—What a transgression is for an organization and how they might respond to it; and
4. "Personal"—What personal stories are being incubated and cultivated within the organization.

What makes stories interesting are unexpected events, provocative ideas, counter-intuitive findings, suspense and mystery, and thematic complexity—the degree to which multiple interpretations lie below the surface. If an organization can make its stories relevant to the listeners' issues and give sufficient information so as to be understandable and coherent, listeners will be able to vividly identify with the characters.

Authenticity is also critical in compelling storytelling. People have to believe you and that's very difficult to achieve if you don't believe the story yourself. Authenticity and transparency become important in social because of the essential underlying trust required to engage others in a low-trust environment. In my experience, most individuals who unsubscribe from an organization's e-newsletter do so because they struggle to find it relevant, pragmatic, or applicable to their unique situations. Communications easily become overly manufactured when they are filtered by everyone from the general counsel's office to the mouthpieces in corporate communications and HR.

What questions can you ask to uncover great stories within your team, organization, and industry? It certainly won't be the stale member surveys you do once every two years. I'm amazed by how antiquated the "pulse check" process is in many organizations. Instead of listening in real time to consumer experiences with a product, service, or event, we wait until they get home and are buried in the minutia of the rest of their lives to send them a survey asking about something that happened days, if not weeks, ago. I can't remember what I had for breakfast this morning much less how I felt about a specific speaker on day three of my eight-day, 5 a.m.-to-11 p.m. conference. Are you *really* surprised that many organizations are either getting very little quantity or quality feedback, or that the same individuals keep asking for the same things they're ignoring?

I often counsel my consulting clients, *unless you excite or disturb them, they'll never get off the dime!* Try asking questions to discover a day-in-the-life story of a typical member, customer, or employee:

- What frustrated the living daylights out of you and what did you do about it?

- What took you entirely too long to accomplish and how could you have done it differently?

- If you ran the organization, what's the one thing you'd fix today and why?

- What are some principles that matter to you? Why and how did you learn about them and their importance?

- What really bothers you—people, events, or ideas?

- What specific projects, engagements, or people you worked with this past year were pivotal events for you?

- How have your views of these scenarios changed and how do these affect your life?

You may be surprised to uncover authenticity and personal connections in stories that make people feel emotionally connected enough that they want to help you achieve your business goals and objectives.

What Got You Here Won't Get You There: Social's Impact on Growth, Jobs, and Prosperity

What Got You Here Won't Get You There (Hyperion, 2007) is one of my favorite books by Marshall Goldsmith. In it he describes, among other things, the twenty habits that hold you back from the top. They include:

- Starting with "No," "But," or "However;"

- Telling the world how smart we are;

- Withholding information;

- Claiming credit that we don't deserve;

- Making excuses;

- Not listening; and

- Passing the buck.

I can't help but see some of the same flaws of personal interactions in how an entire organization might ignore the impact of social. I met an executive once who told me that he had been with an association for three decades, so obviously he was doing something right, and that he saw "no business value" in social media other than to waste his limited staff's time. He added that it is simply a good way for him to keep up with his teenage daughters!

In May 2011, McKinsey Global Institute research found that social is the driving factor in a "vast mosaic of economic activity." From millions of influencer-driven online transactions (e,g., Groupon or Living Social) to downloads of recommended TV episodes on smartphones, the research focused on the internet economies of the G8 nations (Canada, France, Germany, Italy, Japan, Russia, the United Kingdom, and the United States) as well Brazil, China, India, South Korea, and Sweden. Here are some data points that probably didn't make your last board conversation or strategic planning session:

- Internet accounts for 3.4 percent of overall gross domestic product (GDP) in the 13 nations studied. The internet economy, now larger than that of Spain, surpasses global industry sectors such as agriculture and energy.

- In mature countries, the internet was responsible for 10 percent of the GDP from 1995 to 2009. Over the last five years of that period, its contribution to the GDP growth in those countries doubled to 21 percent.

- Most of the economic value the internet and social created falls outside the technology sector; companies in more traditional industries capture 75 percent of the benefits.

- Internet and social are also catalysts for generating jobs. Among 4,800 small and midsize enterprises surveyed, they created 2.6 jobs for each lost to technology-related efficiencies.

What should this mean to you? Unless you sharpen your focus and get a vision for how social may help you lead differently, you'll struggle to remain relevant. Social allows your brand to consistently differentiate itself in the market. It expands your reach beyond what you previously perceived as limited by geographic boundaries or professional affiliation and enables you to listen to customers' wants and needs so that you can develop new and innovative products in real time to match those needs. Social has the ability to disrupt business models by radically changing markets and driving efficiencies. These disruptions will affect your members or customers and their customers. Will you choose to take a proactive leadership role in how social can become an enabler of your organization or industry, or allow social to define it and your role in it?

Can You Find Me Now? The Value of Search

Another important aspect in harnessing the power of social is the fundamental shift in buyer behavior not only relating to products and services but also information that compels us to act. Think about it. The last time you were looking for a product or service, B2B or B2C, did you call an organization and ask them to mail you some of their marketing materials, or send over one of their sales professionals? What do we all do? That's right, we get online to search. Here is the challenge: According to ComScore, the "Neilson" of the web, only 20 percent of those who search know exactly what they're looking for (see Figure 1.3). They're logical and

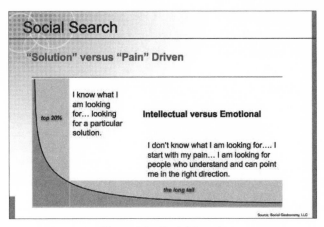

Figure 1.3—Social Search

methodical in the search terms deployed to troll for information about products or to glean insights that will help guide business decisions. The other 80 percent tend to search for an answer to a pain or a fundamental challenge they're trying to solve. The disconnect lies in the fact that most organization websites seldom talk about pain or peer-level challenges. They talk about products, services, events, senior executive bios, investors, and board members.

So what does a preponderance of "long tail" or highly descriptive, pain-centric search results return? Topping the list are conversations from blogs, forums, and discussion groups—social sites where corporate communication isn't—candid, raw conversations of people with similar challenges, from MomsLikeMe looking for reliable babysitters to scientists baffled by the same perplexities of an incurable disease, engineering students trying to learn about companies in advance of on-campus interviews, buyers of recreation vehicles comparing features with total cost of ownership, science teachers looking for creative classroom guides, and global lighting designers collaborating on sustainability options in a LEED-certified structure. In essence, trillions of key strokes are combining to boost productivity, open new pathways to problem solving, or simply make life easier.

A McKinsey research report similar to the one mentioned earlier measured the value of search in August 2011. Beyond brute measures such as the number of searches performed or advertising revenues reported by search companies, it looked at five key economies—Brazil, France, Germany, India, and the United States—and highlighted nine activities that are primary sources of search value: better matching, time saved, raised awareness, price transparency, long tail offerings, people match-ing, problem solving, new business models, and entertainment. It also looked at 11 private, public, and individual constituencies that reap the benefits, from advertisers and retailers to entrepreneurs, content creators, enterprise, consumers, individual content creators, individual information seekers, healthcare, education, and government—many of whom are your members and customers.

Here are some of the findings:

- Total gross value of internet search across the global economy was $780 billion in 2009, equal to the GDP of Netherlands or Turkey, making each search worth about $0.50.

- Approximately 70 percent ($540 billion) of the total value flowed directly to global GDP in the form of ecommerce, advertising rev-enues, and higher corporate productivity. Search accounted for 1.2 percent of the United States' GDP.

- The remaining $240 billion, about 30 percent, was captured by indi-viduals in the form of consumer surplus, lower prices, convenience, and time saved by swift, comparative access to real-time information. That equals to $20 in real benefits to consumers in the United States.

- For the U.S. retail industry, search-related revenues in 2009 were esti-mated at $67 billion, directly from online shopping or from online searches that led to in-store sales.

- In the five countries studied, knowledge workers (many of your staff, members, or customers) experienced search-related productivity gains of up to $117 billion, flowing from faster and more accurate access to independent information.

Is your organization's value-add showing up in one of the 1,500 average U.S. internet user's searches annually or 1.6 trillion searches conducted globally? If social media dominates purchases of information, decisions to attend online or offline events, and buyer behaviors of products and services, and your brand or conversations about your brand are not show-ing up on anyone's short list, you are obviously not a contender for the average internet user's consideration.

Policymakers you must engage within and external to the organization or industry will find themselves challenged as search creates a plethora of issues that are difficult to arbitrate, particularly with the ease with which information, perspective, insights, points, and counterpoints can be accessed through search. Privacy is often an immediate concern, but other critical issues such as copyright, trademark infringement, and censorship make search a tough issue confronting technology policy.

One more piece of good news: Your research will constantly lag behind any attempt to make sense of it all. The last research project you invested six months in developing is often outdated by the time you get around to printing and mailing it.

Other reasons senior leaders gave me to argue the case for members/customers/staff not engaging included: "They just aren't social;" "They're more mature than the 20-somethings;" "They are blue collar, out in the field all day and not tethered to their computers;" "Our profession doesn't lend itself to social media;" and "They're still getting used to email." According to an August 2011 Pew Research Center study, 65 percent of all U.S. adults now use social-networking sites, up from just 5 percent in 2005. Most of last year's growth came from Americans over the age of 30, with seniors accounting for the bulk of it. On a typical day, 43 percent of U.S. adults said they visit sites like Facebook and Twitter, up from 38 percent a year ago. Among internet users aged 50 to 64, social networking on a typical day increased from 20 percent to 32 percent. What does this mean? Your members, customers, suppliers, staff, and stakeholders are a lot more involved in social than you realize.

Evolution of Value-Add Versus Value-Seek

So, why aren't more organizations innovating in how they engage their various constituents via social, mobile, or otherwise? Unfortunately, many organizations are slowed by infrastructure, inertia, and conflicting visions. To make an organization more social, it takes a substantial, concerted, highly focused, and tenacious effort. Conversely, for a customer to benefit from social, he or she just has to buy a smartphone, download a few apps, and go with the flow. The result is that, for the first time, consumers of information, products, and services are able to be "smarter" than companies because of social. They initiate a search for value and often find it, simply because it met their unique need at a particular moment in time. Hence, customers learn to expect a menu of options to choose from and get frustrated with bundled services or products. I've found that social customers want to be served by social organizations, and they become impatient when those organizations fail to meet their expectations. Being a social organization manifests itself in either proactive, value-based off-line interactions or in becoming the purveyor of member-to-member online communities.

Gary LaBranche, FASAE, CAE has been the President and CEO of the Association for Corporate Growth (ACG) since 2008. Unlike many associations, ACG's activity and value is transaction-oriented. The primary role of ACG is to bring people together to do deals: to source, select, and facilitate merger and acquisition activity. Seventy-five percent of its members have done business with another member of ACG in the past year. It is not oriented to standard-setting, credentialing, or professional development. According to Gary, the principle reasons for non-renewals are that the members have left the business or did not find the membership to deliver enough deal-making opportunities. "Member research shows that it takes two to three years before members generate significant business with other members, although the more engaged a member, the more likely and quickly they will generate business," commented Gary. "A challenge is that ACG chapters drive membership recruitment, and some chapters oversell the immediacy of business and under-emphasize the need to become engaged to realize that business. It is important to get

Meet the Association for Corporate Growth (ACG)

ACG has oversight of 56 chapters, each of which are incorporated and affiliated through ACG's licensing agreement. ACG processes their dues, manages their data, handles web transactions and events revenue, manages their websites, advises and trains chapter leaders and staff, issues member communications, provides director and officer liability coverage, handles trademark and domain registration, files the U.S. Federal group tax exemption for all chapters, and provides a range of services to all members. In addition, ACG monitors legislative and regulatory matters and advocates for the middle-market. Twenty-five percent of revenue is derived from membership dues, with the balance of 75 percent from the annual convention.

Founded in 1954, ACG serves 14,000 professionals involved in the mergers and acquisitions and corporate development business. Members are from private equity communities, lenders, investment banks and similar intermediaries, corporate development, law and other environments involved in M&A activities. ACG manages a budget of $12M and employs 20 FTEs. ACG's Mission is to "Drive Middle-Market Growth." In the lower end of the middle market, for deals under $5M, there is the American Association for Mergers and Acquisitions with 600 members. The Turnaround Management Association focuses on distressed companies, and has 9,000 members. ACG is a secondary membership for about a third of it's members, such as the lawyer who is a member of the American Bar Association, or the accountant who belongs to AICPA and their state CPA society.

new members engaged and connected in the first three or four months to meet their expectations," he added. Gary says he has been talking about the issue of disintermediation since 1993. "Social media is another aspect of the disintermediation dialogue because it provides multiple alternative channels for members to connect outside traditional channels of distribution. Associations have been a key mediator between people for 150 years. The challenge in the disintermediated environment is that members don't necessarily have to go through an association," he added.

If members and customers are not sharing their concerns with you, they're certainly thinking about them and perhaps sharing them in social forums. Here are just some of the comments from members and customers in LinkedIn Groups, Facebook Fan Pages, on Twitter, and Yelp:

- "The networking, educational opportunities, and the annual meeting they bundle as my membership 'value-add' are just not doing anything to help me grow my business."

- "I know the players in my own industry; I'm looking for prospective customers and suppliers who can help me launch new products and enter new markets."

- "I can get a much stronger leadership development program at the executive education course offered by (a local) university."

- "The annual meeting is the same stale format it has been for the past two decades and if I attend at all, I'm usually gone by the second or third day."

- "I'm looking for best practices—and best practitioners, in how to use their solution; they offer this roundtable discussion and customer-advisory board meetings that get the same few people talking about the same way they've done things for the past hundred years."

- "I'm looking for the next 'iPhone'-like innovations in our industry and I can't see it in the meetings they keep inviting me to."

- "I'm a 34-year-old president of our company and one of the youngest members of this organization; they've been around for so long and just don't get people like me, how my team and I work, or what we need from them. More frustrating is that they're either unwilling or unable to listen!"

There Is an App for That...

In between the two extremes of social customers and not-so-social organizations is the universe of digital development. Whether by instinct, out of necessity, or just for fun, millions of developers, hackers, innovators, entrepreneurs, and small- to medium-sized businesses around the globe are flooding the market with plug-ins, apps, games, blogs, media sites, and more. When an individual discovers a powerful new productivity app, it takes him less than a minute to download and install it. At that point, he becomes social. He has instant access to far better information than he did 60 seconds ago. When an organization wants to help its employees act social, it must often install enterprise versions of software, acquire new technology with standardized specifications, provide training, institute new processes, and perhaps modify a number of internal metrics. In essence, it's considerably easier for a customer than for an organization to get involved in social. Furthermore, what people experience from apps and conversations in social arenas they expect from organizations they interact with.

An executive shared his experience as a point of comparison in trying to engage an organization where he's an active member. "I can get on an airline's website in the middle of the night, compare and contrast pros and cons of a multitude of destinations via first-hand experience by my friends, pick a destination, select our seats, select our meals, buy our tickets, get a rental car of my choice, reserve a highly recommended five-star hotel room anywhere in the world at a three-star price, and schedule an entire day of excursions and highly unique experiences, and pay for all of it via my PayPal account. Did I mention that I can use their mobile app to check in and get status updates, and they proactively update me if there are any disruptions in my plans? But I can't click-to-chat, schedule a meeting with an association's staff member, or see digitally on their website the latest publication they keep mailing me, where I could interact with other members around a particular topic? I would benefit from this interaction now, not at the next annual meeting! I honestly don't think they get it!"

In many ways, innovation used to be better organized. Before the proliferation of always-connected mobile devices, individuals didn't have access to much real-time information. Most innovation came from established firms. Then Apple and Google came along and spurred the introduction of over one million new apps (and growing). A random assortment of individuals, loosely organized groups, small teams, and start-ups are racing to hyperlink, organize, and analyze the physical world in much the same way that the Web operates. This race will annihilate existing business models even before it unearths better models to replace them. For many, it is both an unsettling and exhilarating time.

The advantage now belongs to organizations that are upstarts or can function with great agility and nimbleness. That agility will allow the organization to uncover opportunities that disrupt the status quo and earn their piece of the value-seek formula. The very nature of success means that established organizations will be slower to recognize and respond to the changes outlined in this book. Besides, disruptive forces always appear first at the edges of established industries, so it is tempting for larger organizations to ignore or minimize them.

In the following chapters, I'll demonstrate why six disruptive forces will require the highest levels of leadership to develop and implement an effective member or customer-centric experience strategy and will share insights regarding how socially enabled organizations are getting even smarter. Organizations that get ahead of these changes will grow rapidly and continue to prosper. Those who react slowly or tentatively will be increasingly marginalized.

Member/Customer–Centric Expectations: 1 to Everything

In the late 1990s, I worked for Bruce Kasanoff, CEO of Accelerating 1 to 1 and former nonfounding partner at Peppers and Rogers Group (PRG). Don Peppers and Martha Rogers are considered the parents of one-to-one marketing. In many ways, they were ahead of their time because they saw the one-to-one future that social and mobile technologies would empower. Bruce, currently CEO of NowPossible, has evolved his thinking into a particularly interesting and relevant model for member-based organizations: 1 to Everything.

The 1 stands for the member or customer. Everything is every other person, device, element, and piece of information on the planet. For example, a cell phone is a device used to differentiate many things. It can be used to identify songs that we just heard on the radio. Using integrated Google maps and augmented reality, cell phones can show which houses are for sale on any given street and include social insights about them. Phones are used to photograph products and get instant reviews and price comparisons both in physical retailers nearby or anywhere a product is sold online. The shift in the customer-centric balance of powers is no longer just organizations' segmenting customers but individual consumers differentiating for themselves restaurants, merchants, friends, experts, media, entertainment, just about *everything*.

Over a decade ago, Don Peppers and Martha Rogers developed a marketing framework to Identify, Differentiate, Interact, and Customize (IDIC). It advocates the need to identify members or customers individually, differentiate your treatment of them based on their unique needs and value-seek, interact individually with members and customers, then customize products and services for each profitable member or customer. It struck Bruce that he could turn IDIC around and use it to predict how members or customers are likely to leverage the interactive technologies that are now part of our daily lives. One-to-one is about looking at individual members or customers through the organization's lens. Here's what IDIC looks like when you look through a customer's eyes. (See Figure 1.4.)

1 to Everything: A Customer's View of the Connected World

Identify	Differentiate	Interact	Customize
anything in the world via a digital device	*options based on my current status and preferences*	*with objects, people, experiences, insights*	*my next interaction based on this one*
• Restaurant	• Which will I like best?	• Intuitive interfaces	• Remember my choices
• Home for sale	• Fairly priced?	• 3D views	• Remember where my favorites are located
• People	• Highest Quality?	• Demos	
• Hotel	• Proximity?	• Data overlays	• Observe how my choices relate to others
• Flight	• Compatible with other components?	• Personal interactions	
• Event	• Friends' or experts' opinions?	• Add pictures to words, or vice versa	• Save me time, money, and effort
• Part number	• Delivery options?		• Reduce complexity
• Health risk	• My physical condition (vital signs, alcohol usage, weight...)	• New games	
• Item for sale		• Deeper insights	
• Plant or flower		• Immersive entertainment	
• Bird		• Relevant news	
• Artwork		• Interesting patterns	
• Song			

Original IDIC framework created by Don Peppers and Martha Rogers. Exhibit adapted by Bruce Kasanoff of NowPossible.com

Figure 1.4—1 to Everything by Bruce Kasanoff at Now Possible, LLC

This framework makes it easier to predict emerging services that organizations could offer in the age of connected relationships. Nearly anything you see out your window—cars, office buildings, people, the weather, birds, restaurants, or billions of other possibilities—can and will be differentiated on your behalf by applications that haven't yet come to market. Visionary organizations could leverage 1 to Everything to segment their members or customers one by one and use IDIC to create a portfolio of products and services particularly useful to each segment.

7 Measures of Success, The Decision to Join, and Race for Relevance

Because social can be a strong enabler of performance, execution, and results, I want to highlight several books published by ASAE that I find particularly relevant to the ideas in *Return on Impact*. Think of them as the foundation to build on as you embrace thinking and leading differently. What my predecessors didn't have access to are the vast reach and innovative models that social and mobile represent in our world today, and I'll highlight that in the next chapter's discussion of social strategy as an imperative first step. In none of these publications is anyone talking about Facebook, Twitter, or YouTube. The tactical means to accomplish broader objectives is in execution—assessing, planning, and, thus, leading differently—because social defines the path to success moving forward.

Originally published in 2006, *7 Measures of Success: What Remarkable Associations Do that Others Don't* is the ASAE and The Center for Association Leadership's Measures of Success Task Force study. Led by Michael E. Gallery, PhD, CAE, the task force was composed of a large group of volunteers and staff who worked for nearly four years to collect, review, and process data and then write and edit the manuscript. Jim Collins, of *Good to Great* fame, acted in an advisory capacity, helping the task force implement the matched-pairs methodology. The project's value lies in discerning the often subtle differences between two well-matched organizations—what one association did or didn't do to give it a performance or financial edge on its counterpart. Many believe the findings of this study are as valid today as they were when the book was published. Below are some excerpts from the book about four aspects of remarkable organizations, followed by some of my observations of their work comparing 18 matched associations:

1. A Customer Service Culture—"Remarkable associations build their structures, processes, and interactions—their entire culture— around assessing and fulfilling members' needs and expectations." Customer service must go beyond customer satisfaction. If you're still asking customer satisfaction questions on those stale surveys, it may surprise you to learn that in my observations of a number of clients, lapsed members often report virtually the same level of satisfaction as current members.

2. Alignment of Products and Services with Mission—"Remarkable associations speak passionately about fulfilling their mission and

constantly test their ideas for products against that mission, using it as a touchstone for everything they do.... To find the right mix of products...remarkable associations engage in experimentation." If the goal for a member- or customer-centric organization is to become an indispensible resource for its constituents, how effectively are you affecting, engaging, and transforming those connected relationships?

3. Data-Driven Strategies—"If there is one phrase that sets remarkable associations apart from their counterparts, it's 'data, data, data.' They gather information, analyze it, and then use it to become even better." As I'll discuss in Chapter 8, social insights and analytics tell a very interesting story—one of a more holistic view of not just what your members say but what they search, click, find, read, and react to. Their observable digital behaviors are considerably more credible if you have the infrastructure to capture and act on that insightful data in real time.

4. Dialogue and Engagement—"Many with the study group would no doubt echo the employee at the Society for Human Resource Management (SHRM) who said, 'We all discuss decisions openly with each other. We have a desire to collaborate with each other, and we do it in mission-driven ways.'" You can't argue with the numbers; SHRM membership is reported to have grown from 36,000 in 1992 to more than 250,000 today. But is SHRM dramatically affecting the HR profession? See the breakout box "2011 Strategic Advice for SHRM" on the next page.

5. CEO as a Broker of Ideas—"While CEOs may be visionary leaders, what's more important is their ability to facilitate visionary thinking throughout the organization." In a knowledge economy, the culture of ideas tends to accelerate at a distinctly rapid pace. In Chapter 4, I'll discuss building a different kind of organization and in Chapter 6, I'll review how to attract and retain world-class talent with the top six most important attributes they can bring to the leadership.

6. Organizational Adaptability—"Our data confirmed that no organization—regardless of how remarkable it is—can predict change with full accuracy and therefore be on target with its response.... Our data indicate that remarkable organizations do not panic.... They maintain a clear understanding of their core purpose." In my interviews

2011 Strategic Advice for SHRM: Make SHRM Matter

Voice of HR invited a number of industry contributors to take a critical look at SHRM and offer their strategic advice to SHRM leadership in a web series, *2011 Strategic Advice for SHRM*. This is a republication of Lisa Rosendahl's response posted on her blog (http://www.lisarosendahl.com).

Make SHRM Matter

So much of my day, I face more competition for my attention than I have time to give. Let's talk about competition for my attention from within my chosen profession—Human Resources. I've been a Human Resource (HR) professional for over 15 years and counting. I progressed from an HR department of one supporting 75 employees to an HR Director with a staff of 14 supporting 1,500 employees. My career has spanned private, public, and federal sectors and is still going strong. I am a Senior Professional in Human Resources (SPHR) and a Human Capital Strategist (HCS), I have more degrees than any one person needs and not nearly enough time. I read. I write. I conference. I search. I choose.

My HR colleagues and friends make a difference every day pushing the envelope, generating new ideas, and challenging the status quo. They manage HR effectively by changing human behavior and rally fellow HR leaders to develop workforce strategies to generate talent. They deliver on the plan; they seek out the tough questions; and they teach. They are in the trenches; they are at the helm; and they practice what they preach. I follow. I lead. I listen. I learn. I am inspired.

I am a card-carrying SHRM member and have been for over 15 years. SHRM, at its core, is technical practitioner HR.

It's a necessary and solid foundation that was invaluable to me at the start of my career. As a one-person HR department, I had SHRM on speed dial and the professionals on the other end of the line were beacons in the storm and my one-stop for questions.

Not any more. SHRM is focusing on and meeting a need—but not my need. I am looking for current, relevant, and emerging ideas. When I have questions or need information, I am online in business magazines, leadership columns, and blogs. I am in Human Capital spaces one day and Talent Management and Succession Planning spaces on another. I live at the Office of Personnel Management and federal HR sites. I seek out conferences beyond traditional and technical HR. HR is a dynamic profession, yet when I think of SHRM, I see a solid, rigid organization.

SHRM, create a new reality. Start conversations and let them flow. Let go of being big, of being "the one," of being in charge. Collaborate with other organizations and do what you have to do to provide resources to your members, even of they didn't originate from SHRM. Encourage new ideas, let go of "knowing" the future of HR, and be open to the unknown. Restructure to be nimble.

SHRM, inspire me. Be the change the profession needs. Make me choose you.

with association executives and corporate CEOs alike, those who stayed in the market and continued to cater to the evolving needs of their members and customers are the ones who have not only survived the Great Recession but have found ways to reinvent much of their business or many of their revenue models. More on this and the "iTunification" of your capabilities in Chapter 5.

7. Alliance Building—"[Remarkable associations are] secure in who they are and what they bring to the table; these associations communicate clear expectations for each specific partnership and do not hesitate to walk away if a win-win situation does not materialize. But they're also willing to admit what they can't do on their own." Isn't it interesting that everyone wants to "partner" with successful organizations? Have you ever stopped someone to ask what that *really* means? Relationships go bad with misaligned expectations, so here is a tip for you: Look in the mirror for a healthy self-evaluation before you propose an alliance! And work diligently from the onset to align expectations early and often.

Published in 2007, *The Decision to Join: How Individuals Determine Value and Why They Choose to Belong* rebutted conventional wisdom that a person's decision to join an individual membership organization is not a cost-benefit analysis. Beyond what's in it for them, the findings offer key insights, refined strategies, and a new look at what's valuable to association members. Co-authors James Dalton and Monica Dignam compiled data gathered from 18 individual membership organizations and nearly 17,000 survey responses to paint a clearer picture of what people value about membership in an association. The book aimed to help:

- Improve an association's value proposition;
- Create and execute more effective strategies; and
- Target member and prospect segments and tailor offerings to appeal to those segments.

Of interest to me in my research for *Return on Impact* were topics such as affiliation and involvement, generations and career level, gender, employer type and level of support, world location, and leading associations that focus on the programs and initiatives that matter to members and thus improve their overall value proposition. In Chapter 3, I'll cover embracing world-class engagements with eight connected relationship buyer-types and their unique buyer behaviors. In Chapter 7, I'll share best practices and relevant case studies about socially enabling your execution, directly from insights from member or customer behaviors.

At the most recent ASAE Annual Meeting in St. Louis, I had a chance to sit in on the *Race for Relevance* presentation. What I found particularly interesting and insightful in the standing-room-only session was Harrison Coerver's (along with co-author, Mary Byers) candid discussion on the obsolescence of the old ways of doing things in associations. Published in 2011, *Race for Relevance: 5 Radical Changes for Associations* presents the radical change that is required to maintain influence and thrive in the new environment and avoid challenges associated with old association models, such as loss of market share, increased competition for members' time, and shrinking revenue sources.

In their presentation, the authors discussed five radical changes that will energize and position associations for better performance. Their 40 years of combined experience with more than 1,000 associations was clearly evident in their presentation on governance, management, and strategy. I found *Race for Relevance* to be well written and timely. Five changes recommended in *Race for Relevance* correlated strongly with ideas in this book:

- Overhauling the governance model and committee operations. A more streamlined and nimbler governance in building a different kind of an organization is discussed in Chapter 4 of this book.

- Empowering the CEO and enhancing staff competence. In Chapter 6, I'll cover how to leverage social to attract and retain unparalleled talent, a staff that is challenged and works in a highly social/collaborative environment with volunteers.

- Rigorously defining the member market. In Chapter 5, I'll discuss the critical nature of expanding your reach to a much broader market while remaining realistic and focused on the value your members or customers seek.

- Rationalizing programs and services. In Chapter 5, I'll cover the "iTunification" of capabilities—desirable and highly beneficial member products and services at the moment and on the device of their choosing, socially enabled to deliver an exceptional experience.

- Building a robust technology framework. While Chapter 8 of this book will focus on social analytics and insights, in Chapter 9 I'll celebrate failure as an enormous opportunity for growth. In social, learning and applying lessons from that failure will undoubtedly be dependent on a robust technology infrastructure.

If you haven't picked up *7 Measures of Success, The Decision to Join,* or *Race for Relevance,* I'd highly recommend them as supplemental to your reading and implementation of *Return on Impact.* I think you'll find that each author's unique background, perspective, and experiences shed unique light on the key challenges *and opportunities facing* member- and customer-centric organizations in the decade ahead.

Here is the QR code to learn more, discuss key points in this chapter, and join the conversation in the IMPACT Community.

## CHAPTER 2

Develop a Robust Social Strategy, an Imperative First Step

T HE SILVER LINING in an economy of contrasts is that visionary leaders and entrepreneurs have the opportunity to question the status quo and explore new frontiers. That's what many member-based organization executives and corporate leaders are doing with the question of social. With the slowing of the economy, the pace of change is accelerating at so many levels in organizations that many people believe how a member or a customer-centric organization will operate in the next decade cannot be imagined today.

Unfortunately, many of my interviews reveal that social is not an integrated topic in an organization's overarching strategic plan. Specifically, in the ASAE Foundation's Delphi model survey we asked, "Do you currently have a social media strategy?" The most frequent response was a resounding "Yes." But upon further examination, most associations actually had a

social media plan, and a tactically focused one at that. For example, many simply send out a monthly electronic newsletter and create a social media corner, perhaps by using a Facebook fan page to drive traffic and awareness of an upcoming event. Some plans were poorly developed, ignoring the power of choice and focus, trying instead to accommodate a multitude of conflicting demands and interests.

It's time to put leadership back into strategy. Strategy is not what it used to be or what it could be when social is integrated in the overall thinking process. In the past two decades, I've observed and facilitated strategic planning sessions as a set of analytical problem-solving exercises. Legions of MBAs and strategy consultants use frameworks and techniques to help their clients analyze key industry trends and position their organizations for strategic advantage. Back in the 1970s, thanks to Michael Porter's Five Forces framework (Figure 2.1, see page 35), we learned about the role of market forces in industry profitability and the critical importance of differentiating an organization from its competitive peers. Several years ago, in the original edition of *Relationship Economics*, I wrote about the 10 schools of strategy and their applications given different internal and external scenarios. The challenge with most strategies is the tendency to become myopic within a set of competitive attributes, possibly disconnecting the organization and leadership from a larger sense of purpose and impact. So how does a visionary leader ensure that the organization's strategy remains relevant? The strategy itself must evolve to more proactively embrace and integrate environmental factors and constantly adjust organizational levers to navigate turbulent conditions. Those levers are choices the leader, the board, and the organization make in their pursuit of evolution and relevancy.

The Best Possible Choices

I was invited to keynote the 2010 Produce Marketing Association's annual Fresh Summit alongside former chairman, president, and chief executive officer of Procter and Gamble, A.G. Lafley. Under Lafley's leadership from 2000 to 2010, P&G focused on consumer-driven innovation and consistent, reliable, sustainable growth. With Lafley at the helm, sales doubled, profits quadrupled, and the company's market value increased by more than $100 billion, making P&G among the most valuable companies in the world. Its portfolio of billion-dollar brands—including Tide, Pampers, Olay, and Gillette—grew from 10 to 24. When discussing what made P&G successful, Lafley highlighted the fact that the company's leadership had a clear strategy and were prepared to put all their resources, people, and money behind it. One of the comments I greatly appreciated about Lafley's session was his definition of a clear, choice-rich strategy: *"the best possible choices for the best possible outcomes with a common mission and set of goals."* He reiterated that too many organizations unfortunately don't have a strategy and are ill prepared to make choices about where they're going to play and about how they're going to try to win, to stick with a strategy backed by all their resources.

A strategy should be a dynamic tool for guiding the development of a company over time. Particularly when it comes to social , we need to think about strategy in a way that recognizes the fluidity of this evolutionary landscape and its impact on existing and potential competitors—not just other organizations but that of mindshare and wallet share—and the critical need for *continuous leadership.* Ann Turner is a good example of continuous leadership when it comes to her organization's strategy. Ann is the executive director of the American Association for Laboratory Animal Science (AALAS), a national organization founded in 1951 to advance the field of laboratory animal science through education and training.

"Essentially, AALAS is the mother ship for the field," Turner says. "I would like to say we have a strategy figured out for exactly where we are going to be five years from now, but our biggest strategy is to stay open to what the next thing is." AALAS uses social media for marketing communication to its members today, and is looking for opportunities where it can be used for broader purposes. Social media strategy is crafted and driven at the staff level, and the point person for social media is the associate executive director.

According to one of my favorite books, *The Lords of Strategy* (HBR Press, 2010) by renowned business journalist and editor Walter Kiechel, 50 years ago the world of business functioned without a corporate strategy. Businesses made

> ### About AALAS
>
> AALAS has 13,000 members, 33 full-time staff, and a budget of $5.5 million. It publishes two journals, two newsletters, and a reference directory and has an annual meeting with an average attendance of 4,500, four certification programs, educational products, and a large internet training program with 180,000 enrollees. Membership is institutional or individual and categorized as gold, silver, or bronze relative to cost and benefit. The national organization is incorporated and operates independently from its 50 branches across the United States. It is affiliated with 32 professional organizations connected to laboratory animal science.

plans, certainly, but without understanding the underlying dynamics of competition, costs, and customers. It was like trying to design a large-scale engineering project without knowing the laws of physics. But in the 1960s, four mavericks (Bruce Henderson, founder of Boston Consulting Group; Bill Bain, creator of Bain & Company; Fred Gluck, longtime Managing Director of McKinsey & Company; and Michael Porter, Harvard Business School professor) and their posses instigated a profound shift in thinking that turbocharged business as never before and produced implications far beyond what even they imagined. Strategy was integrated into the general management curriculum in business schools. In both academic and practice circles, it was often identified as the most important duty of the CEO. As the person responsible for the overall performance of the organization, this vital role encompassed both the formulation and the execution of strategy. The SWOT (strengths and weaknesses within the organization; opportunities and threats external to it) model used by many managers was pedestrian in hindsight. Corporate planning departments emerged and introduced more formal systems and standards for strategic analysis.

The past 50 years have certainly enriched the strategy toolkit. But according to Cynthia Montgomery, head of the strategy unit at Harvard Business School, "Strategy has also lost breadth and stature. It has become more about formulation than implementation and more about getting the idea right at the outset than living with a strategy over time." Particularly when we consider a social strategy as the foundation of building a different kind of an organization, of all the questions CEOs or executive directors and their boards are required to answer, one predominates: What kind of an organization do you want yours to *be*? As strategy has strived to become a science, we have allowed this fundamental point (of the organization *being* not just *achieving*) to slip away. Social is one way we can reinstate it.

Changing the Organization's Purpose

When confronted with a challenge such as social, the CEO or executive director must view the strategic significance of issues on the table, both challenges and opportunities, through a holistic lens. Staying faithful to the translation of an organization's purpose into practice, the CEO must also remain open to the idea that the purpose itself may need to change. The judgments made at these critical junctures can make or break a leader or an organization.

Long before IBM's announcement of Virginia "Ginni" Rometty as its first female CEO in the company's 100-year history, Big Blue was a different organization. In 1993, Lou Gerstner, then CEO of a troubled IBM, concluded a necessary radical shift in the company's mindset to resurrect it. This required taking a fearless and candid inventory of the business, realistically evaluating the firm's core capabilities, and shedding everything else. Gerstner announced that IBM would no longer invent technologies, but rather focus on application. The company went beyond its comfort zone in creating new hardware to provide integrated information technology services and solutions. "History," Gerstner would later write, "shows that truly great and successful organizations go through the constant and sometimes difficult self-renewal of the core business."

If the CEO, the executive director, or the volunteer leadership chooses an organization's identity, they also have the responsibility for declining certain opportunities and pursuing others. In essence, the CEO serves as the *steward of the organization's purpose,* guiding it through a predetermined course, bringing it back to the center, even as the center evolves.

Painful Examples of What Not to Do

Isn't it interesting that when we read about or witness successful strategies at work, we marvel in their simplicity and obvious design? They seldom pop out of a strategic management toolbox, a matrix, a triangle, or a fill-in-the blank worksheet. It's often an astute and talented leader who identifies the pivotal points in a situation—one or two critical issues—and then focuses attention and concentrates action and necessary resources to overcome the challenges and capture the opportunities. Too many organizational leaders say they have a strategy when they really don't. Like a team captain whose only advice to his teammates is, "Let's go get 'em," weak strategies mask their failure to guide the organization through turbulent times by embracing the intellectually lazy language of broad visions, missions, ambitions, and values. Although each of these points is an important part of an organization's lifecycle, by themselves, they are no substitute for a crystal clear *and hard-working* strategy.

What's important to understand is that weak, unclear, or just outright bad strategies affect us all. Think of governments with grandiose goals of hope and change that are less and less able to solve deeply rooted cultural problems; organizational boards that sign off on strategic plans that are little more than wishful thinking; public education systems with an overabundance of metrics and standards but impoverished levels of understanding for combating the sources of underperformance. In each scenario, the outcomes are painful to watch and expensive to experience. The only remedy is for all of us—as members, consumers, employees, investors, and public citizens—to demand more from those who lead, more than teleprompter speeches delivered with charisma, more than "open, transparent, and authentic" linguistic upgrades in policy. Social demands a *solid strategy* as a foundation to leading differently.

When the Strategy Is Wrong, Broken, or Weak

So what does a broken, dead wrong, or even a weak strategy look like? Here are six key attributes. Think of this list as *what not to do* when developing or revising your strategy. I'll add the social components later in this chapter.

1. **Ignore the challenge or frame the problem incorrectly.** I do a series of exercises with my consulting clients where I set up scenarios, and their task is to attempt to both identify the problem and its root cause and *only then* try to solve each. The challenge is a glaring misperception of the actual problem. Not an intentional trap by any means, it simply overlooks the obvious. If the challenge is not defined or framed correctly, it will be difficult, if not impossible, to assess the quality of the strategy. And if you can't assess the quality of the strategy, how can you reject it as weak or improve upon it?

2. **Confuse a plan, a goal, or an objective with a strategy.** I deliver 50 to 60 global keynote speeches each year and am simply mesmerized by senior executives and motivational speakers who deliver rah-rah messages on stage. They are entertaining in the moment but hardly memorable if most audience members can't recite a take-away 20 minutes later much less when they get back to the office. Audiences don't lack motivation; they suffer from a lack of competent, strategic leadership. Planning is an extrapolation of the present. What am I doing today and how can I do more of it? Goals are milestones to measure progress in the plan. Strategy is painting a vision for the future and developing a path to get there. The role of the leader is to create the conditions that will make the goal and plan effective with a strategy worthy of the effort and the resources it will take to execute it.

3. **Insert fuzzy or "blue sky" objectives.** Another glaring sign of weak strategy is the presence of those fuzzy objectives parading as

a laundry list of action items. Let's call it what it is: a long list of things to do, often a byproduct of planning meetings where a variety of stakeholders like to hear themselves talk and keep suggesting things they would like to see accomplished. Rather than focus on a few important items that will undoubtedly move the organization's needle, we mop up the entire day's collection into the strategic plan. To make everyone happy and minimize any actual accountability, we label it "long term," implying that none of these things actually have to be completed anytime soon. One of my Fortune 100 consulting clients actually handed down from the senior leadership team and the board 147 priorities for the upcoming fiscal year! Another equally annoying and weak strategic objective is a simple restatement of a grandiose future state at some unspecified point in time. Beyond the fact that no one actually has a clue about what it means or how to get there, the steps to accomplishing the objectives are as equally difficult as the original challenge, thus creating a weak strategy that adds little value to the effort.

4. **Offer up cotton candy.** Next in the list of weak strategy attributes is a lot of hot air wrapped around superficial abstracts. Who doesn't love a clever ad slogan? My personal favorite is a local, no service, mega bank that touts itself as the "relationship bank." I've been a customer for more than a decade, using at least a dozen of their products, and yet I get a call every six months or so from a revolving door "relationship manager" who doesn't know anything about me! When you read an intercompany memo that says, "Our fundamental strategy is one of a customer-centric intermediation," do you wonder what that *really* means? The phrase "customer-centric" is interesting. I use it to illustrate a clearly differentiated strategy as evidenced by more customized, individualized, personalized, or otherwise unique manner in which a target audience's needs are met and exceeded, not just what the organization has to push, promote, or pitch that particular day. But if true and sustainable differentiation and highly personalized customization are not the intent with the above memo, other than pure fluff, what exactly sets the organization apart?

5. **Settle for lack of willingness or ability to decide.** Decision making is both an art and a science. We face obstacles to quality decision making every day—as consumers, managers, leaders, and organizations. Weak leaders of complex organizations make the mistake of asking

a very diverse group of constituents to reach a consensus around an extremely challenging topic. Because of the vast set of preferences, they can't. So they settle on something like this: "We're committed to providing the highest-value services and being a leader in our industry." Clearly not a strategy, but a political outcome reached by individuals who, forced to reach a consensus, could not agree on which interests and concepts to forego. As A.G. Lafley mentioned, strategy involves focus, and therefore, choice. And selecting the best possible choices means setting aside some goals in favor of others. When this hard work is not done, a weak strategy is the outcome.

6. **Use fill-in-the-blank processes.** Here is one for you from a motivational website selling fill-in-the-blank, template-style systems for strategic planning. (Feel free to search "vision mission strategy.") Ready for the four steps?

 A. Pick any flavor of a transformational leader,
 B. Who develops or crafts a vision,
 C. Inspires people to sacrifice for the good of the organization (change), and
 D. Empowers people to accomplish the vision.

 Enthusiastically adopted by brain-dead organizations, bureaucratic school boards, university presidents who are way past mandatory retirement, and bloated government agencies, this form of intellectual laziness presents the obvious as profound insight. Empty rhetoric and bad examples abound for those who are genuinely interested in devising and implementing an effective strategy. I've actually found a "find and replace" website for social media strategies, with hundreds of examples you can download and then find and replace what you've selected with your organization's name. Try that out with your legal documents or employment contracts and see how it works out for you.

In my discussions with senior leaders, I often talk about the fundamental disconnect between strategy formulation and strategy execution. There is no shortage of mission, vision, values, and beliefs—what I call *wall art.* You walk around enough mahogany rows, and you'll see them elegantly framed in lobbies or hallways. Yet, ask four different people what business they're really in, and they'll give you five different answers! That's when you know you've just met a broken, dead wrong, or weak strategy!

Why Social Should Influence Your Strategy

So much for weak strategy. Let's switch gears to the basic underlying structure of a strong strategy:

- **An Empirical Assessment**—a fact-based explanation of the nature of the challenge, ideal observable behavior (more on psychographics in the next chapter) diagnosed to simplify the often-overwhelming complexity of reality, and certain aspects of the situation prioritized as critical. What fact-based business outcome will the organization's social strategy attempt to address? This salient point becomes particularly valuable in later chapters when we discuss social ROI.

- **A Guiding Plan**—an overall approach to overcome obstacles identified in the assessment. Crisp, crystal clear, and focused, this is your intelligent GPS on steroids that learns from one interaction and applies that learning to the next interaction. In Chapter 9, I discuss social failures, and one of the biggest lessons for many organizations continues to be building a consistent social execution plan where the planning process is as critical, if not more so, than the plan itself. It should challenge key stakeholders to really think about what the organization is and isn't capable of today and where social can dramatically affect its desired outcomes.

- **Diligent Execution**—coordinated steps to support the guiding plan. Freakish discipline to stay the course, not get distracted, and back your actions with an argument. Constantly discover crucial factors and learn from every situation as well as design coordinated and focused action to keep moving forward. Social execution isn't about the technology or the tools. It is the discipline, the organization's mindset, and the initiative to execute key tasks and achieve progressive milestones. I'll say it again: *It's about progress, not perfection.*

From my experience, the best social strategies infuse a childlike wonder and a natural intellectual curiosity for the organization into the structure outlined above, reinforced by analytic rigor for course correction—an incredibly hard combination of intellectual horsepower and execution skills for many leadership teams. So where does social fit and how should it influence your strategy?

Listen to What They *Do*

What would you say are the top challenges within your organization relative to current or prospective members or customers, your value chain's partners, suppliers, and outside resources? How do you know? Beyond what a research report, an industry analyst, or your broad base of constituents may tell you in surveys, what are the observable behaviors online or offline that demonstrate their dissent, dissatisfaction, or discourse?

I certainly don't assume every organization is damaged, so let's look at the positive aspects of your team, organization, or industry. What do the relationships most important to you say about your brand? Where are you as an individual, a team, or an organization creating the most dramatic impact as an outcome for those you serve? What products or services that you've created and delivered in the past year have been most dramatically accepted, used, and applied and have produced value for your members? Which ones have been proactively shared, distributed, or touted as forward thinking by your broad base of constituents? If you cast a wider net than just your current members or customers, who would most likely gravitate toward your value proposition and buy in on your ideas, products, or service offerings? What is the profile of the member or customer who would pay a premium for a product or service you've yet to introduce?

I know. You included some of these questions in your last survey. So, how do you *really* know that's in fact what they candidly *believe or feel* at any point in time? A research firm can survey an industry using statistical analytics to verify the validity of their findings. No argument there. But I think digital behaviors are much rawer, real-time, candid, and forthcoming about revealing true feelings. What is important to embrace is that depending on the audience, it is critical for any organization to balance the social sphere sentiments (often the true feelings of a segment of your audience) with views from more traditional sources to get a holistic perspective of where they're coming from. The above questions are but a few that social analytics can help answer; I'll share more in Chapter 8 when I cover benchmarking, the digital edge, and segmentation.

The Missing Link in Porter's Five Forces

In *The Lords of Strategy*, Michael Porter and his life's work—"taking an extraordinary, complex, integrated, multidimensional problem and getting arms around it conceptually in a way that helps, informs, and empowers practitioners to actually do things"—is highlighted extensively. Porter's Five Forces framework is described as a set of structural factors that create opportunities in an industry that a company could exploit to its competitive advantage. Captured in his 1980 book *Competitive Strategy*, the framework came from his observation that "the essence of formulating competitive strategy is relating a company to its environment," and that the key aspect of that environment was the industry it found itself in and that industry's structure.

The framework defines five factors essential to determining how profitable an industry could be for players and where and how an organization might have room to compete effectively. (See Figure 2.1.)

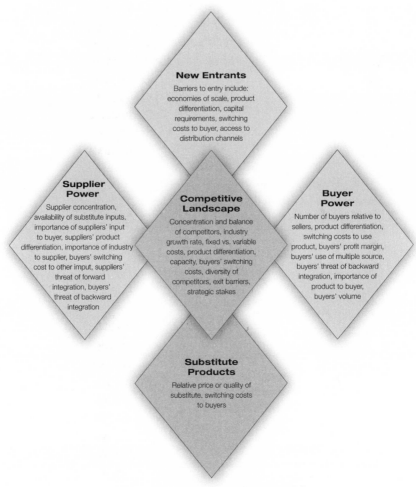

Figure 2.1—Porter's Five Forces Model

At the core of the framework is the competitive rivalry between "firms," surrounded by other forces that determine the intensity of this rivalry: the bargaining power of suppliers and buyers, the threat of new entrants, and substitute offerings. This model has given its users a gratifying thoroughness since it was first developed some 30 years ago, primarily because of the constant motion of forces acting upon one another. You certainly can't argue with success; *Competitive Strategy: Techniques for Analyzing Industries and Competitors* is in its 60th printing. Kiechel writes in *The Lords of Strategy,* "Porter heads the list of authors most frequently cited in the academic literature on strategic management and, since Peter Drucker's death in 2005, of popular ratings of the most influential management guru."

In a 2002 interview published in the *Academy of Management Executive,* Porter summarized his thinking when developing his framework: "Fundamental to any theory of positioning had to be superior profitability. That in turn required competitive advantage, and fundamental to any thinking about competitive advantage was scope, or the breadth of the company's strategic target." In Chapter 2 of his book, he summarizes three strategies a company could choose and reiterated A.G. Lafley's point with, "You'd better damn pick one and stick to it."

1. Low-cost leadership,
2. Product differentiation—making your offering so distinctive that you could charge a premium for it, or
3. Market specialization—Pick a niche and dominate it.

There is no arguing Porter's contribution to the field and discussions of strategy. But here is the missing link in Porter's Five Forces framework: Until some 25 years later, Porter didn't have social networks, media, intelligence, platforms, or engagement. He couldn't have predicted the dramatic effect a more holistic customer lifecycle, influencer marketing, and unique buyer types would have on the bargaining power of buyers. Many of his definitions of buyer concentration, buyer volume, switching costs, buyer information, buyer input, the ability to backward integrate, and decision-makers' incentives were myopic given the information and resources he had at the time (Figure 2.2).

Porter wasn't challenged with the relationship between social influencers, brand affinity, and purchase decisions across different industry verticals; in essence, social influence positioning hadn't been invented yet. Equate this to adding turbo to Ford's Model T. Influencer marketing turns the traditional funnel metaphor on its head; top-down branding becomes

Figure 2.2—Social as the Missing Link in Porter's Five Forces Model

increasingly impotent as social media grows. An estimated 75 percent of buyers (according to a 2011 *Social Business* IBM white paper) no longer believe your marketing, and they tend to heavily rely on personal networks to learn about products and services. Consumers are shaping brands more than the brands themselves. Brands today must develop stronger connections to end consumers than ever before.

Your organization, in essence, is a brand—one that must socialize with its consumers not around just membership, products, or services but information; develop a credible social voice; and provide a return on impact to consumers. For the executives I interviewed who admittedly espoused that social is (just) for communication, I would respectfully point out that it won't be enough to craft powerful messages and push them through traditional channels. You will need to participate proactively in conversations with a broad base of consumers and provide more meaningful value exchanges. Regardless of the industry, organizations will need to focus on developing credible, more engaging, personal, humble, and participatory connections. Loyalty between the producers of information and consumers of it must become symmetrical, where both sides reap equal return from their relationships.

The Evolution of Engagement

Since writing *Relationship Economics* in 2008, I've observed an accelerated evolution of prioritizing and investing in engagements with an expanded base of constituents. Almost every aspect of our decision-making process has become considerably more collaborative and in real time. When we try to solve problems within our organizations, produce innovative products and services, become more effective in our marketing, gain better access to knowledge, lower the cost of doing business, or drive higher and more profitable revenue, we *network* to accelerate the process or enhance the outcome. Successful organizations are elevating the types of technologies they're using, enhancing or dramatically updating their management practices, or optimizing their workflow processes to leverage the "networked economy." Despite the recession, the majority of my clients are increasing their investments in collaboration practices, technical infrastructure, in-house knowledge, implementation, and application of *engagements.*

Inside or outside the organization, reaching key individuals who can influence thinking, perspective, and call to action at the height of the decision-making process has become priority number one. More than a decade ago, Amazon.com began offering targeted product recommendations to consumers already logged in and ready to buy. Complex algorithms integrate a user's digital behavior with his or her propensity to explore *contextually relevant* up-sell and cross-sell options. This is the digital version of "Would you like fries with your order?"

Sales and marketing functions have traditionally used a "funnel" metaphor to describe touch points of influence along a consumer's decision process. Consumers of *information* as well as products or services start

Social Impact @ Work:
Deloitte Australia—Fun Social Experiment Leads to Business Transformation

After reading an article about Yammer in 2008, Deloitte Australia's innovation team began Yammering as an experiment with no plans for mass adoption. The application was free to try and easy to use, and the team thought Yammer might make a nice addition to their email and voice systems but were unsure if/how it would add value. Over the next year, engagement exploded, including among executives, and use quickly spread across 5,000 people and 12 national offices, becoming embedded into core business processes and breaking down communication silos. As use has grown, so have the number of successful cases. The "fun experiment" has helped facilitate a social business transformation that continues to deliver significant value across the company.

with a number of potential options, sources, or brands in mind. Messaging or positioning is then directed at them as they reduce that number and move through the funnel, and at the end they emerge with the one choice, selection, or purchase.

Here is the challenge: The traditional funnel concept is entirely too simple for today's sophisticated and increasingly well-informed consumer. In any geographic market or industry that is online, *connected relationships* exponentially enhance the number of information sources, digital channels, and comparative options. These factors by definition create additional complexities in how we search, evaluate, and engage with organizations. As such, organizations must find new and innovative ways to include their brands in the initial short-list that consumers develop as they evaluate their options while moving along a continuum. The offensive strategy mentioned earlier must proactively take your message to the broader market (more than just your existing "members" or customers) not in the traditional one-way push but with a more systematic and disciplined collaborative intent to engage. The defensive strategy must manage repute, word of mouth, possible misinformation, or competitive FUD (fear, uncertainty, and doubt) about your organization, brand, or value-add. Loyalty will become more challenging to capture and maintain and *perceived* reputation will matter more than ever before.

One final salient point about this evolution: All aspects of your positioning, from strategy to investments, infrastructure, message, channel management, and fulfillment must be integrated across the entire organization. Reaching your target audience with the right value proposition at the right time is half the battle; the other half becomes delivering on the promised experience. Whether they engage with you as an employee, supplier, customer, member, or investor, they want to believe you now and *believe in you*, as they experience working with your organization.

From Monologue to Dialogue to Community

When was the last time you stopped to read a billboard in the airport concourse or train station? Most passive traditional media outlets struggle to capture the attention of people plugged into their smartphones and tablets. Meanwhile, the digitally empowered, keenly critical, ever-demanding, experientially discriminating, yet price-sensitive members and customers are turning in waves to social networks, blogs, and online review forums for independent insights and objective advice. They're not just looking for product or service information, how to get trained, or where to attend an event. They're looking for organizations and brands that are genuinely interested—*and demonstrate interest by their actions*—in building and nurturing a relationship with them. As these touch points continue to multiply, it is critical to elevate the efforts of the organization from monologue to dialogue.

Dialogue for organizations is more challenging than one would expect. Connected relationships benefit greatly from social influence, the impact that our peers have on our relationships with organizations. In years past, members and their associations or customers and their companies built fairly direct relationships with few other parties involved. Connected relationships by definition engage others, learn from others, and ask questions of others in parallel to talking with an organization. Connected relationships have the potential of completely removing some organizations from the equation. Even Facebook finds itself threatened by Google+'s estimated 25 million users in its first month.

True dialogue may represent rather uncomfortable scenarios for some organizations. For example, in dialogue, there is no more fudging the truth. For leaders of these organizations, they'll have to accept that others will openly challenge their claims. Others will very publically review and analyze the quality of their organization's products and services, the degree to which their organization is *deemed* trustworthy (see consumer B.S. radars in Chapter 3), and the degree to which the organization performs as promised. All these factors will be tested, examined, analyzed, discussed, and shared by other people, even as they attend your meetings or sit in front of you to discuss a purchase.

I'm currently shopping for a car. Weekend test drives of at least a half dozen makes and models are part of my decision journey. Recently, while browsing a range of models in a showroom, I began speaking with one of the sales professionals. At the same time, I'm on my iPad2 with no less than eight social sites, forums, and discussion groups of car enthusiasts, car magazines, industry insiders, and consumer advocacy organizations but none by the manufacturer. As the salesperson would talk about key features, I'd simultaneously search online and find reviews. The opinions I found became part of the conversation and an integral part of my decision-making process; I would see a review, mention an observation to the salesperson, and she would respond to it. As a result, I felt considerably more prepared than I would have in the past.

By the way, I also discovered that the specific year and model that I really liked, the one the salesperson said would take four weeks for delivery, was available across town for 10 percent less than at the high-end showroom where I was offered an espresso and a crepe.

The sales professional was up against a formidable, and some would even characterize unfair, headwind. She had to integrate the independent perspectives and opinions offered by my social network, none of whom were physically present in her showroom. I wonder how her brand—or any organization for that matter—is integrating a decision-making process similar to mine into sales training and development? No doubt the purveyors of "Sales 2.0" are salivating to answer.

Communities are far more influential than email lists or chat rooms of vocal customers. They enable the dialogue, consideration, buying, and support of the overall experience. When you attract a community of like-minded individuals based on a common mission, vision, or enemy, they gravitate toward specific conversations and bring their unique experiences and views to each situation. Communities integrate content, tools, and services, which in turn garner attention, participation, lasting or highly engaged interaction, and even more compelling content. If organizations can let go of what they think they know, which I talk about more in the next section, "Uncovering What's Holding You Back," they'll realize that connecting people with one another online is what will last. It's not about the technology; it is about tying the community with CRM, customer support, and dashboards to provide real-time insights.

Communities drive brands and traffic. As content becomes more unique and compelling, the community becomes more useful, which gets more traffic, which creates more links within and external to the community, making the community more authoritative. More loyal users appreciate and are attracted to the authority as the "definitive source or destination," which creates higher repeat visits, more interaction, and even more compelling content (Figure 2.3). This iterative process fuels innovation in products and services, often devised by community members and recommended to their organization, thus creating entirely new sources of revenue.

So how can you create a community? Wrong question. Communities already exist. Explore how you can help a community engage and interact. Instead of becoming a purveyor of information, become a facilitator of member-to-member, or customer-to-customer communities. In the process, you must understand varying factors of motivation to visit and join a community. For some, it's to create relationships based on common interests; for others it's a place to openly share their opinions and

Defining "Community"

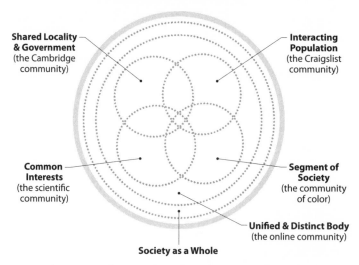

Shared Locality & Government (the Cambridge community)

Interacting Population (the Craigslist community)

Common Interests (the scientific community)

Segment of Society (the community of color)

Unified & Distinct Body (the online community)

Society as a Whole

Figure 2.3—The Iterative Value of a Community at Work

not hold back; yet for others, it's a sounding board or centralized repository of information or opinions they cannot get elsewhere. Jimmy Wales, founder of Wikipedia, describes his community as "one part anarchy, one part aristocracy, one part democracy, and one part monarchy."

What's critical to understand is that the social currency within a community is *value.* Your stature in a community often has a lot less to do with the title on your business card and a great deal more with the value you share openly. As the organization, you must listen and act on feedback, consider it a gift, encourage and be a proactive part of the discussion. Know your audience and serve their agenda, not yours.

One of the most interesting interviews I had relative to the value of a community was with Francis Eberle, the executive director of the National Science Teachers Association (NSTA), an organization that has supported innovation and excellence in science teaching and learning for 64 years. Its 60,000 members are K–12, secondary and higher education faculty, zoos, science centers, preschool groups, researchers, professional developers, trainers, administrators, and corporate members. The total addressable market of K–12 certified teachers is 1.5 million. NSTA considers a community of 430,000 members of the public who opt-in to receive weekly information about NSTA as part of its "family."

NSTA looks for membership trending in the broader community, not necessarily only among dues-paying members. Seven years ago, the board established that NSTA was serving more than just the membership, challenging the traditional membership model. Connected relationships in this community are NSTA's key recruiting engine. For more than 10 years, members have cited colleague referrals as the number one reason they joined. By the way, this opt-in community has paid financial dividends in folds. In 2010, the "digital family" accounted for a substantial $600,000 of purchases. Eberle says, "They came to the website and took a free article and left. We looked if they ever came back to us. And sure enough a certain percentage did and purchased something. So the idea of increasing that digital community and not requiring them to become members has had a positive impact financially."

> **About NSTA**
>
> NSTA employs 110 staff and has an operating budget of $20 million annually. Member offerings include conferences, institutes, and academies. Each year, NSTA publishes 20 books, four journals, and a long list of other materials. Members have access to the NSTA e-portal, which is integrated with the international and urban communities. Advocacy efforts range from federal and state policy making, to helping establish national standards in science, to awards and competitions recognizing excellence in teaching and learning. Its revenue is derived 45 percent from conferences, 20 percent from dues, 20 percent from publications, and 15 percent from grants and other sources.

Uncovering What's Holding You Back

The challenge for many organizations is that the very thing that has made them successful in the past—tight, relatively centralized operational control over a well-defined set of channels and touch points—holds them back in the era of dialogue and social communities. Unfortunately, many associations seldom have had to compete or think of their members as customers. Every part of the association value-chain has reminded me in the past year of how associations are different, face unique circumstances, and cater to a very unique set of constituents who are members, leaders, board members, suppliers, and advocates all in one. Guess what? Social creates that in all of us. Upon closer inspection, even some of the largest industry associations would be characterized as small- to medium-sized businesses. Many are run by professional managers and astute association executives. But if that's the only structure you know, have become seasoned in, and are not proactively learning from the edge of where business really happens, how are you growing personally or professionally as a leader? If you're not a lifelong learner and a student of this evolutionary landscape, how can you ethically expect your members to evolve and remain relevant for their customers?

Many touch points, such as calls to customer service centers, interaction between marketing and member or business development, sponsorship or alliance partnerships, sit in silos with little to no permission to reach into other business functions or operational units. Touch points in associations and many companies alike have been abdicated to specific functions, often disconnected from one another. Yet, a comprehensive strategy across them rarely exists, and if it does, there are no supporting systems to execute, measure, analyze, or improve upon it.

New customer habits also foster new expectations few organizations are prepared for. Some consumers are uncomfortable with click-to-chat, but once they have a great experience with it on a retail site, they look for it in the navigation of your website! Others won't order a product or a service unless they can clearly see feedback and the rating stars displayed prominently. The perception becomes one of, "Well, if eBay and Amazon have customer reviews attached to every product they sell and I can review those before making a purchase, what are you hiding if you don't?" You see, in our current low-trust environment, organizations must heighten their credibility by allowing those who have engaged it in the past to share the good, the bad, and the ugly. That's right, even the ugly! When you allow consumers of your information, products, and services to share their experiences, it highlights that, yes, even as an organization, *you're human!* We all make mistakes; that's not the point. It's what you *choose to do about it after the fact* that separates you from those who simply ignore customer feedback and recommendations or sweep things under the rug like they never happened.

When it comes to connected relationships, you must think beyond marketing, PR, or advertising. Connected relationships aren't about technology, a website, or a place to call your personal billboard. Think of it as an unrelenting mirror of the way your organization touches individual customers and your stakeholders. It's a mirror that will force changes within your culture and your processes, and it is in your interest to make such changes before the connected relationship mirror reveals your organization's flaws publicly.

Think Differently About Social with IMPACT

So, where do we go from here? How do you build a robust social strategy *to think and lead differently*—robust strategy that focuses on *the best possible choices for the best possible outcome?* Let's start with a set of building blocks and conversation starter questions. Sorry, no fill-in-the-blanks or short cuts here. Your final product will take the most difficult kind of work—thinking.

- Start with a strategic approach that places the members at the center of your association operations. A social strategy isn't about you. How can you capture the day-in-the-life of current and prospective members and the value they seek?

- A social strategy should aim to maximize the insight generated through member interactions. If I really focused on member-to-member interactions in a community of like-minded individuals, how could I quantifiably enhance their position? How can I help them be considerably better off with actionable insights?

- It should capitalize on social and mobile information exchanges. People must be able to access you and your content when and where they need to and on the devices of their choice. How can you enable real-time interactions regardless of where they are or how they reach you?

- It needs to synchronize your entire value chain to deliver consistent and predictable outcomes. You don't have to create all the value; you do have to facilitate the collection and dissemination of value from both internal and external resources.

- It must demonstrate short-term value by improving real-time collaboration and visibility for your staff, members, and partners. How can you help people solve problems, overcome obstacles, and think differently about their purposes in the organization?

- It must increase margins by boosting efficiency at every stage of the member life cycle. I'll talk about the member life cycle later, but for now, what are the top two or three areas in your organization where you could boost efficiency? Can you categorize them at the different stages in which your target audience engages you for information, products, or services?

- It drives growth by enhancing, extending, and redefining the value you provide. Go back and review the iterative value-add in the community; numbers don't lie, and intentional growth is driven, not found. If you don't disrupt your value chain, someone else will.

If you conceptually understand the starting blocks, and the conversation starter questions are pushing you to think differently about your value-add, here are three dimensions that will create the greatest movement of your needle in member recruitment/customer acquisition, mindshare and wallet share from each member or customer, and impact in the broader industry/centers of influence where you must create marketing gravity:

- **Member/Customer Profiles.** In the age of connected relationships, you need *deep buyer behavior insights* in real time that you can turn into immediate action. I'll discuss demographics and psychographics information in the next chapter.

- **Member/Customer Value Strategy.** You must rethink how your members define and perceive value and the changes you must make to your capabilities so you can deliver exactly what your members want—profitably! In Chapter 5, I'll cover capabilities.

- **Member/Customer Impact.** You need an approach that allows you to more effectively connect, collaborate, exchange value, and create a differentiated member experience. Membership should certainly have its unique experiences and "privileges."

One of the misconceptions of a social strategy is that it's somehow linear: Go out there and listen to learn, then dialogue what you learned, then support the dialogue that was supposed to come previously, and if you get around to it, innovate. On the contrary, a social strategy is an iterative process that begins with *educating the market.* Compelling and highly unique content provides value, provokes thought, and offers a contrarian perspective. From there, an organization can begin to nurture a trusting relationship with target stakeholders. When you *engage and connect* people with unique interests to one another and facilitate an interaction between them, they learn and grow. If you empower that interaction with an infrastructure and resources—not take over and make it your agenda, but support them—they will become advocates and evangelists. Evangelists will educate other parts of the market on your behalf. Want proof for the power of evangelism? Search "iPod2" and see how many sites listed are Apple's and how many are those that have clearly become evangelists.

The IMPACT model (Figure 2.4) is derived from a careful examination of the membership life cycle and an organization's biggest influence on each critical touch point along the way:

- **Immerse.** Educate the broader market, share value openly, engage, and influence.

- **Member.** Allow them to opt-in to your value-add and pay to join.

- **Participate.** Give them the opportunity to experience the value of the community, where, when, and how they need it.

- **Accredit.** Create definitive value and sustainable differentiation for the members through your affiliation, credibility, exclusivity, brand/legacy value.

- **Community.** Empower them to share the good, the bad, and the ugly.

- **Transform.** Deliver measurable and influential personal and professional growth to every individual your organization touches.

A robust social strategy must cut across the entire organization to be effective, yet focus the right people and sufficient resources of the

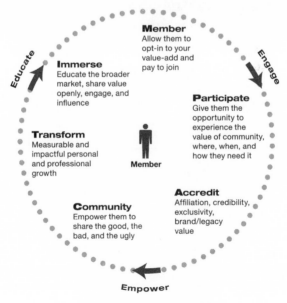

Figure 2.4—IMPACT Model

organization behind it to execute it. Here is what it will take to *lead differently* (discussed individually in subsequent chapters):

- Enhanced Leadership/Board *Mindset.* Broader market reach and current members/customers, review of the microeconomic models, competing to win mindshare.

- Renewed Organizational *Structure.* Distributed accountability, governance councils, cooperative competition, best practitioner board members.

- Elevated Development and Delivery Channels of *Capabilities.* Equally valuable focus on psychographics versus simply demographics, unique buyer-types and behaviors, modularizing the broad base of offerings, "iTunification" of the revenue model.

- Top-Grade Talent. You can't buy intelligence. People must possess creativity, fundamental problem solving, initiative DNA, intrapreneurial agility, pride, and prejudice—not the book—appropriately measured and rewarded.

- Socially Enabled Execution. Keeping your finger on the member pulse, anticipating the unexpected, socially enabled change, smart touches, social currency, and failing forward as an organization.

- Respected and Trusted Monitoring and Analysis. The power and promise of benchmarking those with a digital edge, really leveraging richer data, intense analytics, smart segmentation, and value of immediacy and responsiveness.

The above are not just mantras or clever tag lines. They must become a deeply rooted set of beliefs that you *adopt or adapt* to remain relevant.

## CHAPTER 3

Embrace World-Class Engagement

H AVE YOU EVER been engaged with an organization to the extent you were enthusiastic enough to recommend it to your friends and family? *Really* engaged? How did it make you feel? Did you go back for another experience or to purchase additional products or services? Did you or would you pay a premium for the enhanced engagement? For those who stay at the Ritz-Carlton, shop at Nordstrom, or spend time at Apple's in-store Genius bar, the answers are emphatic: "Oh yes, I went back multiple times, absolutely, amazing, told everyone, the premium was worth every penny!"

World-class organizations unleash their potential for growth by optimizing their most valuable relationships on- and offline. According to Gallup, organizations that optimize engagement outperform competitors by 26 percent in gross margin and 85 percent in sales growth. Customers who are fully engaged represent an average 23 percent premium in terms of share of wallet, profitability, revenue, and relationship growth over the average customer. Actively disengaged customers represent a 13 percent discount for those same measures. In essence, members and customers who are engaged buy more, spend more, return more often, and stay longer.

Ritz-Carlton, Nordstrom, and Apple realize that and proactively work at enhancing each and every engagement. In the process, they have built and rigorously defend the ubiquitous global soft asset of repute and brand. We are probably all clear on what a brand is. How, then, do we interact with it? There's a good chance you will relate to these attributes when you think about your favorite physical or digital brands, destinations, or engagements. A brand:

- *Is familiar*—We immediately recognize and relate to its look or feel and gravitate toward it.

- *Gets attention*—We pay attention to, prioritize, and search for it.

- *Is preferable*—Given the choice, we select it, go out of way to get it, build loyalty toward it.

- *Builds cachet*—Brands provide us comfort and give us status.

- *Exudes quality*—We perceive brands to be of higher quality—made, delivered, and experienced.

- *Is dependable*—We trust products using the brand, expect the same performance over time, and in unfamiliar places or situations, we're reassured by their presence.

- *Is valued*—We willingly pay a premium for the brand, will put up with inconveniences to get it, and forgive their missteps.

- *Is extendable*—We accept and buy new products that fit the brand name.

Of course, we don't feel the same way about every brand; there are varying levels of familiarity or attraction. Some brands we outright reject; economic hardship may force us to move away from preferred brands or re-evaluate our priorities and ability to acquire or experience a brand. Our preference to avoid any association with a brand is based on perceptions or actual experiences. Brands less familiar we tend to dismiss with non-recognition. They are not as visceral as the ones we reject, and the response is simply indifference.

The next stage of familiarity is actually some level of recognition or association. We may have tried the brand once, vaguely recall a neutral experience or key attributes. When we try a brand more than once and have a memorable or otherwise positive experience, we build a preference toward it. We associate these brands with memories of loved ones or other endearing moments, which often trigger *emotional preference.* The ultimate destination on the brand familiarity continuum is an insistence for a particular brand (Figure 3.1). Sociologists tell us that insistence on a brand may be triggered by nostalgia—in other words, a childhood memory or particularly fond association from our past. As adults, we tend to build an insistence for certain brands, predominately because of exceptional experiences.

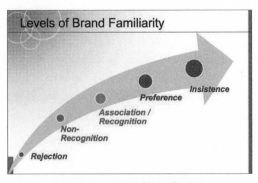

Figure 3.1—Brand Familiarity

That's the desired outcome of a world-class engagement—*exceptional experiences that embed an insistence on a brand in our minds and hearts.*

Another desired outcome of a world-class engagement is trust. With the decline in discretionary time and attention and the accelerated increase of product choices and media clutter, *trust drives transactions.* When we feel authentically engaged and have a vested interest in the improvement of our condition, we develop a comfort, dependence, reliance, and trust in a brand. "I know I can trust this source for credible, reliable, timely information."

Trust is no longer a commodity that is acquired but rather *a benefit that is bestowed,* earned through action, and reinforced by transparency and engagement. Organizations have the opportunity to build an enduring foundation of trust if its leaders commit to a strategy that brings value to both investors and society by addressing the *what* and the *why*. However, given today's low-trust environment, the organization must further explain *how* it makes money, demonstrating a new level of transparency in business practices; for example, revealing ingredients in products or after a sale, listing a service and maintenance process. Finally, it must build relationships across the entire stakeholder universe (the *where*) by engaging audiences across a multitude of media sources—mainstream, new, social, and owned—and joining the conversation by adding value and learning from the critics.

In the wake of the financial market meltdown at the end of 2008, the onslaught of corporate crises in 2010 certainly didn't help our society's perceived state of trust. From the Gulf oil spill to product recalls, the *2011 Edelman Trust Barometer* highlighted a profound shift in the expectation of companies to operate with increased transparency and in a manner that delivers profit while improving society. This research also found unprecedented skepticism—a need to hear, see, or watch news as many as 10 times before achieving belief—plus an increased reliance on those with credentials and expertise.

Here are Edelman's key findings about earning trust (Figure 3.2):

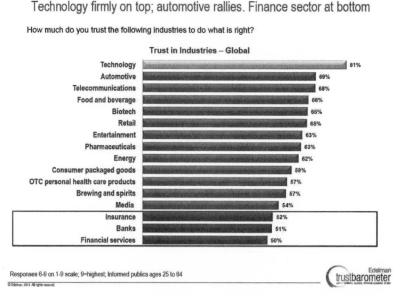

Figure 3.2—Sample 2011 Edelman Trust Barometer in Industries

- Corporate reputation is derived from high-quality products and services consistently delivered by a company that I can trust, one that demonstrates transparent business practices and treats its employees well.

- A "desire for profit and purpose, a stakeholder approach to shared value." According to Edelman, "Fifty percent of the respondents agreed with Milton Friedman's contention that the social responsibility of business is to generate profit." When further probed whether companies could sacrifice shareholder value with efforts that benefits society, 80 percent in developed to developing economies agreed.

- Given the uncertainty in the economy and plethora of sources of information, respondents said that they believe spokespeople with proven expertise in the following order: academics, technical experts from a company, financial analysts, and chief executive officers; in a crisis, the number one trusted source is the CEO as the organization's primary steward.

- As discussed in the social search section of chapter one, more people initially go to search engines than online sources for information about a company. The brands most noted are the familiar mainstream media pillars such as the *Financial Times* and *The Wall Street Journal*.

- If an organization is generally distrusted at the onset of a crisis, it will take only one or two negative stories for an individual to believe negative news about that organization. Conversely, organizations that are generally accepted as trustworthy often need only one or two positive stories to achieve believability. Edelman refers to trust as a "protective agent, a facilitator of action," pointing to the fact that consumers have an increased desire to buy products; recommend products, services, or information; and buy shares in a trusted organization.

Getting Beyond Serving *Us Versus Them*

One of the perplexing challenges I uncovered in my interviews with association executives was a demarcation of members and nonmembers. I certainly understand the financial attributes of "dues-paying, card-carrying members." What I didn't understand was that many admitted to serving only a sliver of their total addressable market yet didn't particularly deem it relevant to proactively cast a wider net. My perception is that with limited staff and resources, the association leadership or the board may think that they would sacrifice quality and frequency of value-add to their members if they attempted to cater similar value to non-paying customers.

I also found advocacy to be a consistent part of the value-add most association executives believe is a key differentiator in their membership

IMPACT @ Work:
Student and Large Employer Engagement at AOTA

Fred Somers, the executive director, and Chris Bluhm, the chief operating officer of the American Occupational Therapy Association (AOTA) are a surprising exception to the recent decline in membership numbers of many organizations. Their members are occupational therapists, assistants, and students. Where other associations have struggled to rebound from the economic turmoil that began in 2008, membership at AOTA is in its seventh consecutive year of growth. The key factor behind their robust recruitment and retention efforts is viewing outreach as a core business function. "We really felt that recruiting and retention—in essence, engagement—needed strategy, focus, and dedicated resources, and we began to implement a number of tactics," Bluhm says.

Meet the American Occupational Therapy Association (AOTA)

AOTA is a society of 43,000 with an annual budget of $18 million and staff of 65 to 70 headquartered in Bethesda, MD. AOTA was founded in 1917. Somers has been with it in different capacities for 25 years. Professional members work in a variety of health and educational settings; student members are enrolled in one of AOTA's 350-plus programs nationwide.

Re-engaging the educational community was one of AOTA's biggest marketing wins. Its educator members are influencing young people entering the profession, promoting the importance and value of affiliation with a professional association throughout an individual's career. Once student numbers were up, that led to a focus on converting those students to professional members when they entered the workforce. According to Bluhm, "Keeping them is a big challenge. We can convert them, but unless

continues on next page

value formula. Yet, when I inquired on numerous occasions, "Aren't you still doing that advocacy work on Capitol Hill for the industry, whether or not these companies are members?" they simply responded, "Yes."

Certainly some aspects of this mentality are also prevalent in the corporate arena: Customers, particularly those with service contracts or service level agreements (SLAs), are prioritized accordingly with support resources. But if you look at how most companies prospect for net new business (discounting natural or voluntary attrition), they're constantly

continued from previous page
we're delivering the value they need in those first few years, they drop out at an accelerated rate." AOTA is working hard to improve its value proposition across all areas of activity, and to more actively highlight its public awareness and advocacy work on Capitol Hill and in state legislatures because those efforts resonate with practitioners.

Another marketing win-win for AOTA has been a national partnership program with the key gatekeepers of occupational therapists—large employers. "Students enter the workforce and if their first boss isn't a member, that's a difficult thing. We'd like to engage supervisors and first-line management in the value proposition and that early engagement process," says Somers. The association partners with an employer to provide professional development and recruitment and, in return, has access to employees to promote membership in AOTA. The program today accounts for 10 percent of the professional member base and growth of emerging practice areas. They've also leveraged the relationship to co-develop professional development products to offer the rest of the membership.

The association is ambitiously testing new notions to increase membership. Testing notions has, in fact, become a hallmark of how they market membership these days: offering discounts, coupons, or free continuing education credits for joining or renewing on time and gathering statistical data to compare results. One highly successful campaign involved mailing 250,000 solicitations per year, with messages relevant to current issues in the profession. According to Bluhm, "Messaging about our advocacy worked very well when healthcare reform was on the six o'clock news every evening. We are always trying to do something new and build on our past success." Being consistent in continually testing new notions has proven to be a winning strategy for the AOTA team.

competing for market share, casting a wider net into the target market. They will invest in proof-of-concepts (POCs) to validate claims, and bring in technical or subject-matter experts from around the country, if not the globe, to attract clients. Meanwhile, associations that have not had to think of members as customers or, in many instances, compete head on with other associations for the same members struggle to see the need for aggressive, consistent, new industry outreach campaigns.

We Evaluate Logically and Buy Emotionally

How do world-class organizations create small wins to gain positive movement in today's competitive and turbulent global marketplace? Whether they are associations like AOTA, corporations, or even academic institutions, high-performance organizations recognize the *emotional drivers* of human nature and leverage them to drive performance, one member, customer, employee, or stakeholder at a time. Instead of focusing on *lagging indicators* such as profit, growth, stock price, or earnings per share—"rearview mirror" metrics of past sales and marketing success— the best organizations concentrate on measuring and managing leading indicators of organic growth, often behavioral metrics. By individualizing their approach, they maximize their market outreach potential and profitability. World-class organizations prioritize their engagements by focusing on the following:

- *Emotional Insistence.* Prospective and current members or customers are not strictly logical; your most profitable members, sponsors, and customers all have strong emotional bonds with your organization. Those bonds must be recognized and strengthened *consistently*.

- *Beyond Satisfaction to Member Delight.* Focusing on creating highly satisfied members and customers is a one-way ticket to mediocrity and poor business results. Simply satisfying customers is not enough. (See sidebar for the Customer Delight Edge.)

- **Effective Touch Points.** The IMPACT model described in the last chapter is a process based on touch points. Every time members or customers interact with your organization, they either become a little more or a little less engaged, but they never stay the same, so you must make every interaction memorable and influential.

- **Culture of Yes.** We have become a culture of policies and procedures. Are they for your benefit or the members? Evolve your culture to one of "of course," "will do," and "taken care of." "Yes" maybe more difficult to say, but it's dramatically more effective and engaging.

- **Local Flavor.** Enduring customer *relationships* cannot be centralized like procurement; they must be engaged locally at the edge of the business where daily interactions happen. Engagement is everyone's responsibility; train and empower your employees to add their individual flavor to an already high set of standards.

The Customer Delight Edge

Associations may conduct annual surveys, asking overall satisfaction questions. Many organizations tout their customer satisfaction metrics, but in today's hypercompetitive world, satisfaction is table stakes. Engagement requires delighting members and customers alike at every possible touch point. Here are five small tips from organizations that create a competitive edge by delighting their members and customers *consistently:*

1. **Unique Free**—When possible, throw in something, ideally unexpected, and create a clear demarcation to elevate yourself from the market noise. Think of Southwest Airlines' not charging change fees and "bags fly free."

2. **One for the Road**—Surprise customers with an experience for the road. Chick-fil-A hands out little cow flashlights for your car from their unmistakable "Eat More Chicken" campaigns.

3. **First and Last**—You have two chances to make an impression: when customers first encounter you, and when they depart. Make the most of both. Ritz-Carlton

doesn't ask, "Checking-in?" when you arrive. Instead they say, "Welcome," with a genuine smile and refreshingly cold bottled water!

4. **Follow Through**—Follow up is a transaction that will satisfy; follow through is a process that consistently delights. A local Italian restaurant hands out recipes, offers cooking classes at a nearby high-end kitchen appliance store, and auctions off their chefs for charity to come to your home and cook for your next dinner party.

5. **Convene Wow**—Think of the engagement or the experience from the customer's point of view. In response to the frustration we all feel when trying to free a product from nearly impenetrable packaging, Amazon created "wrap rage," packaging that is hassle-free and good for the environment.

If you've noticed, many of the customer-delight, cutting-edge strategies don't have to be expensive or resource intensive; they do have to be well thought out and intentional to achieve their desired outcome of truly delighting the recipient.

The Ripple Effect of Buyer Behavior

So how do you transition from engaging people to creating online buyers of information, products, and services? How do you emotionally engage and build a trusting relationship with individuals you can't see, don't physically touch, or interact with in person? You have to think differently about engagement and buyer touch points. Just as the web changed some of your practices, the integration of social into your marketplace will also shift your organization's design. You have to start thinking like a social business, with more effective relationships, operational efficiencies, and workers as the arrowheads and not the feathers in your go-to-market arrow.

Let's start with the individual buyers. We know they're getting smarter and their networks are getting smarter. They're learning from every interaction and association to deliver recommendations and take the next action. So, now we have a globe of highly networked individuals who in real time interact, form relationships, make decisions, buy products and services, and most importantly, get work done. By the way, employees are demanding social tools at work, actively sidestepping traditional and—let's be honest—outdated hierarchies and IT processes to use them. The local megabank I mentioned earlier that claims to be the "relationship bank" yet doesn't know anything about me, despite my having been a customer for 10 years, has developed a Facebook payment application and is spending $60 million to advertise it in multiple channels, yet they block Facebook access from their own offices.

Just as the web matured, so too will social grow from a digital novelty to a platform for business; from social commerce to location-based services, interest, and facilitated networks, crowd-sourced content, live casting, and social bookmarks. For an organization to transform into a social business, it must *embrace networks of online buyers to create business value.* These buyers are looking for you to connect them to expertise. They're looking for engagement, an enabler to identify and connect with, and increased value from interacting with new sources of innovation, fostering creativity, and creating new business opportunities. They have to experience trust to be willing to openly share information. Your organization has to provide these social networks with the collaboration, gaming, and analytical tools for members to engage each other and creatively solve business challenges.

Members are lured by the promise of daily, low-cost interactivity. If you can demonstrate effective member-to-member interactions, the organization can encourage participation in projects and idea sharing, thus deepening its knowledge base. It's not a system, by the way; it's a process. Your organization becomes more valuable because it is strengthening bonds with key parts of the value chain in the industry, improving communication with suppliers and outside partners, creating marketing gravity/pull for new parties in the industry, and giving credibility to the value of membership.

Understanding, segmenting, and catering to unique buyer behaviors translates into measurable business gains, including greater ability to share ideas, improved access to knowledge experts, and reduced cost of communication, travel, and operations. The most engaged organizations leverage the network to accelerate their time to market with products and services, which dramatically improves staff satisfaction and internal engagements as well.

Beyond creating traffic and awareness to your social presence, you have to give customers compelling reasons to come back, stay, and become engaged and involved. You also have to perform. If they can't find what they're looking for, in content and community, they're gone, and it will be considerably more challenging to get them back. This is where social analytics, discussed in more detail in Chapter 8, come in handy.

Demographics Versus Psychographics

So who are your customers, what are they looking for online, and how can you get to know them? The preliminary answers will come from your knowledge of the industry, the marketplaces you serve, and profiles of members or customers you've engaged in the past. Most industries and their member organizations have become fairly astute at narrowing their target market into neatly outlined demographic buckets such as married, male, middle class, age 35–44, with a college degree, who happens to work in the insurance industry.

Demographic profiling is essentially an exercise in making generalizations about groups of people. As with all such generalizations, many individuals within these groups will not conform to the profile. Demographic information is aggregate and probabilistic information about groups, not about specific individuals. These broad-brush generalizations offer such limited insight that their practical usefulness is debatable.

Much more importantly, to a large extent many individuals in the exact same demographic categories *tend to behave very differently online.* The keywords or taxonomies they choose when searching, what motivates them, and the general patterns they pursue are all critical and highly influential elements in how to engage them, which is not as cohorts, but as unique buying patterns.

Equally challenging is the fact that control of the engagement or the brand no longer completely resides in the hands of the organization or the brand itself. The network begins and fuels conversations about their challenges, options others have pursued, and the results, or lack thereof. So, what are the guideposts and markers to help organizations join the conversation and begin to engage proactively? As members or customers move through the buying process, certain constituencies influence their thinking, perspective, and call to action. Sometimes that call to action is a simple interaction, perhaps with other user-generated content such as, "Here is a link to learn more." In other scenarios, the currency of considerably more value is trust, as mentioned earlier. How do buyers build brand affiliation and what do they gravitate toward within various social landscapes? Here are three unique sources of influence as a buyer goes through highly connected stages of awareness, consideration, and action:

1. **Industry/Subject-Matter Influencers.** In every industry there is a set of highly influential bloggers with a strong Twitter following who rarely know their audiences personally. They comment on the state of the industry, key announcements, or trends they're particularly interested in. They hone in on key industry players, partnerships, or competitive threats. Think of these individuals as the "industry analysts" empowered by social.

2. **Social Interactions.** Every day people are active on a multitude of social sites and are often focused on reviews and opinions. They update their own status and comment on the blogs and forums managed by others. In some cases, they know personally the people they interact with digitally.

3. **Known Peers.** These individuals are extremely close to both the consumers and their buying or decision-making processes. Think of family members or close personal friends who recommend a brand or send you an email with a coupon. They directly influence the purchasing decision, predominately based on their close, personal relationships.

When it comes to engaging your target audience online, of greater value than age or gender are what terms they use to narrow their search; the patterns or processes they follow to become aware of information, products, or services; how they evaluate a spectrum of options in their decision-making process; and what influences them to take action. These digital psychographic variables are attributes relative to a member or customer's personality, values, attitudes, interests, or lifestyle. In engagement strategies, the psychographic variables outlined above create a more holistic view of an individual than simply their demographic variables such as age and gender.

Meet Your New Buyer Types

A good starting point in developing a psychographic profile of your target audience is a taxonomy cloud (Figure 3.3). This collection of interrelated terms helps members find and evaluate information that is relevant or of particular interest and value to them. Because of the vast amount of information available via search engines and the natural language terms that most people use to search their individual needs, taxonomy clouds represent a clear and concise path to available options.

Figure 3.3—Sample Taxonomy Cloud

Taxonomy is a framework to:

- Classify and label,
- Identify attributes or facets about information, and
- Represent human understanding of and interaction with information within a logical system.

According to the UXNet—The User Experience Network—a user experience, what your members and customers really want from you, and the vast amount of information within your organization, is the "quality of experience one has when interacting with a specific design." When you combine the collection of search terms individuals use to identify the manner in which *they want to be engaged* with a buying process, you begin to understand their motivation.

A buying process can be simple, with few steps, such as awareness, consideration, and action, or more complex, with distinct phases and barriers. One of the better ones in the market is from Social Gastronomy, LLC (Figure 3.4), in which they have defined the following unique phases and attributes in each stage:

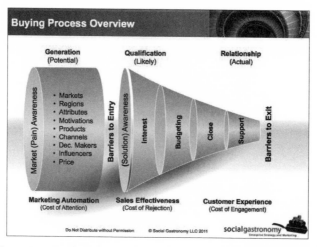

Figure 3.4—Buying Process Overview from Social Gastronomy, LLC

- Generation (Potential)—Awareness versus Motivation
- Qualification (Likely)—Market versus Customer
- Relationship (Actual)—Customer versus Market

When a member or a customer's motivation is integrated with behavioral variables (such as usage rate or loyalty) and variables such as industry, seniority, and functional area unique digital buyer types emerge. Sample buyer types include:

- *Price/Discount/Value Buyer*—seeks to maximize value for the investment of time, effort, and resources; motivated by perceptions of bargains and uses discount, free, low- and no-cost taxonomy; general buying process is online value search followed by evaluations from multiple sites offering similar value; uncovers most favorable bargains in comparative sites.

- *Expert/Educated Buyer*—seeks to be informed and make a deliberate next step in a logical process; motivated by facts and value; uses fact-finding taxonomy; general buying process is online product search followed by a pain search (where specific search language is used to address a challenge) in blogs and forums; uncovers most credible information from forum readership.

- *Cautious/FUD (Fear, Uncertainty, Doubt) Buyer*—seeks to protect and preserve current position or mitigate against future risks; motivated by fear and anxiety and uses specific "precaution," "opinion-seeking," and "product-issue-specific" taxonomy; general buying process begins with online review search and quickly gravitates toward like-minded forums; empathizes and contributes to similar situations on blogs and product page discussions.

- *Caring/Gift Buyer*—seeks to acquire for others and to openly share "gems" or unique finds; motivated by unexpected surprise in finding and providing to others; uses complimentary taxonomy; general buying process is triggered by an event or an in-bound promotion via social commerce, comparative evaluations, and discussions of emotional gratification; contributes to blogs and forums specific to unexpected positive emotions.

- *Instant/Impulse Buyer*—seeks to satisfy an immediate want or a yearning to accomplish a specific task; motivated by need for instant gratification or distractions and uses specific "emotional" and "feeling" taxonomy; general buying process is scattered, unfocused, and reactive to well crafted promotional messages; contributes to blogs and forums specific to decision fatigue, post-purchase remorse, or disconnect between the offering and the experience.

- *Past Buyer (like products)*—seeks to repurchase, very comfortable with cross-sell and up-sell offerings; motivated by continued positive experiences and uses specific "expansion" and "evangelizing" taxonomy; general buying process begins at manufacturer's forums, followed by product forums; finds validation and contributes to blogs and product page discussions.

- *Past Buyer (unhappy)*—seeks to remedy disconnect between perceived and actual value received; motivated by similar experiences of others and uses specific "before and after" taxonomy; general buying process begins at point of perception or initial information source and consistently looks to compare specific mentions of before and after the action or decision point; contributes to blogs and forums alongside other disgruntled or disappointed buyers and may offer a remedy to move forward.

- *Past Problem Buyer (could have used previously)*—seeks to learn from repeat challenge or discussions of similar experiences in the past; motivated by relevance or empathy for others with similar challenges and discussions of option considerations and uses specific "could/should have" references with context to past events; general buying process begins in renewed search for a previous challenge and uncovers new solutions, engages others for compare to original action; contributes to blogs and forums as well as status updates with renewed commitment to an enhanced solution.

- *Unaware Buyer*—seeks realization or actualization and expresses childlike wonder; motivated by uncovering solutions for the first time and accelerating initial learning curve among peers; uses "first time" or "attempted" taxonomy to uncover others with similar dilemmas; general buying process is rudimentary, typically with vast social networks as launching pad to more targeted product information sites; feels empowered by newly acquired knowledge and contributes in sharing videos or photos of its application or implementation with others to expand the awareness influence.

Evolving to a Social Organization

Much of what you've read so far will be extremely difficult to implement if you can't begin to help your organization evolve to think and act more like a social business. As I'll discuss in Chapter 4 on building an outside-in organization, for social to deliver on its power and promise—networks of people to create business value—the conversations, interactions, and value received have to move across the entire organization. Social isn't just a marketing function or a membership-recruiting engine. Social isn't about any one department, function, business unit, or geographic location "owning" an individual. The evolution of your team and ideally your organization will come from the mindset shift of valuing engagements as a series of discrete interactions.

Social organizations shift their lens to really understand what members and customers do: participate in *a set of highly related and relevant interactions that when combined, make up their unique engagements.* This perspective should stimulate much needed dialogue among senior leadership and the board in five distinct areas:

1. **Make Social the Entire Organization's Priority.** Think differently about social as an enabler of your next exponential stage of growth and viability. Remove unnecessary boundaries within the structure and among sources of expertise inside the organization and in the marketplace. Unfortunately, in many circles, "social" is deemed to be beneath the senior leadership's or the board's time or attention.

Nothing could be farther from the tectonic shift that's occurring in your marketplace right now.

2. **Evolve Your Capabilities.** If the touch points of the IMPACT model are to move individual members or customers along a value-based relationship continuum, your capabilities must evolve. Not just for the members or customers you're engaging today but in anticipation of their requirements in the 1 to Everything framework presented in the previous chapter.

3. **Expand Your Definition of Resources and Staff.** Many small to medium-sized organizations become concerned about the bandwidth or talent component. "We just don't have the staff to do more social," was an all too familiar comment in my interviews. First, you have to get from *doing* social to *being* social. Second, we live and work in a free agent nation; capable talent abounds. What you can't afford to do is sit on the sidelines and wait for your competitors or your members/customers to outpace you! Even small organizations can level the playing field by leveraging highly specialized contract labor readily available in the marketplace today via global social engagement sites such as eLance and oDesk.

4. **Make social engagements about *consistent* execution.** Listening, monitoring, and learning while you balance these investments with performance, execution, and results. Agility is extremely important. Your organization must be faster and more mobile, turning time and location from past constraints into advantages. Business can occur when and where it has the ability to deliver the greatest value, allowing the organization to adapt to new market dynamics.

5. **Move with Purpose and Empirical Evidence.** The evolution to a social organization is fueled by the ability to gain real-time insights to make quicker and better decisions, to push valuable and actionable insights to the network quickly, so they can act on it. Appropriate and proactive monitoring and analysis helps the network discover expertise, develop social interactions, and capitalize on valuable relationships.

In the next several chapters, I'll take a closer look at each of these five conversations. The transparency with which you embrace the leadership models—in mindset, roadmap, and toolset to support capturing knowledge and insights from many sources—will allow the organization to quickly sense member or customer moods, staff sentiments, or process optimization efficiencies. It may not be comfortable, but the impact will create a legacy of forward-looking social leadership.

Remember to scan the QR code below to capture practical and pragmatic next steps as well as to engage other readers on the topics discussed here in Chapter 3.

## CHAPTER 4

Build a Different Kind of Organization

ANY AUTOCRATIC ORGANIZATION that ignores constituents tends to ignite revolt among the disenfranchised. I believe protests in the next decade will continue to be less about guns or a flurry of terror and more about tweets, texts, and videos perpetuated by mobile and social. If a Google engineer can create an anti-Mubarak Facebook page and mobilize an army of social media and mobile users into a major protest to topple decades of oppression, what leadership strategies can associations and companies learn about the power and promise of listening, learning, and engaging constituents *proactively?*

"If social [media] can take down the government of Egypt, it can take down your organization," says Doug Chia, assistant general counsel and corporate secretary of Johnson & Johnson, in a recent interview with

Corporate Secretary. So, who should own social? Social isn't a function to abdicate to a 20-something staffer to increase Twitter followers or Facebook "likes." If senior leaders of visionary organizations truly seek not only to develop a strategic direction with social, but also to dramatically affect their organizations and industries, they must examine their structure and governance models, because the immediacy and ungoverned nature of social is in direct conflict with the hierarchical and controlled business structure of many institutions. Culture and community, the cornerstones of social, thrive and perform when trusted and tracked, more so than when commanded and controlled.

Some social media experts have described organizational structures as "distributed, centralized, or coordinated." Frankly, labels such as these depersonalize and create categorical responses that are inevitably inaccurate. You can't lump an entire generation's unique preferences, buying patterns, or specific nuances into a bucket and refer to them as specific to only that generation, such as "Gen-Xer attributes." A distributed structure where social strategy is grown organically from within a department without guidance or institutional support will be challenged to sustain growth and evolve in viability. Its lack of coordination with the rest of the organization, members, strategic partners, or external knowledge assets will cause it to miss strategic insights that fuel the organization into what it could become. A centralized structure, guided by a marketing department where a single group controls the message, allows for very little flexibility across functions. It forces the controlling department to try to understand and keep up with a broad base of constituents. Furthermore, the development of new strategies for other functions screeches to a halt in the bureaucratic approval processes. A coordinated model that hands down rules to the department or functional level for a specific message to a finite audience is often glaringly absent of collaborative culture and may require years to establish.

Does Your Board Have What It Takes?

In my experience in working with corporate and nonprofit organization boards, I'm constantly evaluating key attributes of their input as well as desired output. Consider the parallels of boards in their focus and priorities, structure, role of the staff, interaction with the organization's senior leadership, demeanor, how key individuals are selected for committees or special projects, their governance style, and performance metrics. Let's compare key attributes of two distinct types of boards I've worked with in the past decade. (See Figure 4.1.)

Attribute	Board A	Board B
Focus & Priority	Endless operational reports	Finding another way
Structure	Countless committees	Limited size & scope
Staff	Serves the board	Serves the members/customers
Senior Leadership	Avoids conflicts & fears retribution	Insists on healthy & productive debates
Possible Solutions	Bring in a generic strategy consultant, distribute articles, "meet & talk"	CEO fixes the problem
Landscape	Politics as usual	Politics deemed unproductive
Stature Accelerators	Give a lot of money, bring industry "celebrity power," or has been around for 100 years	Selected based on their ability to create highest impact while working collaboratively with others
Purpose	Something to pad people's resumes	Provide industry guidance and professional expertise
Demeanor	Constantly out of line, doesn't listen, disruptive	Engaging and influential with a consistent vested interest
Selected for Projects	See Stature Accelerators	Based on their understanding of strategy and operations
Governance Style	Micromanagement	Empowerment
CEO	Goes along to get along	Stands up and fights
CEO's Legacy	Street corner	Industry cornerstone
Growing Edge	None	Stay within the bounds of respective roles
Performance Metrics	None	Significant membership/market growth, increased conference attendees; strong financial fundamentals; numerous thought leadership projects
Overall Feeling	Frustration	Pride
Relationships	None	Good colleagues; many are good friends

Figure 4.1—Comparative Attributes of Two Sample Boards

Questions to think about:

- Which board would you like to work with?
- Which board do you believe is productive, efficient, effective, and consistently deemed successful?
- Which board do you believe most senior executives are interested in joining?
- Which board do you have?

- What's your proactive approach to raise the bar for both your board and the senior leadership's relationship with your board?

In my consulting engagements with boards looking to fuel profitable growth, I've found considerable gaps between best-practice goals and processes they would argue are in place. Particularly when it comes to guided strategy, oversight of risk management, structuring executive compensation, and proactively driving bench development and succession planning, there seems to be a consistent disconnect between market definition and acceptance of stewardship versus what's really happening.

Given the caliber of qualified board members in many organizations, best practices simply aren't good enough. A symbiotic relationship between the CEO and the board must exist—one that is characterized by an entrepreneurial mindset, shares a clearly understood realm of responsibilities, and has the right metrics to measure and objectively demonstrate the growth of the organization. In *The Will to Govern Well: Knowledge, Trust, and Nimbleness* (ASAE, 2002; second edition published in 2010), authors Glenn Tecker, Jean Frankel and Paul Meyer argue for the "increased unpredictability, instability, and uncertainty about the future," and the "urgent need for associations to create a unique and sustainable reputation for value among members, customers, and stakeholders."

A reputation for value couldn't be more applicable to key metrics in membership growth, revenue models, and long-term sustainability—all facets of an organization dramatically affected by social. Beyond the generally accepted unique characteristics of associations and the contributions they make to society globally, social will continue to force a reinvention in governance. The shift in the balance of power to members and customers, the aggregate intellectual capital of the membership, the collaborative power of a community to make decisions with a common purpose as well as their credibility as voluntary institutions are fundamental drivers of why social strategy must become fuel for that reinvention.

Experts and association leaders in the past have politely advocated for evolution, which is often synonymous for doings things better (incrementalism). Today, the argument can be made that governance must be reinvented, a more candid term for doing things differently (true innovation). If a population of owners, customers, and volunteers (its workforce) is benefiting from the greater ability to share ideas, improved access to knowledge experts across the industry, and reduced costs of communication and collaboration through social media, a disconnected board will quickly become a dysfunctional one in role and process. By reinventing the governance structure to integrate real-time insights from connected relationships at the edge of where the organization delivers its biggest impact for its customers and members, the organization *thinks and acts in real time*. It begins to function with fewer bureaucratic hierarchies, empowering the senior leadership down to the front-line staff to execute the agreed-upon strategy with an exponentially higher level of agility. A reinvented governance structure enables the social organization to constantly scan the environment for faint signals and trends and to stay ahead of what's happening now, instead of constantly wondering what happened and having to manage crises after they hit the market.

Making Decisions Differently

Continued economic turbulence is highlighting the need in many organizations for strong medicine at both the senior leadership and board levels. Changing the organization and board structure may be an effective way of unlocking better performance. But any such reorganization will be a risky investment of time, energy, and resources and often does little to dramatically enhance the organization if the underlying culture isn't changed in the process. In a December 2010 *Associations Now* article, "Come In, We're Open," the American Dental Education Association (ADEA) is highlighted for eliminating individual membership dues in 2006. Since then, not only have member numbers increased, so have engagement levels, advocacy, meeting attendance, and paid institutional members. ADEA made a wide-open membership model work—a cultural reinvention to do things differently.

An effective social reinvention of the board and senior leadership structure requires a culture characterized by transparency, open sharing of valuable information across the organization, real innovation, and improved decision making. These changes help to create deeper relationships with employees, customers, and business partners, as people inside and outside the organization are allowed to document and share their knowledge and ideas. As others recognize, refine, and promote the value of those ideas and associated content, the social reinvention reaps great benefits.

Imagine a board that is able to:

- Leverage more expertise and a greater diversity of skills and experience;
- Use real time current knowledge instead of more formalized but less current knowledge; and

- Improve their situational awareness and use of social intelligence in decision making.

The most effective reinventions don't just reshuffle the boxes and lines on committee assignments. Instead, they focus on improving the organization's ability to handle its most important decisions. They enable people at all levels to make better, faster decisions while increasing the return on the impact of some or portions of effectively executed decisions. *An organization's performance is the sum of the decisions it makes and executes.* As such, a reinvention won't make much of a difference unless it prioritizes the critical decisions for the organization, specifies who is responsible for crafting the strategic roadmap, and demonstrates how the new structure will help people make and execute decisions better. Reinvention will shift the focus of the board and the senior leadership from documents and project plans to the source of energy, creativity, and decision making that moves the organization forward: people. A people-centric approach relies on:

1. **Networks**—Rich, online profiles of globally integrated networks of members or customers, employees or staff, and partners or sponsors. These trusted experts enable collaboration and agility and allow exploration of expertise and publications to get beyond the boardroom to a network of colleagues to quickly initiate decision-making action or fulfill a real-time business need.

2. **Social and real-time collaboration**—Decision making and problem solving are dramatically accelerated and improved when you connect remote teams of people and allow them to discover relevant expertise.

3. **Mobility**—A social strategy leverages the speed and relevancy of information exchange as an essential enabler of the organization's decision-making process. Individuals can use the device best suited to their needs with real-time, relevant information.

4. **Integration**—Bringing social collaboration capabilities into the processes people use to do their jobs, without overwhelming them, accelerates information sharing within the context of the broader strategy and execution focus.

Social effectiveness also dictates a cultural shift in patterns of behaviors. Beyond expertise or a plan, the board and senior leadership's willingness to experiment, learn, and intuitively shift gears on the fly is a critical behavior in the reinvention process. Many advocates of change begin with exhortations and slogans about the new behaviors needed to think and execute differently, but what they soon discover is that they cannot force or easily persuade people to change their minds. What social does, through connected and trust-centric relationships, is demonstrate how habits can change while maintaining individual views and values.

Social also has the potential to teach incredibly valuable lessons to leaders and board members. Where a leader assumes to know a great deal about an organization's receptivity or the cumulative power of inertia and attitudes, social uncovers whether it is a cultural voice or an individual resistance. Instead of trying to defeat the dissent outright, leaders greatly benefit from the opportunities to listen, learn, and engage proactively. By immersing themselves into the social fabric of their members, customers, staff, or partners, they can develop valuable connected relationships while conducting listening sessions. Many board members or senior leaders know their organizations well, yet that sense of familiarity with their culture can be as much of an obstacle as it is to an outsider. Too much or too little knowledge can lead to inaccurate assumptions about why people do what they do on- or off-line.

Social allows board members and the senior leadership team to really examine and explore the evolutionary culture of their organization, as if seeing it for the first time, ensuring that they're not blindsided at the outset of the reinvention process. Deep, vested interviews, roundtables, and problem-solving group discussions can reveal the existing culture and the specific issues or themes that need to be prioritized.

For many board members or senior leaders, social media represents a formidable information and education barrier. Ask your current board or senior leadership team how much time they spend educating themselves on the business impact of social media and which aspects would most dramatically affect the organization's performance. Many highly competent and capable leaders feel ill equipped to live up to expectations of members, customers, staff, and partners, largely because of inadequate understanding of the business impact of social media.

Three key elements discussed in *The Will to Govern Well*—knowledge, trust, and nimbleness—lend themselves perfectly to reinventing the board's and the senior leadership's attitude toward social as a strategic priority. As mentioned earlier, the ability to make decisions based on collective knowledge rather than opinion, the need to create a culture of trust for staff and volunteers based on a succinct definition of success, and the agility needed to respond effectively to an increasingly complex marketplace represented by the association will be tested and reinforced by social influences.

Social *Is* the Engine for Growth

As outlined in the introduction of the IMPACT Model—Immersion, Membership, Participation, Accreditation, Community, and Transformation—a more social and engaged community sees value in participation. When that participation delivers performance, execution, and results, people are more willing to opt-in for additional products and services. Social drives both personal and professional growth for individuals, teams, and the organization at large. Bain & Company has analyzed executive attitudes and behaviors through a wide range of economic cycles for more than two decades. In its *Management Tools & Trends 2011* research, it compares executive concerns about the long-term effects of the downturn in 2009 and how "seven out of 10 worried about the ability to meet earning targets and growing numbers turned to cost-cutting tools such as downsizing and outsourcing to cope with slowing sales," to a very different picture in 2011. *No organization can cut its way to growth!* In 2011 and beyond, most executives overwhelmingly agree that revenue growth is their organization's number one priority over the next three to five years.

Renewed confidence encourages prudent risk taking. Growth over cost cutting requires innovation that really understands the need to engage in authentic relationships with members and customers as well as employees. Successful growth depends on engaged and productive staff who, in turn, create engaged members and customers. Other stakeholders benefit from the process as a natural byproduct. The same Bain & Company research highlights three tools favored by executives in fueling growth: open innovation, scenario and contingency planning, and price optimization. Open innovation dramatically expands an organization's horizons on sources of competitive and distinct products and services. Scenario and contingency planning can often answer "what if" questions as a strong predictor of future organizational requirements and risk mitigation strategies. Price optimization balances the costs of producing a product or service—both now and in the future—with the perceived value and supporting structure of a price range for that product or service. Social is the enabler of all three: from online forums and discussion groups, to early insights into key market trends, to real-time analysis of buying behaviors and influencer discussions about the price/value ratio.

As boards and senior leaders see the influence of social, often from relevant peer groups, they feel pressured to stress test its promise. Although often very tactical and fostered at the staff level, communities like Facebook fan pages or micro-blogging sites, such as Twitter and Yammer, are built in an attempt to strengthen the connectivity and superficial relationships between members, staff, and sponsors on the association side or customers, employees, and partners on the corporate side. Much uncertainty exists about how to measure the "effectiveness of tools," while the broader and more strategic effects are ignored altogether. Pondering whether social media is a passing fad or a valued engine to fuel growth, many organizations are taking the path of least resistance and merely dipping their proverbial toes in the water. As I heard in many conversations with organizational leaders, the approach is to begin with minimal investment, look at the results (often equally minimal), and up the ante from there.

Two shortsighted pitfalls with this strategy:

1. *Caution in social often leads to a fast-follower strategy.* Attempting to fully understand how a tool will work on a very limited basis before fully investing in it, although logical and understandable in many other aspects of board or organizational governance, is myopic when it comes to social media. If social influence cuts across the entire organization and touches every aspect of how your members or customers, employees, and partners engage the organization, this is not the place for a fast-follower strategy. (See side box *Social Market Leadership: What's Your Next Move?)* Limiting the scope of social involvement, abdicating it to the staff, and consistently referring to it as a communication tool is akin to driving a high-performance sports car only in first gear because you don't understand how the transmission and engine work in concert. Social is the torque or speed, gradient or slope, and fuel efficiency or profitability of an organization's growth engine! If we take just the torque or speed portion of the formula, visualize a wrench connected to a bolt and, when turned, producing torque, a force that loosens or tightens the bolt. The magnitude of torque depends on three factors: the force applied, the length of the wrench, and the angle between the two. The torque or speed of growth from social works similarly in organizations. The bolt is the external market opportunity, such as a new product or

Social Market Leadership: What's Your Next Move?

Here are five reasons a "fast follower" strategy is a losing proposition when it comes to social market leadership:

1. **You start by taking a reactive posture.** As a fast follower, you're intentionally sitting back to see what the rest of the market does. Your ideas, processes, and operation are trained to react. You have abdicated any real vision to uncover new opportunities. How's that working out for you so far? And by the way, how will you ever attract world-class "A-players" when you're positioning yourself as always letting others explore innovative ideas? Without forward-thinking people, processes, and operations, when the disruption comes—and make no mistake about it, social media is disruptive—you won't have the internal capabilities to respond.

2. **You need a highly optimized decision-making and new-product development and launch practice.** As a fast follower, given the incredibly fast-paced nature of social media, you'll need the infrastructure to decide exactly when to enter the market with a social media campaign, re-engineer or re-architect a competitor's campaign in a way that the target customers view them as indistinguishable, and still drive the marketing gravity/pull from your efforts. In the digital relationship maturity model, to go from doing nothing to reactive and cross the proverbial chasm to proactive, predictive, and visionary, there are pioneers, slow followers, and laggards, but I've yet to meet a successful "fast follower."

3. **You'll need a lengthy social market leadership strategy cycle.** As a fast follower, you'll need time to gear up, copy the innovators, and get a strategy, a roadmap, and a campaign put together before the onslaught of competition do the same—not to mention actually building, nurturing, and turning digital relationships into revenues and profits before the window of opportunity deteriorates. While this kind of thinking may have been successful in the past, the pace of change and speed of doing business directly (online) has increased to the point where product/service cycles are much shorter, and influencer marketing today wins market share tomorrow.

4. **You'll need the right people to follow!** As a fast follower, you'll need to listen to the right people online, follow their every move, and hope that the organization has good insights. And revenues/results today are actually lagging indicators of past sales and marketing success, so the results you see today may, in fact, be dramatically different than what lies ahead. Imagine following Wang or DEC computers in the 80s or even the mighty Apple in the 90s, before the iPod. These market leaders suffered great losses, and while Wang and DEC never recovered, Apple did so because of consumer electronics, not computers. Social market leadership requires the same agility to move quickly and learn from experiences for the next campaign if a particular approach doesn't yield the desired results.

continues on next page

continued from previous page

5. **You'll need to change the view.** Years ago when I was at Silicon Graphics (SGI, another market leader that went off the cliff), I remember seeing a poster of a dog sled that read, "If you're not the lead dog, the view never changes." Innovators are constantly in the front exploring new views of uncharted market opportunities. I often ask prospective clients what's the "iPod" of their industry, and their struggle to respond is a telltale sign that innovation, although a desired trait, may not be part of the organization's DNA. Becoming the next anything is really boring— even Google, a market innovator, was just the next Yahoo.

When it comes to social market leadership, it's time to leave the cozy complacent mindset and become the "first something." What's your next move?

service launch, a new member or customer acquisition campaign, or expansion into a new geographic territory. The force applied to the market opportunity is a combination of the organization's staff, resources invested in training and development, a repeatable predictable process, market research, competitive analysis, and marketing communication. The length of the wrench connected to the bolt is the organization's physical proximity to the market opportunity. Lack of physical proximity is what makes it difficult to parachute into a new geography and why field-marketing campaigns are seldom effective when run from a distant headquarters, where there is little knowledge of the village on the ground. The angle between market opportunity and force is the organization's social network of connected relationships. If the organization builds a robust portfolio of highly connected relationships that provide unique and actionable insights and reciprocate value to accelerate the organization's ability to get things done, it will infinitely enhance the organization's torque or speed of growth.

Why does torque or speed of growth matter? Ultimately, it is the difference between first mover advantage and a fast follower. In many markets, there is an inherent window of market opportunity and a very real and often substantial opportunity cost of not getting the torque or speed of growth right.

2. *Just because "someone else is doing it" or you "read about it" shouldn't be mistaken for sufficient and compelling business drivers.* Unfortunately, both market hype as propagated by countless articles in the business or industry press and the market posturing of

embarking on an initiative simply because the competitive landscape is doing it are equally flawed reasons for implementing a social strategy. Unless an organization invests the capital (time, human, and financial) to fully understand how to align social with the strategic objectives of the organization, the engagement and the experience discussed in the previous chapter will fall dreadfully short of broad expectations.

Drivers, strategies, and tactics of business goals should lead the strategic alignment of the organization's focus and its social strategy (Figure 4.2). Only when business goals are aligned with the desired relationships, relevant content, appropriate process, and anticipated adoption of the shareholder value experience can an organization begin to plan its social strategy.

Figure 4.2—Strategic Alignment of Social Market Leadership

Clearly I'm not talking about a staff function or a tool here. Facebook and Twitter are the means to an end. If the board and the senior leadership are to embark on true social market leadership that encompasses strategy, tactics, innovation, capital, and architecture, it must clearly understand certain definitions:

- **Social Networking Sites,** such as LinkedIn, Facebook, YouTube, Twitter, are about presence, having a personal, professional, or organizational presence on these websites.

- **Social Media,** such as blogs, forums, and discussion groups, are platforms for individuals, teams, and organizations to listen to and initiate conversations.

- **Social Market Leadership** is about an organization's purpose, to dramatically enhance its abilities to make dynamic decisions and fuel its profitable growth through incorporating social strategy into its business processes.

Social should not be viewed by the board or the senior leadership team as the management "flavor of the month," similar to business process reengineering or total quality management tools of the 1990s. Only with a thoughtful analysis of why to use it, investing in making it successful, and developing an accountable plan to measure its return on impact on the organization and its key constituents will social fuel the next phase of growth many boards and their senior leadership teams seek. As such, several key questions executives and boards can ask themselves include:

- What early and often faint market signals/trends can the organization identify as growth enablers through social and its connected relationships of staff, members, and customers?

- How can the organization develop a highly streamlined and expedited collection, analysis, and action-park-or-dismiss process for the inbound ideas?

- How can the organization efficiently develop pilot products or services to test the market validity of certain ideas?

- How can the organization effectively learn from every pilot project and commercialize the more viable ideas?

- How can the organization create an iterative process where the real-time analysis is fed back into enhancing the product or service as well as the experiences members or customers have with the organization and its capabilities?

Leadership Competencies and Growth Fueled by Social

If social is to become the engine fueling the next phase of an organization's growth, competencies and quality of board and leadership will be critical. Executive search firm Egon Zehnder International has created a database of performance appraisals from more than 100,000 senior executives and board members, focusing on eight leadership competencies in three critical categories (Figure 4.3). All involve social strategy's fueling organizational growth.

Thought Leadership	Market Insight
	Strategic Orientation
People and Organizational Leadership	Change Leadership
	Developing Organizational Capability
	Team Leadership
	Collaboration and Influencing
Business Leadership	Customer Impact
	Results Orientation

Figure 4.3—Egon Zehnder Leadership Competencies

What specific competencies do these board members and leadership teams of high-performing organizations have in common? How are they cultivating competencies within their existing teams or seeking new talent with needed skills? Social intelligence, as a competitive organizational differentiator, is a leadership competency, one that can fuel growth through two key attributes:

- **Be Customer Relationship Centric.** If members and customers can be synonymous (a leap for many associations), the organization that seeks a launching pad to improve performance will use social to deliver that customer impact. Today's fast-paced market dynamics require an organization to always be "on." A brand can be strengthened or destroyed in a fraction of the time it once took because of social media's instant feedback. Most executives understand this—88 percent of all CEOs who participated in the 2010 IBM CEO study selected "getting closer to the customer" as the most important dimension to execute their strategy in the next five years. Social bridges that understanding with a path to execution for boards and senior leadership teams.

  As I'll discuss in the next chapter, consumers of information, products, and services become aware of, research, purchase, and obtain support for purchases in various ways. They're relying on peer evaluations, social interactions, and after-purchase/acceptance support to make decisions about which brands to continue to invest in. Boards and senior leaders of organizations who don't offer a consistent, compelling brand experience across multiple delivery channels will continue to struggle in getting through the market noise competing for mindshare and wallet share. Messaging alone will not suffice. In the context of leading where customer relationships are the fundamental focus, a socially enabled organization integrates business processes to listen to the information its customers volunteer to share, which is more dynamic than any survey and more intelligent in contextually aware experiences.

When relationships go bad as a result of misaligned expectations and experiences, social strategy must be used to fuel the after-the-sale component. Real people must show personalized profiles, not the organization's logo, in click-to-chat functionalities, community blogs, or web conferences. A flexible model of customer self-service capabilities, such as chat forums and communities, can dramatically increase responsiveness and decrease costs.

- **Align Talent and Expertise with Growth Priorities.** Every organization, regardless of size or governance structure, must pursue a diverse set of growth strategies. Approaches vary by industry, business segment, or unique circumstance. How social can become a unique and effective differentiator heavily depends on the caliber and range of leadership skills at various levels of the organization. Consider an organization's existing and new members/customers and its existing and new offerings (Figure 4.4) below:

		Organization's Members/Customers	
		Existing	New
Organization's Offerings	Existing		**B**
	New	**A**	

Figure 4.4—Existing and New Offerings to the Market

What many consumers don't want is more of the same; over time, existing offerings become considerably less attractive and perceived as commodities. Conversely, where the organization is a credible, trusted source and existing members/customers are very receptive, new offerings become a momentum growth strategy (bottom left quadrant—A). Board members and senior leaders who truly understand the organization's core strengths will see that change and team leadership thrive within as well as outside the organization.

In contrast, growth strategies and priorities of existing offerings to new members/customers (top right quadrant—B) require board members and senior leaders to excel at a broad range of skills. The bar for performance, execution, and results becomes focused on market insight and net new member/customer acquisition and adaptation of the organization's core competencies to a new set of market requirements.

In essence, for social to become a viable enabler of growth, the organization must not only assemble a critical mass of talent at its board and senior leadership ranks—covered in upcoming chapters—but also align leadership's realm of responsibilities and skills with the organization's prioritized growth strategies. World-class organizations consistently assess talent requirements at multiple levels, for current as well as anticipated requirements of the organization. With this assessment they then map clear board enhancement and leadership development targets and integrate the accountability and performance expectations into their recruitment, succession, metrics, and reward/compensation processes. They don't make excuses about organizational size or inability to attract great board members or leaders. They systematically attract and build exceptional board members and excellent leaders with the skills necessary to drive consistent and profitable growth!

Five pillars of change in the reinvention of the board will be critical to any success:

1. Distributed accountability
2. Governance councils
3. Co-opetition
4. Heightened insights
5. Intense social analytics

Let's take a closer look at each.

1. Distributed Accountability

As connected relationships—those characterized by increased quantity and quality of digital integration with and among members and customers—become more pervasive, the board and the senior leadership will increasingly be accountable to a set of tightly defined responsibilities. They will also assume responsibilities distributed across functions and groups strategically placed to manage and use insights generated by connected relationships. These may become more challenging to board members and senior staff, as responsibilities will span geographic boundaries, reflecting the global nature of social, and increasingly the roles will be filled by newly created positions with unique and borrowed skill sets—borrowed via highly specialized senior leaders or board members "on loan" from other organizations or brought in as sources of independent and highly unique insights for a specified period in the organization's lifecycle.

Regardless of the organization's structure—from membership-based, to service-delivery nonprofit, to an advocacy network—social will redefine what it means for associations to be accountable, not just during a scandal in their sector or in their organization, but to contributors and volunteers who demand resources be allocated properly and to regulators who pressure associations to demonstrate consistent service to the public purpose to merit tax-exempt status. Similar to a venture-capital-backed firm where investors demand prudent stewardship of the organization's limited resources, it may be tempting to accept the popular point of view that more accountability would be better. The world of social media demands prioritized and highly distributed accountability among competing demands of the organization. The organization, its board, and senior leadership, mindful of *to whom and for what* it is accountable, owe accountability for disclosures, performance evaluations, self-regulation, active participation, and continuous adaptive and comparative learning.

Because social accountability is strategy-driven, it can help organizations achieve their mission. Furthermore, as connected relationships tap into an organization's core and distributed activities, board members and senior leaders will be held accountable for the performance of groups that don't report solely to them. The very definition of accountability in holding people responsible for their actions, or the means by which individuals and organizations report the selection and performance of their actions, is being challenged by the immediacy and responsiveness required by social. In the *International Encyclopedia of Civil Society,* Professor Alnoor Ebrahim identifies four core components of accountability as:

- *Transparency*—collecting information and making it available and accessible for public scrutiny;
- *Answerability or Justification*—providing clear reasoning for actions and decisions, including those not adopted so they may reasonably be questioned;
- *Compliance*—through monitoring and evaluation of processes and outcomes, combined with transparency in the manner which those findings are reported; and

- *Enforcement or Sanctions*—for shortfalls in compliance, justification, or transparency.

Social interactions in particular highlight both the "external" dimensions of accountability for an organization in terms of an obligation to meet or exceed prescribed standards of behavior, and an internal sense of responsibility expressed through individual action and organizational mission. Connected relationships make the fundamental questions surrounding accountability—to whom and for what—more complicated. *Upward* accountability refers to relationships with donors, sponsors, foundations, government, and investors. As such, it is often focused on the use of resources. *Downward* accountability refers to relationships with groups receiving services such as members, customers, communities, or regions directly or indirectly affected by the organization. *Internal* accountability refers to the relationships within the organization and the organization's responsibility to its market focus, mission, board stewardship, senior decision makers, and front-line implementers in the field.

Accountability is a litmus test for connected relationships. If it is skewed to simply satisfy the interests of the most powerful or the biggest donors, it loses its credibility and the trust bestowed upon the organization. Conversely, if the voices of members are heard through social interactions and their loyalty is earned through really listening and responding to perceived value—starting with the board—this distributed accountability becomes a source of power for the organization. Social fuels distributed accountability, which in turn influences who is able to hold whom to account for their decisions, performance, and actions on behalf of the broader constituents of the organization (versus a select few behind closed meetings or exotic "strategy retreats").

Most constituents would include financial and procedural governance, meeting or exceeding performance by key leading indicators, and the mission of the organization as key areas of expectations and distributed accountability. As generally described by professor Ebrahim, board members are responsible for:

- Seeking and considering adequate information on which to base decisions (care),
- Disclosing conflicts of interest and placing the organization's interests over personal ones (loyalty), and
- Acting within the organization's mission while adhering to internal organizational protocols for decision making (obedience).

The financial turmoil caused by mortgage-backed securities and financial derivatives markets in 2008 certainly forced many boards to focus intensely on the financial stewardship of their organizations. Beyond the board's fiduciary responsibility to focus on internal controls and legal compliance, however, connected relationships are expanding accountability to the broader purpose of the organization: performance that meets or exceeds results. *Distributed accountability enhances the focus on linking goals to outcomes.* Particularly for nonprofit organizations, it's not an either/or scenario of the mission versus performance but rather a mission-centered performance with a long-term view characterized by listening and learning as well as reflecting on and adapting to challenges and opportunities.

From a tactical standpoint, distributed accountability will reinvent board meetings so that there are broader discussions of performance, not as a sequential series of events but as a complex web of solid- and dotted-line relationships in designing, developing, and delivering value-based touch points for members across the entire organization. The chart will show how social strategy has been embedded in other functions of the organization: membership redefined as value-add to the broader community of practitioners, capabilities aligned with the membership life cycle, and retention as a direct result of engagement and peer-level accountability.

2. Governance Council

In many organizations today, digital interactions are spread across multiple, complex silos that are isolated from each other. There are scores of redundant copies of member or customer information, and how an organization uses that data is just as redundant and tangled. In the complex web of solid- and dotted-line relationships to design, develop, and deliver value-based touch points for members across the entire organization, a core team has to manage, organize, and optimize this focus on linking goals to outcome. As the second critical success pillar of change in the reinvention of the board, governance councils with greater representation from a broader set of functions will replace traditional committees.

Traditional committees seldom function or succeed *as a team.* Independent agendas by individual committee members create distractions from the focused stewardship of the organization's strategy. An individual can succeed, yet the committee can fail to deliver the desired outcomes. Consensus building and defending the status quo is often the norm. Tenure in the organization or the industry, name recognition, level of financial support, or favoritism may be the traditional nomination or selection criteria. In many organizations, decision-making and intentional actions become unnecessarily complex and can take entirely too long, largely because of the structure and governance rules of traditional committees. The committees' realm of responsibilities may be disengaged from the daily challenges of staff members, hence the detrimental disconnect between strategy formulation and execution.

Conversely, governance councils function more like a sports franchise—an American football team for example—with a singular focus: to support the leadership *in real time.* Governance councils are composed of highly specialized individuals intentionally selected for specific functions, often directly relevant to their unique expertise. (Most would agree that a defensive lineman doesn't have the physical makeup or the skills to be a wide receiver or vice versa.) Governance councils are composed of a hybrid of outside expertise, functional leaders, and front-line staff members who can bring their unique perspectives to the discussion of possible choices and the agile decision-making process.

Organizations want to leverage information to maximize their performance and the level of engagement from each member or customer. They want to assess the value of data as a balance sheet asset, and they want to calculate risk in all aspects of their operations as a competitive advantage in decision making. It is for these reasons that governance councils are emerging as a strategic priority for organizations of all sizes.

One example could be a digital governance council where all member- or customer-facing functions are represented to discuss the ways they engage and influence each member or customer. If touch point details are shared across functions, the organization has a dramatically higher chance of ensuring the same level of experience and engagement, regardless of how people interact with the organization (website, mobile, local chapters, or regional or national conferences). Furthermore, all supporting functions could clearly understand their roles in support of this unified experience and engagement.

At the board level, developing a governance council to more effectively understand and leverage value-added touch points across the entire organization is a quality control measure that adds new rigor and discipline to the process of managing, using, improving, and protecting organizational information. Effective governance in this evolving area can enhance the quality, availability, and integrity of an organization's data by fostering cross-organizational collaboration and structured policy making. It balances factional silos with organizational interest, directly affecting the four factors any organization should care about most:

- Increasing revenue per member or customer,
- Lowering costs of acquiring a member or a customer,
- Reducing risks associated with member engagement, and
- Increasing data confidence in each value-added touch point.

Within a common forum for board members and senior leaders to explore challenges and solutions, the governance council can become instrumental in developing benchmarks, best practices, and guidelines to successful member engagement. If the goal of the organization is to maximize its impact, a governance council would also benefit from insights from outsiders, industry partners, and thought leaders who can bring unique perspectives to the table.

3. Co-Opetition

Another pillar of change in the reinvention of the board will be the mind shift that more robust formal and informal external partnerships will be critical in enhancing those value-added touch points. Often, external partners create very logical sponsorship opportunities for member-based organizations, such as sponsoring an event or a research project. Unfortunately, that's myopic when it comes to broader member engagement or user experience. Most board members have certainly heard of mobile applications; many probably use several on their smartphones. Yet, mobile applications are not part of the strategic planning process in many organizations. Starbucks is using a website to generate thousands of ideas from its customers about how it can enhance their daily experiences. Procter & Gamble is using a website to generate thousands of innovative ideas from a broad base of constituents who interact with its products on a daily basis. Virgin Atlantic Airways has developed a taxi-sharing app for smartphones and incorporated a customer forum where the company can gain key insights about behaviors once customers land at specific destinations.

These are just some of the examples of unified, cross-business, cross-functional collaboration responsible for every touch point from in-person interactions, to promotional campaigns, logistics in getting the right information to the right person at the point of need and on the device of their choice, innovation from the most unlikely sources, and the design and delivery of unique products and services. When trust is nurtured and insights from these touch points are openly shared among external partners, both the partner and the organization benefit from a stronger understanding of, and engagement with, end members and customers.

Sometimes, an external partner may be a traditionally perceived competitor, if not for the same set of products or services, certainly for mindshare and wallet share of the target audience each organization is attempting to attract and engage. When two seemingly competitive organizations agree to participate in a joint discovery process to analyze key market trends and collaborate on a solution, the results benefit not only both organizations but the overall industry as well. Why would two competitive organizations collaborate? That's where *co-opetition* comes in.

Co-opetition, a model in which networks of stakeholders cooperate and compete to create maximum value, is one of the most important business concepts of recent years. By enabling connected relationships through information sharing as well as integrating and streamlining processes, mobile and social technologies have made it even more necessary for organizations to both cooperate and compete. In today's networked economy, co-opetition is a powerful means of identifying new market opportunities and developing strategy. Adam Brandenburger and Barry Nalebuff, professors at the Harvard Business School and the Yale School of Management, respectively, expanded upon the concept in their book, *Co-opetition*. They asserted that business is simultaneously both competition and cooperation. There is a duality in all relationships with respect to win-win and win-lose interactions. The success of most organizations is dependent on the success of others, yet they must compete to capture value created in the market and protect their own interests.

Given a common mission, vision, or enemy—think of unfair business legislation—it is in the best interests of both organizations to pool resources, insights, and industry or subject matter expertise to collectively uncover new market opportunities. Particularly in the association industry, this model is applicable to national, regional, and statewide organizations.

4. Heightened Insights and 5. Intense Social Analytics

The final two pillars of change in the reinvention of the board are logically intertwined: heightened insights and intense social analytics. I'll cover both topics in greater detail in Chapter 8. In today's overabundance of digital interactions it will become more challenging and important for organizations to capture and effectively use rich member or customer

IMPACT @ Work:
Creating Market Needs

In my experience, three unique types of market need create growth opportunities: existing, heightened, and created. Existing needs drive much of the natural demand and supply curves. Periodically, the need exists but requires additional awareness campaigns to be heightened in the minds and hearts of the intended audience. Sometimes, an association has to simply create a market need previously unrecognized by the target audience. According to Alan Sparkman, the executive director of the Tennessee Concrete Association (TCA), "National organizations tend to focus on advocacy at the legislative level, which is very important, but they aren't necessarily responsive to strategic needs at the state level. In some cases, the national organization is resistant to the efforts to promote and market new products. At the state level, members are closer to the ground and can see the possibilities and, in many ways, have more freedom to try things because the cost of failure is much lower.

During Sparkman's 15-year tenure, the promotion of two concrete products, ultra thin white topping and pervious concrete, has had the most impact on creating value for TCA's members and the industry. In the late 1990s, the concrete industry began to experiment with the process of using concrete as an overlay, and TCA became active in developing that market. Tennessee now leads the nation in

continues on next page

Meet the Tennessee Concrete Association (TCA)

The Tennessee Concrete Association is a 501(c)(6) trade association for the ready mix concrete industry. TCA was founded in 1986 and has 170 company members representing approximately 75 percent of the Ready Mix concrete producers in Tennessee. TCA's annual budget is $500,000. Revenue is 40 percent dues, 40 percent certification activities, and 20 percent meetings and miscellaneous. It has a small staff—3.5 full-time employees, one of whom is fully devoted to certification. TCA promotes and markets concrete products to expand the market for their members and raise the profile of the industry. It also responds to technical, regulatory, and safety issues in the ready mix concrete environment, sponsors several national certifications from the American Concrete Institute and the National Ready Mix Concrete Association, and offers TCA members discounts on these national certifications.

continued from previous page
the number of ultra thin projects.

Pervious concrete is a solution for storm water pollution. It was first used in the 1970s in Florida, but as the storm water environment changed nationwide it became a real solution. TCA has spent a decade promoting the concept of pervious concrete to its own members who initially said, "Why would I want to do that? There's no market for it." TCA educated its members about the product and promoted its use as a solution to cities, counties, and engineers. As a result, the market is growing significantly, says Sparkman.

insights. The vast number of touch points mentioned earlier highlight agile movement in meeting members' unique needs at specific points in time. They desperately need access to key pieces of information this afternoon, but tomorrow the same information isn't nearly as vital or useful. Analyzing and extrapolating patterns of behaviors and the ability to respond quickly to changing needs isn't a low-level staff function. The board must realize this adaptive learning opportunity and provide the supporting environment, capacity building, and foresight in the value of information sharing with a broad base of constituents. Supportive leadership can reinforce learning by encouraging dialogue and debate and providing resources for reflection.

Capturing and leveraging these insights isn't a marketing or an IT function. Information from value-added touch points is a *strategy enabler* that can help redesign core organizational elements such as membership pricing, partner or sponsor targeting, and the selection of key advocacy priorities. The board's stewardship of these touch points will create an exponential increase in volume of member or customer-centric data and a certain intensity of analysis required to effectively process and make decisions from it. Cross-functional collaboration on touch points and distributed accountability mentioned earlier will enable the organization to gather, collate, gain impactful insights from, and disseminate data that streams in from every member or customer interaction.

Not every organization will be capable of creating or effectively using sophisticated data analytics—think of the financial services or the airline industries where a massive amount of information is used daily to calculate pricing formulas. That's where creative business and revenue model partnerships with outside firms will create opportunities for visionary organizations to exchange data and constantly test alternative tactics to engage and influence the behavior of members or customers.

The fundamental barrier to any organization's ability to dramatically leverage social as an enabler of exceptional member engagement or customer experiences is not understanding or implementing recognized best practices. It's rather the lack of organizational stewardship. Staff functions such as marketing, communication, or IT cannot be responsible for the vast number of touch points where members or customers interact with the organization. Boards and senior leaders must collaborate in adapting their organizations to be consistent with how members and customers behave and, through connected relationships, redefine traditional organizational structure.

"iTunify" Your Capabilities

THE MOST PROFITABLE, sustainable way to build and scale an organization is to find a group of individuals (never forgetting that relationships are between individuals) who have problems that drive them crazy and who are willing and able to pay for solutions to solve them. If the organization becomes a student of those problems—studying where they come from, how they manifest themselves, what the alternatives and risks associated with addressing them are—and is obsessed with solving them, it can create a clearly differentiated value proposition, one that many individuals are often willing to pay a premium for versus the alternative. Member-based organizations have been somewhat insulated from the competitive forces of most businesses, but social networking is dramatically and increasingly challenging the perceived value of member-based organizations to those "customers"

with problems. Many leaders forget this simple proposition; businesses have fallen in love with their own products and services, and many associations are drinking way too much of their own Kool-Aid, completely losing touch with the problem-solving or quantifiable value-adding side of the formula.

A recent issue of *Time* magazine illustrated a particularly interesting and relevant concept around how Steve Jobs extended Apple's influence beyond Macs. Jobs, Apple's late CEO, had the vision that Apple would be more than gadgets. He understood that devices drive consumption, or as we used to say years ago when I worked at Silicon Graphics, "Hardware is a necessary evil." Consumers of entertainment, products, and content have made Apple a player in music and video distribution, retail, and publishing. Industry giants in various sectors have bet their digital presence on apps in the iTunes store, with its estimated 250 million plus users and their buying patterns. The ease of use in researching, reviewing experiences from peers, downloading, and paying for apps along with the accelerated time to use and receive value has reinvented product development and distribution. Long gone are the days of extensive and expansive applications; they've been replaced by simple, agile, and highly accessible points of information, insights, and entertainment. The current generation doesn't have to wait for shows or movies to appear on the TV schedule as many of us did growing up. Anyone can download or stream almost whatever content they want on an iPhone or an iPad from anywhere in the world where there is an internet connection.

Consumers, members, and customers accustomed to that kind of flexibility want products and services but are cynical about marketing and advertising. They do not want to spend an hour online ordering, days waiting for a purchase to arrive, another few hours assembling it, or time on hold with customer service trying to figure out why it's not working properly. The price of an offering often includes features or functionality consumers have little interest in, which begs the question: When was the last time you and your team went through the portion of your business that is meaningless to your members and customers?

Doing so often has far greater positive impact on most organizations than any single strategic planning item from some off-site meeting. By stripping away obstacles that surround an organization's products and services, including the unwanted junk mail, the unnecessary and wasteful repetitions, the unwelcomed attitude of overworked and stressed staff, and the senseless bureaucracy that we tend to bucket as "policy," you can create value for your target members or customers. *By focusing on providing less of what they dislike, you create greater value and impact in what they're really looking for!*

Dennis Tomorsky has been the CEO for the Wisconsin Institute of Certified Public Accountants (WICPA) since 2006. Annually, WICPA provides 100 to 150 seminars, 10 conferences, and 50 to 75 breakfast meetings, discussion groups, and lunch meetings. The depth and scope of educational offerings are far greater than any of its competitors in the profession. Forty to fifty percent of WICPA members are geographically dispersed outside the population-dense Madison/Milwaukee/Green Bay areas, so providing greater access to educational programming is a challenge and a key priority. Technology is providing some solutions, which have led to a 700 percent increase in online educational programming in five years. Members also struggle with keeping current with the increasing and complicated regulatory issues involving technology, taxes, auditing, and financial statements in public accounting.

In response to member feedback, WICPA *compacted and customized programming to add as much value as possible to the educational experience.* For decades the association had operated on the premise that the best education model was an instructor-led, eight-hour presentation and a three-ring binder. However, very often the program might have only three hours of specific content that related to a participant's area of expertise or need. Today, WICPA's conferences are organized by subject areas, such as nonprofits, tax accounting, or specific industries, and for the generalist CPA in the corporate environment.

Meet the Wisconsin Institute of Certified Public Accountants (WICPA)

WICPA is 106 years old, employs 15 people, and has a membership of 8,000 individuals, of which 6,000 are licensed CPAs and represent 55 percent of the addressable market. The remaining members are CFOs, controllers, retirees, students, educators, and government professionals. WICPA provides advocacy on behalf of the CPA profession at the state level. At the national level, in collaboration with the AICPA, the association makes itself available to the legislative, executive, and judicial branches if there are questions in areas of member expertise. WICPA's annual budget hovers between $2.8 and $3 million, derived approximately 50 percent from dues, 33 percent from educational events, and 17 percent from vendor advertising and sponsorships.

Modularize Based on *Their* Needs

The more adaptable your capabilities become, the more competitive your organization becomes. So how can you focus on modularizing all that you offer based on the unique needs of your target audience at various touch points? How can you *really* understand what they need (a fundamental problem), when they need it (event driven), the easiest manner to deliver it to them (distribution channels of real-time insights), and the most effective way to apply your value-add to solving their problems (outcome-focused execution)? Because if you can ask the right questions and frame the right challenges for your organization, you can focus on key metrics such as:

- Speed of delivery,
- Flexibility of delivered components (keeping in mind that they don't want to know everything you know or need every aspect of what you offer),
- Internal ratings by staff, and
- Actual usage by members and customers.

In the IMPACT Model—Immerse, Member, Participate, Accredit, Community, and Transform—the critical touch points in the immersion stage heavily depend on your ability to quickly segment the broader market and modularize your offerings based on the unique needs of key segments. Keep in mind that these are increasingly sophisticated consumers—of information as well as products and services—for whom "push" advertising is irrelevant. They no longer separate marketing from the product but rather see their online experiences with the organization *as the product.* As such, every employee and leader of your organization must think first and foremost about marketing, not traditional push marketing, but the immersion of the target audience in the experience and value of the organization as a purveyor of actionable insights.

In-bound calls or emails are now marketing opportunities; when people walk into your office or visit your website, that's a marketing opportunity. When they search for and download one of your position papers, that's a marketing opportunity. When they subscribe to or purchase your magazine or a publication, that's a marketing opportunity. When they read your blog or watch a video of your CEO being interviewed, that's a marketing opportunity. Their experiences before, during, and after attending your online educational sessions or your annual conference are all marketing opportunities. In essence, every touch point in the immersion stage is an opportunity to engage and influence your customers' thinking, perspective, and next logical call to action.

Notice, I didn't say, "sell them," or otherwise require them to fill out an extensive online form asking information about their third-grade teacher or grandmother's maiden name! Marketing and selling are distinctly different functions, and if you confuse the two with connected relationships, your efforts will backfire. The goal is to *stimulate interaction and dialogue while you educate people.* To educate them effectively, you must begin by understanding where they are in *their* journey. Is this an impressionable student evaluating your industry as one of several or a recent graduate eager to shed his student stigma and embark on the next chapter in your industry as a "professional member"? Is this a recent transplant in your industry because of economic conditions (think of people who change fields, subtly or drastically) or one who has a few years under her belt looking for opportunities to advance through personal and professional growth and development? Is this a seasoned veteran highly concerned about having an impact on the future and leaving a legacy in the form of a foundation (helping the same student mentioned earlier with a scholarship)? These initial impressions influence the people who may become the future pillars of your industry.

If you expand your mindset and begin to engage a much broader audience, every piece of information you can learn about their needs, expectations, and desired relationships helps you manage that relationship more effectively. Each interaction and exchange of value has that much more impact on their personal and professional growth. Your often-limited time together seems more productive and the resources shared between the two parties are used more efficiently. Sociologists refer to this as being *ambient aware.* The goal in modularizing your capabilities is to not only become ambient aware as an organization but to match the information and behavioral insights you capture from every touch point with the education people seek to help them move to the next stage of their uniquely selected journey.

On Air

You surely have seen the "On Air" sign in a film or on television. When the sign is on, it's the signal that a live broadcast or recording is in progress. When the light has been turned off, the recording has stopped and it is safe to go about other business. The challenge with social and connected relationships is that this sign is *never off.* Your organization is "On Air"

365 days a year and 24/7. Not being able to access information on your website during the holidays is an absurd situation for your members or customers. Access to relevant and timely information has become part of our daily lives, and as consumers, we struggle to understand or accept being without it. With ever-pervasive mobility, discussed a little later in this chapter, come expectations and responsibilities. Members and customers expect service, speed, and availability in a variety of forms, and your organization has to be committed to delivering the products and services they are looking for, at the point and in the manner that they need.

To adapt your capabilities to their needs, you have to become more efficient in using both your time and their time to learn from each other. Train and empower the entire organization to listen intently and hear what customers have to say—at every touch point. If you truly value this information, let them know by demonstrating your ability to listen and tailoring your products to meet their wishes, 365 days a year, 24/7.

Arlene Pietranton is the executive director of The American Speech-Language-Hearing Association (ASHA), an 85-year-old professional, scientific, and credentialing association based in Rockville, Maryland. She has been with the organization since the mid-1990s and has been its executive director since 2004. Most members are clinical service practitioners in schools or healthcare settings, but some are researchers, professors, and instructors in academic programs.

ASHA's organizational culture is such that staff and volunteer leaders have an explicit understanding that the organization exists for the benefit of its members. According to Arlene Pietranton, "Within our strategic pathways, we are explicitly looking to increase the opportunity for members to be engaged with the organization: for them to provide input to policies and resources the organization is developing, to provide articles for our communication vehicles, to be presenters on topics, to give perspectives on decisions the organization is making, and to use social media to comment and engage with us."

Maggie McGary, online community and social media manager for ASHA, says Twitter has really taken off with members. "Our role was to follow members' lead and start using it more as we saw them adopting it. Our members are using Twitter to market their businesses, or as what they call their 'PLN' (Personal Learning Network). Our role is to try to be instrumental in helping them connect with each other, and to use the conversations we see among our members there to inform new products and services." Another opportunity for social within ASHA has been a community outreach program. In one campaign, ASHA used Twitter to collaborate with the *Washington Parent* magazine for a Twitter chat with two speech language pathologists (SLPs). During the chat, parents had access to member experts so they could ask questions about speech and hearing issues they were having with their kids. Maggie McGary then drove concerned parents to ASHA's website to locate certified SLPs and audiologists in their area. "On Twitter we have more than 7,000 followers, but they tend to be SLPs, audiologists or students rather than consumers. For us to host a chat geared towards parents and consumers on our own, we probably wouldn't reach the audience we were trying to target. Being able to identify partners who have that consumer audience we were looking to reach and connect them with our members was helpful."

Anticipate Member Evolutions

Referring back to the IMPACT Model, if you immerse an audience with value-added education, the next logical step is to help them see the unique opportunities available to members or customers of the organization. Recognizing patterns of behavior, usage, and performance helps prioritize those who feel engaged and see not just the one-time, but ongoing, value of your interaction. Think about it, if they visit your website often, subscribe to the RSS feed of your blog, interact with your Facebook page, follow you on Twitter, subscribe to your YouTube channel, download research papers, or attend an upcoming webinar, you can *anticipate their interest*. This is when you proactively reach out and invite them to a local chapter event. The challenge for many organizations, large or small, association or corporate, is that they simply don't have the infrastructure to recognize who is coming to their various touch points, and much more importantly, the connection between the offline or online touch points as described above.

This is where social customer relationship management (CRM) can be a strong asset to an organization, helping followers and fans become members, customers, and advocates of your unique value-add. As more individuals and communities of common interest share conversations, while leaving out organizations, the new channels they rely on for their decision making outpace the organization's resources and ability to keep up. Beyond the social strategy and a different mindset of placing members or customers at the center of the organization's focus, social CRM is the evolution of customers' interaction with the entire organization, through an agile set of processes, at the time and through the dynamic channels of their choosing, focused on the insights from those multiple avenues of conversation. The 2010 Altimeter Group report, *Social CRM: The New Rules of Relationship Management,* effectively captures the more compelling uses of social CRM. (See Figure 5.1 below.)

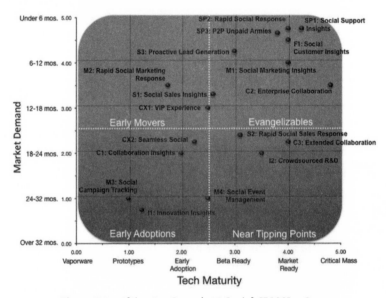

Figure 5.1—Altimeter Group's 18 Social CRM Use Cases

Anticipating member or customer needs in advance has more to do with the organization's focus and attitude about connected relationships than the digital touch points mentioned. If you know something is going to happen a day, a week, or a month from now, accept the responsibility and the organizational accountability to tell customers rather than making them reach out to you. Engaging them *proactively and intently* is one of the most effective ways to gain mindshare and wallet share.

As a society, we're creatures of habit. Look for patterns on your website, in calls to customer service, in orders for various products and services, or in requests for more information. Most organizations can get a good idea of what is going to happen next, so they can begin to anticipate member or customer needs. More importantly, share the insights from these patterns to prevent annoying incidents from happening at all. If you know that 60 percent of members who attend an event come back weeks later to order a digital download of the conference presentations, save them time and effort and tell them about this pattern up front.

Anticipating member or customer evolutions extends beyond the initial interaction with a product or a service; think about the next several steps. For example, what might you recommend to them to *stop doing* or do *instead* of their current set of actions? They're coming to you for your products, services, and market insights. Those insights could include suggesting alternative paths that are more effective or persuading them to think about something else instead. The value comes from saving their resources—time, effort, capital. Why not create a resource box on each page and *contextually recommend* similar information, products, or services other members or customers have explored or purchased previously? If they're reading an article, why not recommend the next topic in the series or a video explaining the applications or implementations of the idea you just presented? Take a closer look at the *Harvard Business Review* Blog (Figure 5.2) with key up-sell/cross-sell of information sections in the "Editor's Picks," "Top Magazine Articles" by most recent timelines, and "Featured Products" for sale.

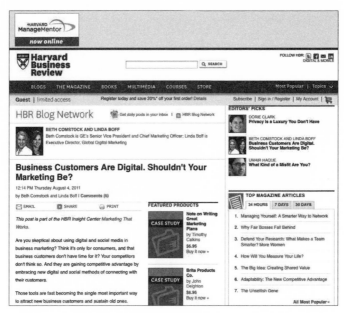

Figure 5.2—HBR Blog with Recommended Top Picks, Top Articles, and Featured Products

Thinking Beyond Membership Dues

Connected relationships and social interactions that fuel an organization's growth extend beyond getting an individual or a company to become a member or a customer. Organizations must move beyond just marketing, communications, service, and support applications of social media connectiveness—described by others in the association industry as "crawl, walk, run" steps—to key business processes critical to moving members and customers along a growth continuum. Here is how the IMPACT Model and key touch points along the way must map to a broader set of six business processes and specific applications of social interactions, from member and customer engagement perspective, to internal collaboration opportunities, to heightened insights and social analytics. (See Figure 5.3.)

1. **Immerse: Engage to Educate**—If they feel engaged, if key employees they interact with treat them as individuals and aim to have a dialogue focused on their unique needs and wants for personal and professional growth, they will take advantage of and benefit from the educational opportunities.

IMPACT Model			Social Business Applications	
	Business Process	Customer/Member Engagement	Internal Collaboration	Heightened Insights/Social Analytics
Immerse	Engage to Educate	• Augmented Events • Feedback Loops • Lead Generation • Loyalty Impact • VIP Experiences	• Campaign Creation • Resource Staffing • Insight Collection	• Sentiment Analysis • Social Media Monitoring • Campaign Performance • Reputation Capital • Engagement Effectiveness • Advocacy Response • Reach Breadth and Depth
Member	Interest to Member	• Save a Join • Steal a Join • Partner Member • Multi-channel Commerce	• Collaboration Forecasting • Lead Source Matching • Prospect Augmentation • Crowdsourced Relationships	• Geographic Penetration • Product/Service Profitability • Membership Campaign Effectiveness • Distribution Channel Efficiency
Participate	Passive to Active	• Issue Escalation • Peer-based Support • Reactive Support • Proactive Support • Predictive Support	• Insight Source Creation and Curation • Support Escalation and Resolution • Project/Initiative Forecasting • Issue Resolution	• Service Level Performance • Incident-type Analytics • Channel Optimization • Member Delight • Member Retention
Accredit	Learn to Earn	• Partner Collaboration • Crowdsourced Innovation • Learning Performance • Game Theory • Earning Advancements	• Internal Design • Internal Ideation • Accreditation Process • Application Approval • Certification • Standards Development	• Testing Behaviors • Accreditation Brand Perception • Accreditation Acceptance • Application to Accreditation Ratio • Certification Renewal • Market Acceptance of Standards
Community	Growth Through Collaboration	• Project/Initiative Idea Generation • Benchmarking Best Practices • Polling and Data Collection	• Project/Initiative Staffing • Collaborative Workspaces	• On-time and On-Budget Project Delivery • Project/Initiative Collaboration
Transform	Apply to Elevate	• Board Regeneration • Foundation and Legacy Creation • Success Sharing/Industry Advocacy	• Recruiting and Retention • Compensation Design • Feedback Loops	• Employment Elevation • Compensation Benchmarks • Reputation Capital & Professional Net Worth

Figure 5.3—Connecting the Dots Among IMPACT, Business Processes, and Social Applications

2. **Member: Interest to Member**—The value-add from the education reinforces the unique value of membership, not available to them elsewhere.

3. **Participate: Passive to Active**—Although the organization can encourage participation, members must experience sufficient value to elevate themselves from passive observers to active participants

4. **Accredit: Learn to Earn**—As they learn, they join an elite group of professionals based on a set of higher standards and qualifications most relevant to outcomes in the industry.

5. **Community: Growth Through Collaboration**—Personal and professional growth is earned through sharing, stewardship of key initiatives, and servant leadership.

6. **Transform: Apply to Elevate**—The application of the gained knowledge, as well as the broad portfolio of relationships within and external to the industry, will create the changes in behavior that affect members and transform their desired outcomes.

Top of the Box Split with a Corner Strike

The above heading describes one of my favorite soccer plays. It's a corner kick by one team to the top of the opposing goal keeper's box, where the ball actually goes through the first intended player's split legs as a fake and a second player runs behind from the opposite direction to strike the ball to the open goal post. In the youth soccer I coach, we run that play 100 times at practice in any given year, in anticipation of one of a dozen opportunities when it can be executed for the competitive edge. That's exactly how organizations need to think as well: Have a set play that equips you to respond to—or anticipate—what a member or a customer may need. Think of member or customer situations where they need you to execute a specific set of actions, well planned and rehearsed, in concert across the entire organization.

So how can you create opportunities for your members or customers to tell you that they're interested in only a select few offerings at that moment and not all that you have to offer? Have you ever noticed that Ritz-Carlton staff won't simply give you directions to a meeting room, a pool, or a restroom but walk you there personally? Beyond how you engage members in person, you also need to create set plays into your website, mobile, and social presence by establishing guidelines and empowering your team to respond expertly when they recognize a member's situation matches one of the plays at their disposal. Here are a handful of set plays for your connected relationships online:

- Infrastructure that remembers people's pertinent contact information, including shipping, billing, and delivery addresses, so they can order items with a single click;

- More intuitive navigation, from their perspective and eliminating ads in key areas where customers want less clutter;

- An intelligent search function that helps them narrow their searches in natural language and the ability to constantly learn from what they're searching and what content you can recommend next;

- Offering them value-based options based on key information they've shared with you;

- "Click-to-call" or "click-to-chat" functionality on every page to minimize their efforts—this nonintrusive manner of being there if they need you creates great reassurance;

- Desktop sharing functionality—amazing how much easier it is for you to show me where something is on the site versus telling me about it; and

- Interactive scheduling—instead of back and forth emails or voicemails about availability, why not put staff schedules (not necessarily details, but simple availability) online, so members can propose schedule times?

Simply having five or six set plays based on the most common scenarios, where members or customers engage you with their most pressing needs, is a great starting point. Are they "rushed," "looking for these specific three things," "really interested in what's fresh in the industry," or simply "mad as hell"? By the way, being interested in what's fresh is the exact opposite of being "rushed." Exploring what's fresh takes time to wander around the site, read articles, or watch new videos, so feed their hunger for new and interesting things. Your efforts to be efficient and hurry them along will have negative impact. Instead, offer tools to help members collaborate with others, ask questions, and, if possible, try an experience. Really think about the experiences desired and anticipate what else they may be interested in, such as special offers, an upcoming event, or a chance to give something back.

"iTunification" of Membership Models

The brilliance of Apple's strategy isn't simply in the devices such as iPod, iPhone, or iPad. It's the enabling distribution mechanism of iTunes that keeps the users constantly educated, engaged, and empowered. Apple knew that the path to the initial customer or member acquisition had to be a platform that would keep them coming back, allowing them to squeeze more value from their investments, learn about expanded capabilities, and buy more, depended on an ecosystem that was intuitive, easy to navigate, and centralized. It is a platform with guidelines for third-party developers to create compelling applications, many of which are still free and offer consistent up-sell/cross-sell opportunities, from which Apple generates multiple sources of revenue. "Apple envisions a world," Forrester Research analyst James McQuivey told the BBC recently, "in which people don't consume any kind of digital media without its help."

So let's take the same model to your membership. Do you really believe one size fits all? Are you forcing a broad base of constituents, from staff to individual and corporate members or customers, to sponsors and partners, to fit into your select few options? What does it really mean to have "silver, gold, and platinum" membership packages and what specific observable behaviors determine which value should be included in each? Much of what I've learned about membership models reminds me of the rigid rules some industries apply to their members or customers:

- Are hotel check-in and check-out times highly restricted for the guest's benefits or for the hotel's?

- Why do car rental companies force their customers to return cars with the gas tanks full when they have gas stations on site as well as enormous buying power as global organizations?

- Why do I have to cut the bar code off the package and mail it in with my original receipt to get a rebate for buying a scanner?

- Why do airlines charge me $150 to change my ticket when I'm a "plutonium" member, and why can they use each other's reservation systems and seats on empty planes, but my membership status with one "partner" means nothing to the others?

- Why do I have to sign my credit card charge form when I buy something in a store but not when I buy online or over the phone?

- Why do I have to be home between 8 a.m. and 3 p.m. for the cable company to come fix their service—often a connection issue outside the house?

Many organizations justify such practices as "policy." What they don't understand is that these incongruous policies are incredibly aggravating for the very members and customers they're trying to attract. In other words, have you worked really hard to create awareness for your brand and to interest and engage your audience, yet you don't care or haven't invested the time, effort, or resources in making the entire experience easy rather than annoying? Let's go back to the iTunes example of membership offerings; based on what you've learned about people through multiple touch points, you can offer individuals value-based options to create a highly *customized and personalized* membership package. The best part is that they're actually willing to pay a premium for services you've never thought about offering. You haven't thought of that, of course, because you've been so worried about member or customer satisfaction surveys that you've missed the bigger picture and upside potential. There are plenty of satisfied customers who never come back, primarily because you did the minimum level of work to satisfy their needs. What keeps a member coming back to iTunes is not only the painless manner in which it updates the software and more than 100 choices for applications, but it also recommends "noteworthy" and "staff favorite" new applications users should consider.

iTunes remembers an individual's contact and credit card information and emails the member a receipt within minutes of a purchase. The access ramp to this amazing world of information, entertainment, productivity, and outright coolness is a user ID and a password. As a point of comparison, most association executives I interviewed reported that on-demand education was a priority for their organizations. Similarly for Apple, one of the fastest growing areas for iTunes is on-demand education captured in the "iTunes U" section.

Fueled by hundreds of global educational institutions, iTunes U has thousands of audio- and video-based courses for a broad base of members. Is your organization one of the content providers or do you really still feel that you have the market cornered on education and credibility?

"iTunification" also means giving your members or customers less of what they don't want! They don't want shipments of CDs or reams of paper in an outdated report; they just want to download that podcast or research PDF right now. Nor do they want to purchase the same thing over and over again; just let them download the same purchase on multiple devices of their choosing. They don't want clutter, so give them the ability to organize music, applications, and books in a logical library and sync purchases with multiple devices. They don't want paper (printed instructions), details (step-by-step processes about how to use an application), worries, bureaucracy, disrespect, fear, rejection, repetition, stress, or similar headaches. Don't get me wrong; support is a necessary resource, and Apple provides plenty of it on iTunes Tutorial, iPod User, iPhone User, and iPad User as well as Apple TV User setup instructions under the Help menu. But when was the last time you asked your most loyal members or customers what they wanted less of? You may be amazed at the response. They know you much better than you think, and social media is the perfect platform to engage them for these types of conversations. What do they want less of in your industry?

If your organization is obsessed with solving your members' or customers' biggest headaches, eliminating what they want less of could be the most effective thing you can do. Creating modular capabilities and delivering them to your customers' fingertips makes you an invaluable resource. By developing the infrastructure to capture what your customers really want and need, you can learn from them and eliminate annoying or redundant processes and technologies or minimize the need for customers to jump through multiple hoops to work with you. Members and customers alike also greatly appreciate assurances from their connected relationships. Orbitz offers you a refund check if the flight you purchase is available for less before you travel. Why can't your organization offer the same assurance on product and service pricing or delivery dates?

iTunification of your business model also extends to corporate partners or sponsors. Instead of predetermined sponsorship packages for your next event, why not allow sponsors to choose from a menu of options, or better yet, tell you the types of sponsorship or partnership that would be most effective for their business? I've never understood why advertising so often is a separate package and the sponsor has to commit to an entire year's worth of magazine ads, instead of being able to choose a combination best suited to their needs, such as fewer ads for publication, a booth at the annual meeting expo, and/or a webinar series on a particular topic with a thought leader of their choosing.

Five Low-Cost Ways to Learn What Members/Customers Want Less Of

So, how can any organization learn what its customers or members want less of? Here are five simple ideas, often ignored or underestimated, to consider:

1. **Look at what they leave behind.** We leave behind that which we don't see value in: the silly bags full of useless brochures at conferences, binders in training sessions, warranty cards in packaging (since I can register online), instruction manuals, CDs (since I can download updates), excess papers, packaging, and reference material (much of which becomes outdated tomorrow).

2. **Ask for their notes.** Most individuals take notes of what they want to capture, retain, remember, or share with others. If a set of instructions, websites, reference points, events, dates, rates, times, and places are not captured in their notes, they don't care! Create an incentive for them to email or fax you their notes and discern that which they found of value to capture and much of what they didn't. The online version of this is to watch the online FAQs or chats, tweets about key topics, or consistent inquiries into a call center.

3. **Frame the root cause.** The organization plans, designs, develops, and delivers what it thinks is a great event, but the participation is lackluster at best. Beyond the obvious schedule conflicts, weather, traffic, or bad timing, really try to understand the root cause of the poor attendance. Was the promotional copy relevant and compelling? Did it create a sense of curiosity? Was the program perceived to have impact? We typically ignore online or offline events that miss the mark in effectively conveying the content and the community who will be there.

4. **Ask about their experiences in real time.** The highlights tend to be top of mind. If they forget or don't mention a particular point, it didn't have impact. "Top Lists" also force people to prioritize what they valued and leave out what they didn't.

5. **Don't include it next time.** It's human nature not to miss something until it's gone. Next time you offer the same product or service, don't include some of the side items and see how members react. If few notice or ask for those things, they weren't that important, or participants found other ways to satisfy the need.

Bonus: Look around your own life and experiences as a consumer of products, services, and information. What are you constantly getting that you could do without? Do we really need fax cover sheets if they're going electronically into someone's direct email inbox? Do we really need printed boarding passes for our flights, stickers on our luggage (versus RFID tags unique to each piece), or much of what we receive in the mail, the preponderance of which is thrown in the trash?

Digital Migration of Human Knowledge

Johannes Gutenberg, a goldsmith and businessman from the mining town of Mainz, Germany, invented the printing press with replaceable/moveable wooden and metal type in 1436. This method of printing spurred a revolution in the production of books but also fostered rapid development in the sciences, arts, and religion through the transmission of texts. The written word has always been at the heart of capturing and disseminating human knowledge. By 2015, eReaders, multipurpose tablets, and other digital devices are expected to be in the hands of 20 percent of the world's developed population. This new delivery channel is triggering a profound evolution in publishing and trends in the creation of content.

Many associations depend on publishing as a critical component of their value-add as well as their business and revenue models. At initial glance, the publishing industry seems unlikely to suffer the same jolting upheaval as the music industry when Napster arrived. Although several factors suggest a smoother evolution of digital print, such as consumer attachment to paper (thank you for reading the print version of this book, by the way), the complementary nature of e-books and paper, and limited electronic piracy at the moment, organizations that rely on traditional publishing must take notice. According to recent Bain & Company research involving 3,000 consumers across six countries and three continents, "readers tend to read more when equipped with digital readers."

For organizations that capture and disseminate knowledge in print, social and connected relationships will force them to rethink their business models and relationships with authors, distributors, and consumers of content. Consumer behaviors and direct relationships will be more critical to each stage of the value proposition than ever before. There are also enormous opportunities for every organization with unique and compelling content to benefit from the emergence of paid digital content.

The challenge is one of human behavior, as most online readers want to continue to get information for free. They will, however, pay for premium content, which today is mostly financial information, local news, and deep analysis. Creating value will not come from simply reformatting content from print into digital but rather from experimenting with new formats such as adding motion and sound and directing readers through technology (similar to the QR codes integrated in this book) to interactions that provide accelerated knowledge.

Printed publications won't go away anytime soon. Most consumers are not willing to abandon the paper experience, devices and e-books are perceived to be too expensive, and reading on a screen can be tiring.

But because more reference content is migrating to digital formats and many references are available online for free, print sales of such works have dramatically been decreased. The static nature of first-generation electronic reader (Amazon Kindle, Apple iPad, B&N Nook) technology is also not taking advantage of what is possible, such as real-time collaboration around specific content, cross-referencing unique content, and integrating social interactions with the content. The publishing arm of an organization's business or revenue model will not benefit economically from migrating to digital formats without a fundamental evolution in the distribution of value across connected relationships.

The consumer-centric practices of Amazon, Apple, or possibly Google in the near future illustrate a set of data-mining algorithms based on consumer insights, making each platform an advisor with relevant and timely recommendations. This is where your organization's brand will become a strong competitor against the commoditization of content collection and distribution by a multitude of virtual content aggregators and distributors that can upend the traditional publishing hierarchy across the globe. Only by focusing on the specific needs of your members or customers throughout the evolution of their membership life cycle can you create the greatest economies of scale while redeploying resources to digital channels and creating new services for consumers of that information. One interesting example, although limited in its scope, is the ASAE *Associations Now* Interactive Extra. (See Figure 5.4.) The entire publication may need to evolve to further enhance member-to-member interactive options/discussions.

Figure 5.4—Sample *Associations Now* Interactive Extra

Several interesting examples replicate successful models. Vook.com, a leading enhanced digital publisher that brings content to life with greater interactivity and connects people around stories and ideas, recently announced TextVook, animated apps and eBooks that deliver short-form content on a range of topics including history, science, psychology, law, economics, and music. TextVooks can benefit anyone wanting to learn on the go and on their devices, such as teachers seeking new ways to enhance their lesson plans.

"TextVooks make learning fun and accessible—and all of this in under 30 minutes," says Brad Inman, founder of Vook. "Brush up on the Civil War during your lunch break, learn the fundamentals of psychology while waiting for a flight at the airport, or get a crash course in the history of the Middle East over coffee."

Connected relationships among members and customers not only stimulate demand for published content but also establish stronger direct links between producers and consumers of compelling insights. Organizations have an opportunity to redefine this module of their business to expand beyond simply sharing information to providing actionable insights to targeted members/customers in the form of opinions and moderated debates, integrating on- and offline dialogue, and pushing the limits between free and paid content.

Organizations must also reinforce the "perceived value" of digital formats to unlock profitable growth. What will members and customers be willing to pay and for what features and services? The digital shift is further placing the member or customer at the center of inventiveness. Multimodality formats that can integrate video, sound, and music as well as various degrees of interactivity and collaboration into the reading experience include:

- **Hybrid**—The "Vook" mentioned earlier adds a set of high-definition visuals to the reading experience.

- **Nonlinear**—Understanding science through textbooks can be challenging. Xperica brings the experience of touch to various science experiments to foster better understanding. Users can interact with various elements to see how the experiment as a whole reacts.

- **Interactive**—In the Amanda Project, the reader is engaged in writing a collaborative script after a provided starting point. The user is prompted to continue the story and the best contributions are then published in paper format.

- **Social**—Authonomy.com, a new community site for writers, readers, and publishers, conceived and developed by book editors at HarperCollins, aims to "flush out the brightest, freshest new literature around," helps hopeful authors create their own webpage and upload their manuscript for visitors to vote and comment, which prioritizes taste and preference for HarperCollins to publish.

Three Initials After My Name for *My* Benefit or Yours?

In the IMPACT Model, after immersion and membership, participation and accreditation become the critical stages where unique and value-centric touch points must engage connected relationships. iTunification of your capabilities can also translate into taking the digital evolution of the printed word to your target audience. Why not create compelling content in a highly interactive manner to engage a community of passionate individuals focused on a common cause or a mission? Most accreditation processes require tenure, accumulation of knowledge, perhaps applications of that knowledge in real world environments within various projects or initiatives, and eventually some kind of a testing or evaluation process. How much of that experience within your organization is social or interactive today? How are you empowering members and customers to learn from the experiences of others and develop a preference for your brand because you have abandoned the antiquated paper process—which they want a lot less of—in favor of a highly engaged and highly interactive process?

A strong market validation for the value of accreditation is paying customers. In other words, does the accreditation create market pull or gravity for the members? Will they see a dramatic impact on their current or prospective business because they have your three initials after their name? An organization that I formerly was an active member and a passionate advocate of for close to a decade has an accreditation that it touts on its website as:

The Certified Blank Professional (CBP) designation, conferred by the National Blank Association and the International Federation for Professional Blanks, is the industry's international measure of professional skill. The CBP designation is earned through demonstrating competence in a combination of standards:

- Professional skills,
- Professional business management,
- Professional education, and
- Professional association.

Professionals must be members of NBA for at least three years and complete a rigorous application process to earn the CBP designation.

Here are the fundamental challenges for me as a former member of this organization:

- I've been in that industry for the past 10 years and have yet to lose business because I didn't have this certification. Although some of my buyers recognize the credentials, the market isn't asking for it and, candidly, the association never did a very good job in building a compelling value proposition in the market, in other words, marketing gravity or pull through economic buyers.

- The process is extremely paper- as well as labor-intensive; many individual members engage third-party resources (that have become thriving businesses) to help the collection of the required verification and navigation of the excessive steps.

- Other than three initials after my name, a special meeting at the annual conference, and maybe a few conference calls throughout the year, I can't see how I am better off as a member of this accreditation community.

- As a professional in this industry, I have not seen competence demonstrated by others with those initials after their names versus those without it. If the bar is set that this group is the best of the best in the industry, it certainly isn't evident when they're "On Air."

- Outside of North America, this accreditation is an unrecognizable asset. It is nontransferable in international markets where I actively participate in a global practice.

Don't misconstrue my comments. I deeply believe in the value of life-long education and the legitimate professional accreditations that keep ill-prepared practitioners out of the gene pool. You will not hear me argue against the validity of an MD, a JD, a PhD, a PE, or a CPA to name a few. But if you examine what they have in common, each professional accreditation is:

1. Globally recognized, not simply by the accrediting body (self-preservation) and a set of industry peers (misery likes company) but by the target industry or the general public as the utmost level of professional standards in a given industry;

2. The attainment is rigorous and (ideally) a hybrid of education and practice involving theory, application, and implementation;

3. Requires a formal mentorship/apprenticeship to reinforce on the job training and development;

4. The achievement of the accreditation is focused on the outcome (improving the holder's condition, the current or future organization served, and the industry); and

5. Continuing education is required and tracked rigorously to evolve the role, the profession, and the industry with elevated insights, changed procedures, policies, updated market research, and enhanced best practices of the most qualified practitioners.

As the leading organization in your industry, what are you doing to make sure your accreditation is perceived by the market and by members as the highest level of professional accomplishment, knowledge, applicable expertise, and predictable results? Now is the time to raise the bar internally and externally when it comes to your organization's credibility and repute.

Mobile Capabilities—Separating the Biz from the Buzz

Three attributes are leading the mobile revolution: enhanced utility of mobile applications, the accelerated computing and graphics capabilities of mobile devices, and the expanded breadth of data networks. Smartphones and tablets are invading the domain of PCs as the preferred devices for web browsing, email, content streaming, commerce, and social media. A recent McKinsey study found that nearly 50 percent of U.S. online consumers are now advanced users of smart phones, social networks, and other emerging tools—up from 32 percent in 2008. They are already more accustomed to paying for digital content and services than traditional online users are. Three quarters of iPhone users, for example, now pay for one or more apps each month. Developers are constantly competing for design, ease of use, and new mobile payment options.

These findings are particularly valuable for organizations that empower their members or customers to research key topics, compare value of products, tap into the opinions of other members or users, and solicit advice from friends and colleagues, all in the midst of decision processes. New sources of trusted information are emerging as user-generated content and user interactions increase in online forums. But becoming mobile is more than reformatting your website to be displayed on mobile devices. You must consider a "day in the life" of a mobile member or user.

Most users access information on their mobile devices in short, browsing spurts, often driven to a destination in response to a specific event or need. Most common consumer-centric examples are travel and vacations, tech products, financial products and services (stock prices), cars, insurance products and services, entertainment (movie tickets), and media (music, movies, and gaming). From a business user's perspective, access to quickly discernable insights tends to be most valued in between appointments, leading up to and during business travel, and in preparation for upcoming events.

As such, mobile content must be a unique and insightfully filtered touch point. Users simply won't go through a 400-page research document on their smart phones, so the organization needs to focus both its content and delivery channels with the following strategies in mind:

- Create unique access points, such as m.yourdomain.org, specific to mobile users with simplified and highly intuitive navigation as well as optimized and accelerated content delivery. The customers' or members' navigation of the content they deem most compelling will also be valuable to analyze later.

- Create highly focused search functionality, front and center. Remember, mobile users tend to wander less and are often looking for very specific content. Condense the information into its most insightful and actionable pieces; mobile users are browsers, not readers, so boil it down.

- Consider multimodality. Mobile is perfect for audio and video files— not for three hours of it, but for a collage of the most valuable sound bits from across your entire content library.

- Provide options to learn more. For example, give customers the option to send a link to their email address, forward mobile info they find to others, or share the insights with their social networks.

- Consider your members or customers and their professional maturity levels. Similar to college courses, can you offer 101, 201, 301 material?

- Allow sponsors to partner with you and align their value-add with your content in a nonintrusive manner. Don't clutter the already limited mobile real estate with ads. Rather explore unique opportunities to engage users of the content with advocacy marketing. (See the advocacy marketing section later in this chapter.)

Another viable value-based touch point is SMS-based strategies. Mobile calls to action featuring an SMS keyword and short code allow much of traditional media to be actionable and measurable. Savvy organizations can spread the word about unique products or services to members and customers via SMS, mobile Web, and branded applications. The answer to elevating an organization's message above the market noise is to trigger a consumer behavior—everything from opting into SMS alerts (try texting "RETip" or "ROIBook" to 90210), downloading a coupon application to sharing links with friends. Why not incorporate these consumer behavior triggers into mobile, local, and hyper-targeted keyword search along key IMPACT touch points? In a recent interview with *Mobile Marketer*, Maria Mandel, vice president of marketing and media innovation at AT&T Advanced Ad Solutions, said, "Mobile media is a great channel to break through the clutter, because you can target your exact audience by demographic, contextual, behavioral, and even location-based targeting."

Particularly for organizations that may find it difficult to reach and readily connect with members and customers, mobile marketing can be used to effectively reach target consumers with the right offer at the right time and place, not just for product promotions but to engage and influence them with the right actionable insight. Think of great mobile tactics to engage, such as chapter or local meeting destination locators, discounts, shopping/wish lists (perhaps for that upcoming accreditation), gift suggestions, product information, or tips. Mobile pay-per-click and pay-per-call ads can be efficient ways to convert "intrigued" into "interested and engaged." Mobile alerts, offers, and coupons can be powerful in reaching last-minute information seekers/insight shoppers. Mobile advertising and search can be effectively used to drive product awareness.

After exposure to a mobile campaign, increases in purchase intent average five points and even up to as high as 10 points for the best-performing campaigns, according to Dynamic Logic in the same *Mobile Marketer* article mentioned previously. Like any other marketing medium, cross-promotion and a seamless transition for members and customers between the different touch points is critical. Site promotion codes should work from every touch point, but having special mobile coupons to increase adoption is becoming more common.

Consumers are starting to get more comfortable with using their mobile phones for purposes other than calls and texting and are willing to experiment with relevant mobile offers that provide a clear value exchange. Geographically targeted coupons and ads have much higher redemption rates than online versions and can potentially convert a nonmember into a member by adding that extra incentive. Also, since social and mobile typically trend close together, having a mobile site with share-to-social abilities and vice versa is an easy win. Organization leaders who think creatively about their brand and what the member or customer would want can create endless possibilities.

Schema Disruption in Advocacy Marketing

Because connected relationships convene in communities of advocates and are frequently replacing traditional information sources, organizations are losing their stronghold on the control of information flow or specific sources of "user advocacy." Cultivating advocates through blogs, forums, and mobile applications has become a critical way for organizations to deepen their relationships with members and customers. In a recent report by the Boston Consulting Group, former Tremor CEO Steve Knox describes advocacy marketing as a "form of marketing that harnesses the power of recommendations from third-party individuals who are not affiliated with the brand." Knox believes that tapping into trusted social networks to disseminate and amplify relevant messages to target audiences allows consumers to participate in the development of products and services while providing valuable and candid feedback to the organization about new offerings and marketing campaigns.

So how does an organization create messages that will get advocates engaged? The research shows a direct correlation between key principles of advocacy marketing and cognitive science and the concept of *schema disruption*. Mental models of how the world works allow us to absorb and process information using a set of expectations. Advocacy is ignited when we encounter an experience variance of expectations. It is natural to want to share our experiences at dinner gatherings with friends, around the water cooler, and on blogs and online forums. If that experience variance is significant enough, we tend to prioritize and amplify it—which is the secret of advocacy marketing.

In our current low-trust environment, members' and customers' trust in brands and brand marketing tends to erode, allowing advocates to have greater impact. Social media and relationships also act as conductors and accelerated transmitters of advocate messages. Connected relationships become that exponential scale in advocacy marketing and have the potential to double the revenues of a new product launch versus traditional marketing channels alone, according to the BCG analysis.

The key to success in advocacy marketing is not only aligning the organization's strategic goals but integrating current marketing plans with *thinking differently* about traditional "reach-based" marketing models and moving to new "relationship-based" models. By integrating the various sources of advocacy, organizations can distinctly and dramatically elevate themselves and their unique value-add above and beyond the market noise.

## CHAPTER 6

Attract and Develop Unparalleled Social Talent

W HEN BAGGAGE HANDLERS at United Airlines broke musician David Carroll's guitar and then rejected his damage claim, he didn't just tell a few friends. He told 10 million people in "United Breaks Guitars," a catchy YouTube video trashing United. When Maytag fumbled multiple service calls over several months for Heather Armstrong, whom the *New York Times* recently dubbed "Queen of the Mommy Bloggers," she was so upset that she used her mobile phone to tell her million-plus followers on Twitter they should never buy a Maytag. There are endless examples that demonstrate how one individual and his or her connected relationships have the ability to instantly damage a brand's repute after a poor experience.

It's not just upset customers who wield authentic power that create impact online. Employees are equally capable of being digital defenders of the faith. At Stanley Black & Decker, Rob Sharpe used homemade videos for online sales training, much like how David Carroll used video to scream at United. Frank Eliason, now senior vice president of social at Citi, launched a one-man mission at Comcast to solve customer service issues via Twitter. The team has grown to more than 50 individuals today, engaging thousands of productive customer interactions while reinventing the role of a "call center." Eliason's maverick status has garnered him a flurry of media attention, and a number of corporations have followed his lead by using Twitter (and sometimes other microblogging services such as Jaiku and FriendFeed) for reaching out to their own consumers and resolving complaints. On his personal website, Eliason recently commented:

> This coming year, we will see more companies embracing their own employees' use of social media. The fact is employees are the most passionate about the company and they are the best ones to represent the company to customers. We will also see companies focus on the customer experience. This will not just be a marketing message, but rather a shift in the way they conduct business. There will be a major change in cultures for companies and those who embrace these aspects will be the long-term winners.

Paul Vienick, senior vice president of product management at E*Trade, made it possible for the company's Mobile Pro application to serve customers and build loyalty, just like Heather Armstrong used it to demonize Maytag. The Mobile Pro application for the iPhone was the number one downloaded application in the financial section of the iPhone's app store for several weeks after its debut and has consistently been in the top five downloads, according to Vienick.

Social's impact reaches beyond products and services. It can be an equally effective advocacy enabler. Mark Betka and Tim Receveur, of the U.S. State Department, unwilling to be stopped by a lack of funding, used Adobe Connect to create a public diplomacy outreach project called CO.NX for facilitating webchats with U.S. government officials and businesspeople. With tens of thousands of international participants, and more than 600,000 Facebook Fans, it sheds a different light on the role of the State Department and its realm of impact. The U.S. Chamber of Commerce and its Campaign for Free Enterprise measures one aspect of its social impact by proactively reaching out to citizens to encourage them to engage congressional representatives on hotly debated legislative issues.

Sample Social Media Job Titles

In summer 2011, Idealist.org reached out to thousands of nonprofit organizations to learn how they had been affected by the financial crisis that hit the sector in the fall of 2008 and, more importantly, about how they were feeling about the future. Three thousand organizations from all over the United States responded with "cautious optimism." While the economy is still fragile and while the whole sector is being very careful with its spending, this survey tells us there is reason for optimism. Although social specifically was not segmented, communication and fundraising were. So what are some of the sample social media job titles that have become vernacular and what do different realms of responsibilities entail?

Check out Figure 6.1 by MindFlash.com for key job descriptions and average salaries based on posted positions in 2010.

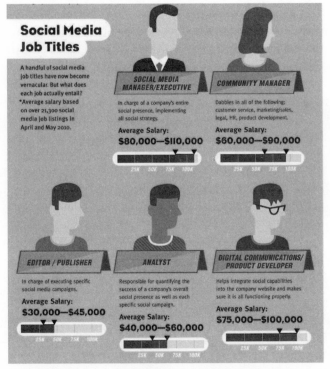

Social Media Job Titles

A handful of social media job titles have now become vernacular. But what does each job actually entail?
*Average salary based on over 21,300 social media job listings in April and May 2010.

SOCIAL MEDIA MANAGER/EXECUTIVE
In charge of a company's entire social presence, implementing all social strategy.
Average Salary:
$80,000—$110,000

COMMUNITY MANAGER
Dabbles in all of the following: customer service, marketing/sales, legal, HR, product development.
Average Salary:
$60,000—$90,000

EDITOR / PUBLISHER
In charge of executing specific social media campaigns.
Average Salary:
$30,000—$45,000

ANALYST
Responsible for quantifying the success of a company's overall social presence as well as each specific social campaign.
Average Salary:
$40,000—$60,000

DIGITAL COMMUNICATIONS/ PRODUCT DEVELOPER
Helps integrate social capabilities into the company website and makes sure it is all functioning properly.
Average Salary:
$75,000—$100,000

Figure 6.1—Social Media Jobs via MindFlash.com

"Ten years ago, our goal was to encourage constituents to write letters to their congressmen, which would take a while. Today, we can activate an army of concerned digital citizens to email, tweet, or post on a multitude of social sites to reach their legislative representatives *instantly*," says Bill

Miller, former senior vice president for political affairs and federation relations and national political director for the U.S. Chamber.

Talented staff members who are empowered to *really* use social to solve internal and external challenges as well as to take advantage of opportunities they uncover every day are the fuel to implement your social strategy. Buyers beware; it will change your organization from inside out. Freeing employees to experiment with new disruptive technologies; make high-profile decisions on the fly; build processes and systems that the members and customers see, touch, and feel; and essentially become the voice of the organization in public is not something most companies or associations are comfortable about allowing. They are concerned about how employees will use the technology.

Far more important than trying to block employee access to social is to acknowledge that with smart phones and broadband, they're equally connected. So why not recruit, train, develop, and empower them differently to harness their intelligence, creativity, problem solving, initiative, pride, and surprisingly entrepreneurial mindset as a strategic asset, and by doing so, elevate your organization's performance, execution, and results? Arm the right employees with the technology and let them build solutions at the speed and demands of today's connected relationships. But if you're like most organizations, this last paragraph might as well have been written in ancient hieroglyphics, because your organization isn't set up to make these decisions and activities possible. It can be—if you think and lead differently.

From Best Practices to Best Practitioners

The transformation process of any organization in becoming more socially enabled has to start with the manner in which it identifies and attracts world-class, social talent. Attracting and retaining world-class social talent is a painstaking challenge for many small- to medium-sized organizations. This is especially true for those with limited financial resources, such as early-stage ventures, nonprofits, and associations that are trying to add social as yet another "must-do" on their existing overflowing plate of action items. Many such organizations recruit less experienced talent and ask them to learn social on the job, attend conferences, or get self-educated through trial and error. That may work in many other functional areas, but for an organization to evolve in its strategy, embrace engagement as a core competency, and modularize its capabilities, it will need a different type of talent. It will require intelligent employees with the drive to take the initiative and combine personal characteristics with natural creativity and curiosity, an accelerated learning curve, no fear of failure, and the ability to learn from every interaction to execute the organization's social strategy.

Associations must find creative ways to tap into a global workforce, passionate about both the organization's cause and the will to create an exceptional social presence for that cause. How? By focusing greater attention on engines that can dramatically alter the talent pipeline flow into nonprofit, civic, and public service sectors. The Civic Ventures Purpose Prize™ and the Partnership for Public Service are two good examples of such initiatives.

Companies can also do more to mentor nonprofit leaders and offer internships in nonprofits for current and future employees. Businesses can also provide incentives for retirees and alums to go to work for nonprofits. Bridgestar has emerged as exemplary in enhancing the flow and effectiveness of passionate and highly skilled leaders into and within the nonprofit sector.

Despite any given period's unemployment rates, the global talent risk is imminent; that risk of the gap between required skill sets and the abundance of talent to fill it grows exponentially when you factor in the understanding, application, and implementation mindset, skill set, and roadmap of social in key individual roles. Talent gaps threaten the economic growth of companies, industries, and global economies today and will continue to in the future. It will be a struggle to remain competitive as social helps fuel the displacement of financial capital with human capital as the engine of prosperity.

According to a recent *World Economic Forum* study, "The U.S. will need to add more than 25 million workers to its talent base by 2030 to sustain economic growth, while Western Europe will need more than 45 million." The highest demand will be for those who have experience in engaging internal and external networks through social applications—often socially educated professionals, technicians, and managers. The best and brightest will continue to be highly employable because of their cross-industry, cross-cultural, and highly transferable skills. Identifying and cultivating an ongoing talent pool is also going through transformation. Traditional means of sourcing and recruiting talent, such as personal referrals, headhunters, sourcing, job boards, and print, have dramatically shifted to social networks, search engines including job aggregators (sponsored links), career sites, talent community, and social referrals.

Beyond leveraging social to source and recruit great talent, what are key attributes of employees who fuel an organization's social presence? What unique characteristics should you suddenly infuse into your hiring process? What magical quality in your human capital formula will make your organization an overnight success in the social sphere? Unfortunately, there is no magic pill. You have to think beyond mediocrity to meritocracy. Intelligence can't be taught, and educated staff will quickly identify opportunities for enhanced operations through social insights. Creative employees will understand where to find the answers—a big contributing factor to organizational knowledge. Intuitive problem-solvers frame problems correctly and discover disparate pockets of information created across organizational or industry silos. Employees who take initiative can often locate specific subject matter experts quickly and efficiently instead of constantly trying to reinvent the wheel. Intrapreneurs understand that time is an individual's most valuable asset and use social networks with powerful search capabilities to expedite connections and increase knowledge and service capabilities.

These employees will engage their counterparts—both inside and outside the organization—in conversations. Although a great deal of attention is placed on the public conversations of social media, according to interviews with hundreds of chief information officers (CIOs), more social media projects are fueling business processes behind the firewall than in front of it. These conversations connect employees with their colleagues globally, whether they're employed by the same organization or not. Organizational conversations facilitate efficient resource connections,

---

Attributes of a Socially Optimized Business

How do you define a social organization? According to Dachis Group's Social Business Council, a collection of practitioners from global organizations who are at the leading edge of social's impact, "It's a business alive with energy and big ideas. It's collaborative, authentic, customer-centric, trusted, open, and real-time."

After decades of what they perceive as "mechanistic, process-oriented management dogma," it seems that visionary organizations of varying sizes are waking up to the fact that a creative, global workforce (not always employees within the organization) can dramatically affect business results. Only when organizations embrace passionate, socially savvy individuals and empower them to blossom will they be able to create a social organization.

This XPLANATiON from the collaborative knowledge of the Dachis Group has been turned into a clean, clear visual (see Figure 6.2) focused on the benefits and the impact of an organization's social talent.

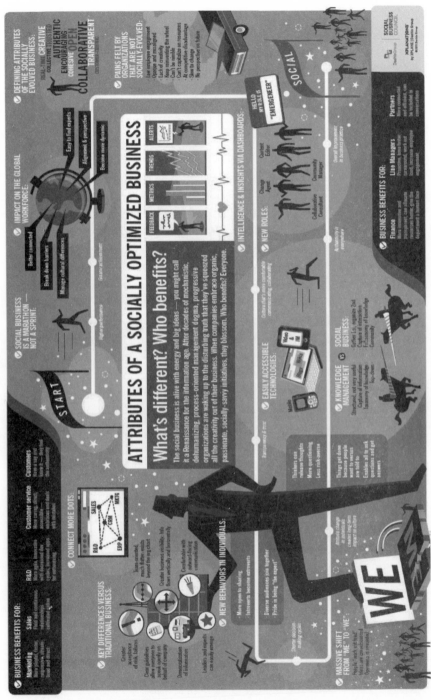

Figure 6.2—Attributes of a Socially Optimized Organization

allowing practitioners to browse Facebook-like profiles, resumés, availability, utilization, project experience, white papers, presentations, team information or reporting structure, firm activities, and contacts. Equally valuable are the parallel universes many employees function within. Cross-access to portfolios of relationships, not limited by physical connections, gives social exponential reach within the organization as it overcomes geographic, functional, and time zone boundaries.

Beyond Mediocrity to Meritocracy

If content is the king, context is the emperor! Context allows knowledge workers to coordinate activities, report status, keep managers and leaders updated, gather help, and help others. The addition of digitally savvy employees into the workforce, particularly those comfortable with sharing and transparency, combined with the geographical distribution of more teams as organizations attempt to moderate real estate costs or give employees more work-life flexibility, makes productive collaboration that much more critical. Forrester Research notes that in five years, almost half of U.S. workers—about 63 million people—will work virtually. This will change everything from designing workplace information strategies for collaboration, to delivering content experiences to people across channels, to engaging the next-generation workforce to serve customers better. In essence, social is challenging various forms of hierarchy while demonstrating that expertise matters more than credentials and that hierarchies can be developed from the bottom up.

Social forces every leader to ask a series of questions, specific to the caliber of talent the organization needs to attract, develop, and retain; specific to the policies or procedures it is willing to create with a new level of agility; specific to metrics and compensation plans that measure more the value received from the outcome of efforts than any input. Questions such as:

- What kind of association or company do we want this to be?
- What is our comfort level with transparency, intellectual property, and self-management?
- Are we willing and able to create meaningful metrics and reward individuals for different behaviors?
- What does it mean to lead in a highly connected world, where people can learn, adapt, and apply their learning without being told to do so?

- How will leadership development and succession planning change, if fewer highly talented knowledge workers will want to work for your organization full time?

If candor is infused in the subsequent discussions around these questions, the organization and its leadership will arrive at a set of philosophical underpinnings. They may include universal truths such as:

- Bureaucracy is oppressive and stifling, dramatically limiting people's personal and professional growth possibilities.
- Enabled people become more effective when they can apply their talents where they can be used best.
- Most people are thinking, energetic, creative, and caring human beings of integrity.
- A culture of information sharing builds trust and encourages social interactions as essential factors to driving a social change in the workforce.
- Empowered knowledge workers foster innovation and growth through quick access to information and collaboration, which stimulates creativity, ideation, and problem solving.
- Social supports people's innate sense of "belonging" when they are recognized for their contributions and are encouraged to build stronger communities and relationships across the organization.
- Leadership development is a byproduct of strong and highly supportive communities, expertise infusion along a personal development pathway, and personal brand management.

Kelly Koczak is the vice president of marketing communications at the Produce Marketing Association (PMA) in Newark, Delaware. I first met Kelly back in 2008 at the ASAE Annual Convention in Toronto, where she was speaking about how key members of her organization—the growers, logistics or transportation companies, and retail buyers of produce—could use Google Maps to more effectively engage each other in streamlining the supply chain process. A fairly clever idea, if you think about the perishable nature of produce and the timeliness of when produce is picked and how it's transported and delivered to end consumers.

Ever since that first presentation, I've found Koczak and the PMA team to be particularly astute in exploring how social can dramatically enhance their market presence and the value they bring to their members. More recently, she led the development and deployment of the PMA's

Fresh Magazine mobile application. Look at the manner in which PMA describes the impact of this publication for its target audience:

> Unlike most trade pubs, *Fresh Magazine* is a focused read, written for busy business leaders with buying power. Centered on innovation, *Fresh Magazine* covers the latest in hot issues impacting the industry, PMA people and initiatives, innovative companies, business and marketing trends, and technology. Written through a lens that is fresh and informed, *Fresh* offers a perspective that only PMA can provide. It prompts the kind of dialogue that makes industry's decision makers connect. And it has shelf life. As a PMA publication, *Fresh Magazine* has the "keeper" exclusive stories and interviews with PMA experts and thought leaders around the world.

Beyond integrating Twitter, Flicker, and YouTube into their annual events, Koczak and her team have also joined with United States Department of Agriculture (USDA) to create ChooseMyPlate.gov, "a fruits and veggies video challenge" to educate their market on the nutritional values of healthy foods.

"Kelly has been an incredible asset to our organization's social footprint," says Bryan Silbermann, PMA's president and CEO. "She's creative, takes incredible initiative, and is constantly exploring how we can continue to add tremendous value to our members," he added.

"I see social [networking, media, etc.] as a huge enabler of not just my role but our entire organization's ability to remain relevant and add consistent value to members who rely on us for market leadership and advocacy," says Koczak. "I love exploring new ideas, yet make sure we, as an organization remain grounded and balance creative ideas with real impact for our members—not doing things that are just cool or fun, but those that deliver real results and engage our target audiences as well."

Time to get a CLOU

The Self-Management Institute, founded in 2008, has an interesting perspective on organizational structure: that it is simply a set of relationships that individuals have with other individuals. It propagates a general business philosophy, particularly relevant to social, that self-management is the most effective and efficient method of organizing people. It believes self-management "is the way families are organized; it's the way community relationships come to be; it's the way that the most prosperous economies are organized. Is it possible to capture that effectiveness and efficiency in commercial relationships?"

Chris Rufer, creator of The Self-Management Institute, is also the founder of the Morning Star Company, a leading vertically integrated food processing company, which he began in 1970. Morning Star was recently recognized by the joint Harvard Business School/McKinsey M-Prize for its innovative application of social technologies (See Figure 6.3.) to Chris's early vision of a framework for a document that he called the Colleague Letter of Understanding (CLOU). Used by Morning Star colleagues primarily as a tool to coordinate and organize themselves, individuals within the enterprise would have a CLOU, which they would be personally responsible for crafting in collaboration with key colleagues. It would include:

- Personal Commercial Mission. Each colleague within Morning Star is responsible for crafting a mission that represents his or her fundamental purpose within the enterprise. This is intended to be their primary guiding light, the statement that should be the direction for all of their commercial activity within the enterprise.

- Activities. The key activities that the colleague agrees to accomplish in pursuit of their Personal Commercial Mission.

- Steppingstones. Identifying the key measures by which colleagues gauge their performance in accomplishing the activities they commit to as well as the accomplishment of their mission.

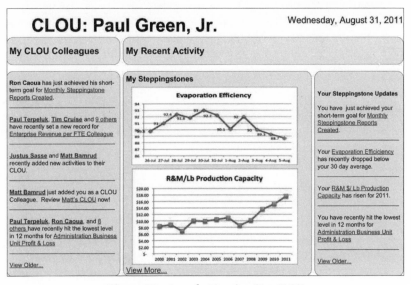

Figure 6.3—Sample Morning Star CLOU

- Time commitment. The amount of time colleagues agree to commit to the accomplishment of their mission.
- CLOU Colleagues. Those colleagues to whom they make these commitments. Your CLOU colleagues were to sign off on the CLOU, indicating their agreement with all of the representations therein.

The network of relationships forged through the various CLOU connections serves as the "org chart." It's not based on any appointed hierarchy, since there are no titles and no formal hierarchy within Morning Star. It's an organization chart based on real relationships within the enterprise—a portfolio of highly interdependent and connected relationships. It's highly *dynamic,* since it changes based on changing circumstances, and *contextual,* since important relationships depend on the nature of the current situation.

Collective Intelligence, Social Creativity, and Problem Solving

Wikipedia defines collective intelligence as a "shared or group intelligence that emerges from the collaboration and competition of many individuals and appears in consensus decision making." Within the social context, it is connecting global relationships with unique perspectives to create systems of network effects and feedback loops that improve framing key challenges and opportunities, exploring creative solutions, and accelerating problem solving as use increases. What are network effects? In essence, the greater a network application's usefulness and value, the more people will use it. The more people use it, the more useful and valuable the network becomes. In their books *The Wisdom of Crowds* and *Smart Mobs,* authors James Surowiecki and Howard Rheingold describe the three types of collective intelligence as cognition, cooperation, and coordination and provide examples of each. (See Figure 6.4.)

When the right people are encouraged and enabled to share information, seek resources beyond the organization's perceived boundaries, and become a part of a community where the currency of the realm is impactful ideas, they tend to flourish in the organization's social communities. Rich with information sources, as the number of members in these social communities and the productive capacity of the organizations continue to grow, the lines between external, internal, social, technical, or subject matter issues begin to blur and overlap with current and new business models.

According to Greg Jarvis in *Social Networks: Managing the Impending Chaos—Social Networks are Coming to Corporate* (Deloitte Consulting,

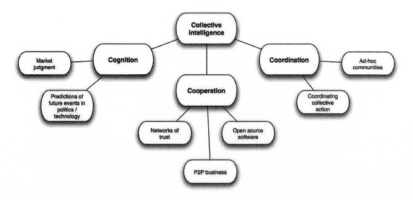

Figure 6.4—Types and Examples of Collective Intelligence

LLP, 2011), internal social networks connect current and former employees and personnel with similar interests, projects, and affiliations. The member-based organization is an example. Internal-to-external networks establish vertical industry relationships through continuous dialogue across the entire value chain—manufacturers, distributors, integrators, consultants, end users, and employees. The organization can learn from external networks where members or customers interact with each other.

A September 2009 McKinsey Global Survey, *How Companies are Benefiting from Web 2.0,* highlighted measurable gains within the organization as well as with external partners from the context of social networks mentioned above. They include:

- Increased speed of access to knowledge,
- Reduction in communication costs,
- Increased speed of access to internal experts,
- Decreased travel costs,
- Increased staff satisfaction,
- Reduced operational costs,
- Reduced time to market for products/services,
- Increased number of successful innovations for new products or services, and
- *Increased* revenues from new or reinvigorated business models.

But have you ever thought about why we *really* have to collaborate? Most people know their jobs. If you do your job and everybody else does theirs, won't you all be doing the organization's job? To paraphrase a recent conversation with a client, "I'm not sure why we have to work with all of these other people anyway!"

Many of today's organizations, regardless of their size, are actually complex systems that require continuous, responsive coordination to be effective. Work is much less repetitive than before. Job roles, realms of responsibilities, and economic cycles force more work to be performed by fewer staff members and make work a set of highly connected tasks, not separate actions. Work instructions can never be complete descriptions of what needs to be done. What we do is often all about links. Who needs to connect and the context of what they need to connect about cannot always be planned in advance. Interdependence is *contextual* and *situational*. To successfully frame a challenge or an opportunity and explore creative options, the constantly changing people forming the organization have to connect. Work is communication between and among interdependent people. In the age of connected relationships, the days when we could just do our own thing are over.

When it comes to understanding the organizations in which we work, most of us understand best our own myopic roles and the work groups we have been part of. As a result, most people are unaware of the larger network they affect. When problems arise, this unconscious interdependency often leads to short-sighted problem solving and suboptimal solutions. Issues are resolved in favor of just one point of view or the short-term "quick fix," versus the longer-term impact on a much wider set of relationships. This unintentional consequence causes most individuals, teams, and organizations to work considerably harder. And to do what, really?

When the circle of involvement is larger, many changes occur. When people see where they fit in the bigger picture, they are able to see the interdependencies and are able to respond much, much faster to changing conditions. In my consulting work, I've observed that when creative solutions consider broader impacts on the organization or the industry and are presented in transparent processes—open innovation occurring within an organization's social culture—they are more than four times faster than corresponding processes where people see just their own part.

That's where the power and promise of social collaboration comes in. No one person or one function can meet today's challenges alone. We need a community of intelligent, creative problem-solvers who willingly participate and provide their insights to address increasingly interdependent issues. Positive and productive social collaboration is necessary because no one person ever has the most complete answer. Answers reside in the interactions between us.

Widening the circle of involvement also means expanding who gets to participate within and outside the organization. It is about inviting and including contextually relevant, new, and different voices and perspectives. We may not like or even agree with their perspectives, but in a transparent arena of connected relationships, civil discourse is a critical ingredient in thinking differently.

Misperceptions of Social Collaboration

We all have the experience of teams discussing among themselves about what is and isn't working. "If only *they* would get their act together!" This kind of thinking never produces learning, responsiveness, and agility in social collaboration. Bringing more people into the conversation is essential. By widening the circle of participation, a leader or an organization also widens the conceptual framework of the challenge or the opportunity at hand and the range of possible creative solutions.

There are several myths and misperceptions about social collaboration within an expansive circle of internal and external participants. Let's take a look at a few:

1. **All social collaboration is good.** Bad collaboration is about collaborating without a strong focus on results. Collaboration for the sake of collaboration creates infighting and disagreements about agenda and metrics, often distracting from the real work. "There is a right way and a wrong way to collaborate," says Morten Hansen, professor of management at the University of California at Berkeley, and author of *Collaboration: How Leaders Avoid the Traps, Create Unity, and Reap Big Results* (Harvard Business School Press, 2009). Some of the barriers include "not invented here," hoarding, search difficulties, and transfer (including geographic limitations). A related concern is that collaboration can elicit regression to the mean. Remember when the White House asked the public to vote on what they thought were legislative priorities and the number one answer was legalizing marijuana? Clearly, the wrong arrow was in the crowdsourcing quiver.

2. **Social collaboration requires managers to lead the conversation.** As managers contemplate widening the circle of involvement, they sometimes believe that it means having less ability to provide input based on their knowledge and experience. Paradoxically, engaging

more people requires more from managers than the current management paradigm. Instead of being responsible for identifying both the problem and the solution, they are now responsible for not only identifying the problem and the people whose voices need to be heard but also enabling others to reach and engage them. Who else needs to be a part of this conversation? How do we invite and engage people who do not report to me? How do I invite people from outside our organization who can contribute? Successful social collaboration today is increasingly a result of skillful management of online participation: Who is included and who is excluded?

3. **Productivity will surely suffer if larger numbers of people are involved in social collaboration.** The new social platforms and interaction technologies have dramatically reduced the cost of participation. Temporary communities can be formed to solve a problem or tackle an opportunity more easily, cheaply, and faster than ever before—if people are invited and want to engage.

4. **Great decisions are natural byproducts of collaboration.** An August 2010 study of hundreds of nonprofit employees by CommonGood Careers underscores an argument against this point. It found that when staff is not involved in or aware of an organization's decision-making practices, they express confusion, disempowerment, and dissatisfaction. The study also highlights that organizational decision making falls on a continuum, with traditional top-down on one end and highly distributed (let's get everyone involved) on the other end. Without a perceived right or wrong approach, what is certain is that organizations must be clear about the process by which the decision will be made, by whom, and in what context. Beyond obvious, a transparent decision-making process is often absent in many organizations, even those with a "collaborative" culture. Social collaboration tends to create yellow flags of concern sooner if any of the decision-making processes (by whom, and in what context) are missing, and red flags tend to spread alarm at an accelerated rate.

5. **Consensus finding will benefit creativity.** In *Is Gen Y Teamwork Killing Creativity?* blogger Rebecca Thorman acknowledges the great many positive aspects of teamwork that younger generations are bringing to the way organizations work, but questions whether the manner in which they're doing it limits innovation and the individual voice. She writes, "All this teamwork makes it incredibly easy to

live in society but also threatens the individual mind, intuition, and originality. Consensus isn't all gravy." What is the appropriate solution when less consensus and a legitimate "fight" is warranted? Social collaboration brings unique perspectives from multiple sources to the same point to provide different points of view and alternative options. It also tends to nurture an attitude that says, "We agree to disagree, yet let's move forward," rather than traditional attempts to square a circle and get nothing accomplished in the process.

Professor Hansen from UC Berkley points to innovation, cross-selling of customers, and efficiency as viable goals of good collaboration. He highlights Procter & Gamble's White Strips teeth-whitening product as a result of three units coming together to create an affordable product. Oral care identified the market need; home care provided the bleaching technology; and corporate R&D contributed the film technology.

It is also particularly interesting how concerns about abuse or bad behaviors come up in many discussions involving social collaboration. These are likely to surface whenever there is a new medium. However, these abuses seem to rarely occur inside the organization, unlike on the Web. Think of it this way: No one is likely to do bad things in a well-lighted parking lot with security cameras monitoring every move. However, in the dark alleyways of email, such behavior is more likely to occur.

Social collaboration is a means to an end: a process, a management style, or an approach to deriving *clear, concise, and informed decisions.* When done well by well-intentioned individuals, it integrates open-innovation principles that allow visionary leaders and their organizations to enhance not only their products and services, but their core business processes as well.

Let's Convo

Convo, abbreviation for conversation, a noun describing:

1. Agile strategic exchanges embedded in a learning loop that spins and accelerates; and

2. Adaptive conversations, designed to inform, immerse, and co-create solutions.

That's a description of what Stuart Henshall, chief strategist and facilitator at Convo.org, refers to as his work with organizations to "uncover new possibilities, frame opportunities, and design solutions that accelerate business growth." Through what Henshall describes as "creating immersive learning environments," the firm aims to expose its clients to new perspectives and jointly develop insights through research that fosters lasting change. Of particular interest in thinking of the ideal social collaboration framework that spurs more effective decision making is Henshall's diagram of the Convo process. (See Figure 6.5.)

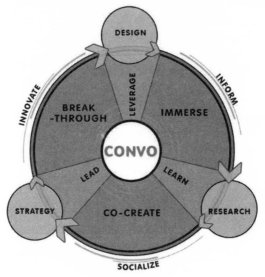

Figure 6.5—The Convo Process

Their "strategic conversations platform" has three distinct, yet highly interrelated, components:

- Immerse: people, lives, context, behavior, needs, pain points, and challenges;
- Co-Create: sharing and learning, collective discovery, conversation spaces, tool kits;
- Breakthrough: convos that stimulate innovation and grow your business.

Social collaboration is open innovation and should transform the manner in which global organizations develop new products and services, in essence, exposing internal R&D to outside ideas in a highly iterative process. Think of a "convo-like" process as an accelerator of getting knowledge workers to flow toward asking better questions, challenging the status quo, and seeking external ideas from people in a variety of industries, disciplines, and contexts and then combining the resulting lessons in new applications. This "collective" process/collective intelligence can be harnessed, making an organization that is collectively more aware, more responsive, more open to new and upstream thinking. Convo is a virtuous circle to help people focus on changes that matter and questions which often can lead to breakthroughs.

The Impact of Initiative, Intrapreneurship, and Pride

Social is changing the face of collaboration as more organizations find creative ways to use communities—public communities such as LinkedIn Answers as well as private ones behind the corporate firewall—to pair internal "seekers" with external "solvers." If one aspect of social collaboration is to optimize processes in more effective decision making, nearly any activity a company is challenged with, from hiring and development practices to optimizing global supply chains, can be characterized as a process. Many such processes tend to be generally more alike than different across organizations and even some industry sectors, making social collaboration insightfully rich. The collective know-how of millions of managers is now at the fingertips of the right talent within any organization.

That's where an individual who has the initiative to tap into this wealth of experience can create enormous positive forward motion for the organization. To borrow an adage from industrial designers at design consultancy IDEO, the best source of new ideas is old ideas. Creative designers often take a familiar structure (a hinge, for example) from an existing product and apply it to a completely new service or context. Another highly powerful application of a "convo-like" process could be a project team that initiates a conversation with a social community of knowledge workers willing to discuss their experiences to serve an immediate need, and then combines those external ideas with internal ones to improve the organization's process. *That initiative tends to improve something in an organization, even if it isn't broken.*

Intrapreneurs, or entrepreneurs within or around the ecosystem of any organization, also have a dramatic impact on social collaboration. Corporate psychologists often look at a key individual's role and contributions within an organizational structure. Now take that same individual and add 5 billion friends and their connected brains. The very essence of "we" discussed in organizational meetings includes those connected people. This global community has the potential to build a structure that's truly different from traditional large organizations. Big organizations will continue to get bigger. However, more and more talented people will choose not to function exclusively within a large organization but rather as global entrepreneurs, as barriers to entry are lowered and social connectability is accelerated. More and more people will want to create, collaborate, and evolve themselves personally and professionally. So the challenge for any organization becomes how to pick talent from within the surrounding ecosystem, instead of imagining that any current or prospective employee in the immediate vicinity will want to be married to the organization for years.

The last, but certainly not least, unique attribute of talent within or around any organization is social pride: pride in the diversity and quality of connected relationships, in seeking compelling challenges, in creating unique solutions, and in productive and pleasant interactions within social communities. In consulting with global clients, I've also observed pride in expanding one's portfolio of digital relationships with a certain contrarian perspective on the status quo. Highly engaged and empowered talent view issues from an unbiased perspective, use reversal-thinking processes (bring the restaurant to the people), and often have the courage to sail against the great, mediocre mainstream.

Meet Me with a Better Question in the LOFT

Have you ever wondered how we've arrived at a place in our society where organizational training and development looks more like corporate speed dating than an investment in the development of a person as a future leader of the organization or someone worthy of being passed the baton? Training and development is often one of the first areas to get cut in economic belt tightening. Much of the global training material that exists is a stale binder of rehashed content, written by disconnected people who, respectfully, have never sold anything, advised anyone, developed a process, or operated a function.

In many of my consulting engagements, I observe that as individuals, teams, and organizations, we have become very good at problem solving and often very bad at identifying or framing the correct problem to solve. Both my parents are retired teachers and as long as I can remember, test-driven educational systems have measured a teacher's effectiveness at imparting the right answers to students, but they do a very poor job of equipping students to find the right questions. The same challenge lies within how we hire, train, and develop our staff and employees and work with partners, members, and customers.

Knowledge sharing through a peer-level structure at the edge of where business happens must become transferable, coachable, practical, and applicable. Most frontline staff members don't want to know everything the organization knows or even everything the organization thinks they should know. They want actionable insights—another disconnect from much of the training and development content and processes out there—at the moment where they can apply it with the greatest impact.

Two recent books in particular, *A New Culture of Learning: Cultivating the Imagination for a World of Constant Change* (CreateSpace, 2011), by Douglas Thomas and John Seely Brown, and *Make Just One Change: Teach Students to Ask Their Own Questions* (Harvard Education Press, 2011), by Dan Rothstein and Luz Santana, articulate practical applications of how we can modify the learning formula to encourage people to ask their own questions. If applied in our organizations, these ideas could help introduce new products and market opportunities; access recipients' knowledge to see what they need to understand better about a product, service, or process; and help employees themselves to learn differently.

Social learning can dramatically affect increased participation from the group and within peer learning environments, improve content and context delivery management (remember value-add versus value *perceived, received, and applied* mentioned earlier), and enhance efforts to address varying levels of effectiveness across sizes/depths of learning and development capabilities.

In *Make Just One Change,* the authors recommend six steps in traditional education that, when combined with social, can help any organization to train and develop its broad base of constituents differently:

1. **Experts Design a Question Focus.** The Question Focus is a prompt that can be presented in the form of a statement or a visual or aural aid to focus and attract participant's attention and quickly stimulate the formation of questions.

2. **Participants Produce Questions.** Participants within and external to the organization use a set of rules for producing questions without assistance from the instructor. The four rules are: ask as many questions as you can; do not stop to discuss, judge, or answer any of the questions; write down every question exactly as it was stated; and change any statements into questions.

3. **Improve Their Questions.** Participants focus on an iterative process to improve their questions by analyzing the differences between open-ended and closed questions and by practicing changing one type to the other.

4. **Prioritize Their Questions.** The instructor or subject matter expert, with the end result of the training and development process in mind, offers criteria or guidelines for the selection of priority questions.

5. **Collectively Decide on Next Steps.** At this stage, participant and instructors work together to decide how to use the questions for constructive purposes, such as formulate a topic for a subsequent in-depth discussion, roundtable, or seminar.

6. **Reflect on What They Have Learned.** The instructor reviews the steps and provides participants with an opportunity to review what they have learned by producing, improving, and prioritizing their questions.

For many organizations, this is a significant shift in practice. The organization's role in social learning and development is simply to facilitate the process and allow participants to ask all the questions. Refocusing challenges away from traditional problem solving to framing the right questions could help the airline industry spend fewer resources strip-searching people at airports and more resources on identifying potential terrorists; it could help organizations design, develop, and bring to market more products and services that members and customers actually want and need and leadership teams to worry less about satisfaction and more about engagement, experience, and delighting the broad base of constituents they must engage.

Collaborative and *informal learning* are more than just sound bites. They're core beliefs in blending learning and performance. If real learning and, more importantly, adoption and adaptation of that learning, is to help individuals grow in their current and future realm of responsibilities, organizations must find ways to integrate accidental, informal intersections of learning and performance into the process. That intersection requires real people in real time, hence, the impact of social mentors, coaches, masters, guides, power users, subject-matter experts, and communities of best practitioners sharing informal moments of knowledge transfer. Social fuels collaborative learning environments that integrate the theoretical with the application and implementation context of applied knowledge.

Workers at world-leading ophthalmic lenses manufacturer Essilor International can trace their training and development to European apprenticeships with masters of lens design, casting, and polishing at the beginning of the industrial revolution. As experienced Essilor workers are retiring in mature markets, the company often hires people with mechanical or chemistry backgrounds because there is minimal higher education dedicated specifically to this industry. New hires in growing markets often have little awareness of what is involved in the production of ophthalmic optics, because other industries (earlier adopters of digital and nano-technologies) are attracting more resources and driving higher education to address their own specific needs.

In 2007, Essilor executives wanted a set of cost-effective, basic, standardized e-learning tools. But thanks to feedback from the participants in 10 training pilots on three continents, by 2009 the organization had created LOFT (Learning Organization for Tomorrow), a dynamic internal, collaborative program that uses Web 2.0 technology to disseminate knowledge and transforms shop floor workers into peer trainers and coaches. The LOFT harnesses a collection of training tools from multiple sources that transmits passion, pride, and best practices throughout the world.

A highly social corporate university encapsulating a global ecosystem, the LOFT initiatives include components such as continuous innovation groups, a trainers and coaches community, social networks, private networks, professional and personal pages, a complete training system, a bi-annual engineering and human resources best practices week, and a collaborative, online sharing space where e-tools are posted, updated, translated, and improved.

Because shop floors are continually evolving at Essilor, so must the methods for training and development of new workers across this global enterprise. Shop floor workers cooperate in continuous innovation groups and report best practices and new discoveries to their locally hosted social networking and personal pages as well as to shop floor operators who have been selected as trainers. These trainers are in charge of the initial skills transmission for new hires, and they follow a very detailed script to help them develop their trade. Meanwhile, coaches focus on the personal development of both new hires and trainers. Coaches take care of the newly trained during a ramp-up period, which leads to official certification if the new hire reaches the necessary quality, productivity, and autonomy goals. These coaches also coach the trainers on their training skills and behaviors.

Though many of the workers or factories do not have internet access, the best of their innovations and ideas—say, a specific game to get understanding of difficult points or, in one case, a personal tag system to identify helpful certified colleagues—are shared by management on a collaborative internet space, translated into other languages by volunteers, and transmitted to the local networked pages read by trainers and coaches in other countries. (See Figure 6.6.)

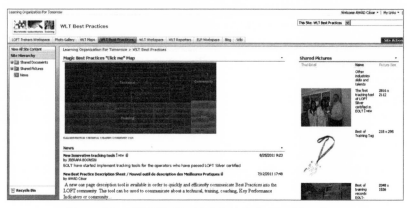

Figure 6.6—LOFT Worldwide Lab Training Best Practices

What can your organization learn from 810 volunteer trainers and coaches spread over 102 sites in 40 countries? Operational leaders and subject matter experts can do extraordinary things with a focus on the customers and a true sharing of their voices. In a time of economic crisis or budget constraints, limited resources in the war for globally capable and highly transferable talent may instead be successfully used to more effectively train and develop knowledge workers within the organization as well as those you seek to attract to it. In essence, learning and development is *social, global, and based on a real-time mindset.*

A Different Kind of *Race for Relevance*

One of the questions for senior leaders earlier in this chapter was, "How you will lead in the age of connected relationships?" The answer is a central point in recruiting world-class talent. Every employee must feel *relevant to the future of the association or company.* Unfortunately, in many highly structured, command and control organizations, good ideas only flow top-down, even though management always asks for ideas from the "rank and file." Is it any surprise that most ideas from the top are seen as holy and the ones from bottom of the organization as incomplete? As I wrote in *Relationship Economics,* even though organizations of all sizes across a multitude of industries claim "people are our biggest asset," it's often a transactional relationship: You work, I pay you; you follow the rules, you can stay.

The age of connected relationships, fueled by knowledge workers across the organization, accelerates employees' need for relevance. Beyond your tenure and pay grade, which correlates directly with your level in the organizational pyramid, your relevance in the past had little to do with your intelligence, contrarian perspective, or vision to do things differently (real innovation). Social widens the digital gap between the generations just entering the workforce and those looking to exit it, causing a legitimate concern for organizational brain drain. Those retiring may only understand remaining relevant in retirement. Through knowledge-tethering, where relevance is a game of intellectual capital investments for retiring knowledge workers who have spent their careers gaining "village knowledge" that can help shape the future of the organization and the industry they deeply care about, the organization can continue to keep the retiring engaged.

Because of connected relationships, age and tenure matter less than good ideas—regardless of where they come from—unbound by organizational structure. The hierarchical pyramid of command and control must yield to track and trust fueled by innovation—*daily!* The challenge for many organizations is two-fold: First, how do you "institutionalize" innovation by tapping into the collective knowledge and insights of the entire organization, past and present? And second, how do you balance a management structure with enough control to operate as a responsible, profitable, and sustainable entity while creating enough flexibility and freedom for individuals to spark, fan, and fuel new ideas across the organization and throughout the industry?

Consider as an example the efforts of Rite-Solutions. Founded by three partners in January 2000, Rite-Solutions, a software/system engineering company based in Middletown, Rhode Island, builds advanced, mission-critical software for the U.S. Department of Defense. Rite-Solutions embraced a mission to create an organization in which ideas and people flourish and new products, technologies, and directions are freely generated and deliver tangible rewards to all involved.

To fuel this mission, Rite-Solutions had to think and lead differently in both its organizational structure and innovation process. If you compare a traditional organizational structure—full of boxes in an antiquated reporting triangle—and a neighborhood where people like where they live, there are distinct behavioral differences. In the former, open positions become organization-wide turf battles to fill in the box, while in the latter, friendly neighbors step up and help when they're needed to do what they can for the well being of the neighborhood. As "motherhood and apple pie" as it sounds, there is considerably less drama and trauma in a good community than in a traditional organization structure.

So Rite-Solutions focused on building a company of good neighbors. How? It started by making every employee an owner of the company; it's 100 percent employee-owned. Instead of a job title, every employee's business card reads, "One of FEW" ("friends enjoying work"). "We all share offices (including the cofounders and all the top executives), with all the work getting done in team-based environments where each person plays multiple roles and can work on multiple teams, many on a volunteer basis," says Jim Lavoie, one of the founders. Information is shared widely and often, as it is very clear that every person is important to the future of the company, that they are cared about and that nobody needs to tackle a challenge (or for that matter, ever feel) alone. "We discuss that our success will be through One of FEW producing the Power of We," adds Lavoie.

On the innovation front, the founders recall growing up in business cultures where good ideas had to go in front of a "murder board." A poor soul presented an idea under the interrogation spotlight of a committee committed to "help you with your idea" but that, in fact, did more to fire hose and shoot down its relevance. Like many leaders who try to swing the pendulum in the other direction, Rite-Solutions founders tried everything and quickly learned what doesn't work in today's innovation-as-a-buzzword corporate mentality:

- Innovation as an annual ritual at the Innovation Retreat where staff "trust fall" with each other.

- Just-in-time innovation, a jam, blitz brainstorming, or an innovation meeting off site because you're stuck and have to come up with something—*anything*—to present to higher ups.

- The "innovation war room," an unstructured white space where you put up whiteboards and the ideas will magically come. Don't forget to write, "Do not erase," so the cleaning crew doesn't erase your brilliance overnight.

Ultimately, Rite-Solutions turned to what they knew as a core competency of the organization: games and software. They wanted people to invest intellectual capital in ways that they felt would benefit the community. That led them right to the stock market as a good game platform for the innovation engine. In 2005, they launched a state-of-the-art "innovation engine," Mutual Fun (Figure 6.7), designed to provoke and align individual brilliance toward collective genius. The goal was to connect on an emotional level where all employees are entrusted with the future direction of the company, asked for their opinions, listened to, and rewarded for successful ideas. The quest continues to be for each employee to feel more relevant and turn that relevance into forward motion toward a future state that they all create.

Figure 6.7—Rite-Solutions' Mutual Fun Innovation Engine

Rewarding Social Behaviors

Social expands traditional compensation models and pays teams for the right behaviors. Sociologists and psychologists have reinforced the notion that an individual's motives are unbelievably interesting. People are not as easily manipulated and predictable as organizations may think. Let's look at two prevailing thoughts when it comes to rewarding behaviors:

- If you reward something you get more of the behavior that you want, and

- If you punish it, you'll get less of what you want.

A July 2011 MIT study *Is Pay-for-Performance Detrimental to Innovation?* researched a group of individuals and gave them a set of challenges. To incentivize their performance, they offered three levels of rewards directly correlated with performance, essentially a typical motivational scheme within most organizations—reward the very top performers, ignore the lowest performers, and the middle gets something in between. Here are the flaws they discovered, defying the laws of behavior:

- As long as the task involved only mechanical skills, bonuses worked as expected: the higher the pay, the higher the performance.
- Once the task involved even rudimentary cognitive skills, a larger reward led to poor performance.

The Federal Reserve Bank sponsored a replica of the same study in rural India, where the compensation ranged from two weeks' to two month's salary. The people who were offered the medium reward did no better than those offered the smallest reward; the people offered the top reward did the worst of all. This is actually not that big of an anomaly and has been proven over and over again. For simple straightforward tasks (if you do this, you get that), this performance-based compensation is great.

Social tasks are more complicated and require conceptual, intuitive, and creative thinking. As such, traditional incentives often don't work. The best use of money as a motivator is to pay the social talent enough to take money issues off the table and get them focused on the work. Once you do that, three factors lead to better performance and personal satisfaction:

- **Autonomy** is our desire to be self directed. Traditional management is great if you want compliance; if you want engagement, self-direction is considerably stronger. Working on what you want, when, with whom, and how you want (one day of pure undiluted autonomy) tends to lead to incredibility interesting results. Try this with social instead of an innovation bonus.

- **Mastery** is our urge to get better at key tasks and functions. This often isn't driven by money but by having fun, overcoming challenges, and making a contribution. These knowledge workers have challenging jobs, and yet during their weekends or after work in their limited discretionary time, they do equally interesting things, not for their employers but for the masses, for free. Think Linux, Apache, and Wikipedia.

- **Purpose** is our desire to make a difference. If an organization creates a transcendent purpose, the talent gets more excited about coming to work and making a difference. Great products and services are created when the knowledge worker is engaged in doing interesting work in an interesting and engaging organization. Niklas Zennström, the

Skype founder wanted to be disruptive while making a world a better place. Steve Jobs expressed a desire to put a ding in the universe.

Social forces organizations to think beyond carrots and sticks. Can you allow your social talent to do the type of work that stimulates their minds? Can they build something? Do they believe they are contributing or just slogging through the minutia of the day? Are they working with people they respect? Are values shared? Do they believe in the organization's mission? Do they think the organization has a vested interest in them as individuals?

## CHAPTER 7

Socially Enable Your Execution

I F YOU TURN on the television or scan a newspaper's business or op-ed sections of late, it is hard to miss the focus on the economic volatility. Even the generic newsletter from my large and disconnected major financial institution had general statements assuring me that this activity is not normal and that, as a valued investor with their firm, I should not make any irrational decisions and should stay the course with their investments. Of course, they never defined what *stay the course* really meant.

The economy was in a similar state of flux in 2009. Headlines and organizational messages were the same: Stay the course and don't do anything rash in these *unprecedented times.* If the unprecedented happens more than the precedent, maybe it's time for a new precedent?

That's where we are with social engagement. The recent launch of Google+ and its phenomenal acquisition of 50 million users in 88 days (Figure 7.1) surpassed even the most impressive of similar user/member acquisition campaigns by MySpace (remember them?).

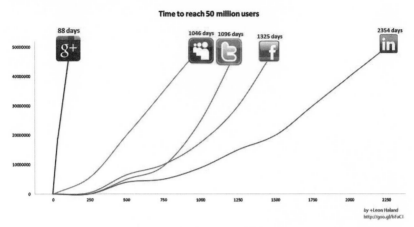

Figure 7.1—Google+ to 50 Million Users

Some argue that MySpace was ahead of its time and that its creators faced considerable headwind in educating consumers about the new social sphere, thus making their feat more impressive than Google, which already had millions of highly engaged search customers. What's notable is that Facebook realizes that it's not just the member acquisition that matters, but renewal and retention. The number one factor for renewal and retention is engagement—or *stickiness.* According to Citi Investment Research and the 2011 analysis compiled by ComScore Media Matrix, it seems both Facebook and Google are doing anything but staying the course (Figure 7.2).

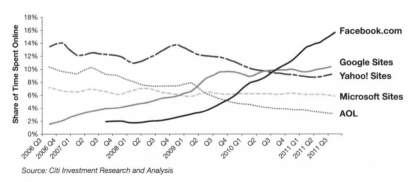

Source: Citi Investment Research and Analysis

Figure 7.2—U.S. Share of Time Spent Online

Don't Lose Your Compass

No one can predict the future, and if we were able to, perhaps we'd be spending our time differently. We hypothesize the current economic volatility will subside at some point, that the political landscape in our nation will improve or we will fail as a nation, that the European debt crisis will subside or the euro will fail as a currency. Despite these musings, volatility is here now, and it stirs up emotions that can cloud the decision-making process and impair an individual's, a team's, or an organization's ability to execute. Keeping execution focused is imperative in these uncertain times, so either make the investments and stay the course, or get on a course that makes you more comfortable executing a socially enabled strategy more consistently.

Social involves some of that same volatility. Formation of strategy alone won't suffice, nor will the tools matter all that much. We marvel at technology's features and functions, weigh its pros and cons, and in becoming mesmerized with shiny new toys, lose sight of defining and staying the course. That course is *execution, performance, and results* within, among, between, and around highly connected relationships. Engagement through social channels helps individuals and organizations improve their communication; drive innovation; bring good ideas together; combine complementary expertise; make serendipitous connections; discover ideas; stand on different and highly connected shoulders; and watch ideas as they are refined, expanded upon, and transformed into a desirable product or a service. Social interaction drives greater operational speed and efficiency and helps control spending; you could say that social creates a *new precedent.*

Critical to our increasingly complex team, organization, and industry structures is balancing execution and performance with exploring and learning in constantly evolving social spheres. How does an organizational leader balance a multiplicity of demands with the need to make better decisions without much thinking about them, yet knowing the impact of a wrong or a poorly made decision? Whether an association employee's specific role is focused on member or customer acquisition, delivery of products or services, provisioning, member or customer service, media or legislative relationships, what enduring principles can lead to choices that reflect openness, integrity, and authenticity in the age of connected relationships? How can you consistently deliver the results demanded by your members, customers, staff, partners, board members, or investors?

Here are 10 supporting execution pillars for the IMPACT model mentioned in previous chapters (***bold italic for your reference***). Think of them as scaffolding for your social renovation or as universal truths. Without particular attention to these strategy *execution* best practices, your efforts to engage, enable, and empower connected relationships within the organization or external to it, will falter:

1. **Challenge status quo, certainty, and critical assumptions.** When you as an individual, a team, or an organization think that you're undeniably right, that is exactly the right time to ask: What might we be missing? What questions are we not asking? Which critical assumptions that are mission makers or breakers are we ignoring or taking for granted? Comfort leads to complacency. Complacent thinking makes you lazy. In the age of connected relationships, lazy performers get left behind. When you ***immerse*** an industry in your value-add, that's exactly the right time to think about how to do things differently.

2. **It's not about perfection; it's about progress.** The relentless pursuit of diverse opinions promotes the evolution of novel ideas. Building focused communities that help improve the quality and speed of gathering business insights will accelerate your ability to generate new ideas and to constantly improve upon them. If ***membership*** in that community is not right for an individual or an organization at a specific point, incremental value-add delivered over time and reinforced by social interactions is more likely to help build acceptance of the unique attributes of membership.

3. **We evaluate logically but decide emotionally.** Smarter touch points, such as monitoring real-time sentiments in a social dashboard (described in more detail in Chapter 8), interwoven throughout your members' or customers' interactions with you will help you better understand not just what they think but *how they feel.* Gather compelling and important requirements from their emotional attachments and they'll do more than just write a check; they'll ***participate*** and, over time, become advocates and evangelists. The combination of high-quality ideas and frequent real-time feedback from those eager to share their experiences give you a much stronger sense of the member's, customer's, or industry's pulse than an annual satisfaction survey. The nature of real-time information both

challenges and grows an organization's ability to be agile, responsive, and predictive.

4. **When in doubt, take the high road.** What do you believe fuels world-class start-ups? Most successful companies that were once start-ups began with *indispensible* (Google) or *addictive products* (Facebook). To quote Paul Buchheit—creator of Gmail, developer of Google AdSense, and founder of FriendFeed (acquired by Facebook)—"You don't have to be good if you're great." Combine your great products or services with *obsessive service*—inside and outside the organization—and you build unparalleled barriers to entry for your competitive landscape, such as **accreditation** by choice. The high road is to instinctively know as an organization what it means to do the right thing, even when inclined to do the opposite. If people find it impossible, in a challenging moment, to envision how they'd behave at their best, it's helpful for the organization to develop a staff culture that tries imagining how other individuals or organizations they admire would respond.

5. **Infuse love for the organization and its purpose.** We don't often hear about love for an organization, but social **communities** are about deeply passionate people who genuinely love what they do, who they do it for, who they do it with, and the results they create as a community of like-minded individuals. It may be wishful thinking to assume people will be rewarded with riches for following their hearts. But those who love what they do seldom need to hit the snooze button in the morning. They seldom believe that their willingness or ability to perform is a chore or that they have a "work life" versus a "personal life." They simply aim to live a richer life. Nonprofits can compete for world-class talent even though they may not offer material riches. When individuals in a community feel unappreciated or unloved, that's when they begin to explore alternative options. If Google and Apple can give engineers up to 20 percent of their time to work on whatever they want as long as they account for it and report on their progress, so can your organization. Reduce the labor intensity of all that you "have to do" to give the staff discretionary time to read, write, explore, and do what they live—consistent with the mission or the purpose of the organization. If you don't tell them how, they may just surprise you! One of my entrepreneurial clients has designated the first Friday of each month

as a "learning and growing day." The staff goes off site every first Friday and spends half the day talking about key lessons they learned last month as individuals, teams, and the organization. Then they spend the second half of the day doing something fun together— never terribly expensive, but always memorable, including building homes for Habitat for Humanity.

6. **As individuals and organizations, we're richer than we think.** From our educational foundation to our professional pedigree, *transformation* evolves our positions, possessions, and perspectives. Compared to much of the rest of the world, we're richer in all three. Our society leads us to believe that more is better, bigger is stronger, and complexity is a byproduct of prosperity. We somehow conclude that "keeping up with the Joneses" is the path to beat our competition to the finish line. In a social world where sharing information is dramatically more influential than hoarding it, this mindset is a prescription for disaster, disappointment, and discontentment. Visionary leaders and front-line contributors are guiding their organizations to consider: How much of what we already have truly adds value to others in our daily interactions? What could we do without, and what can we reduce, reuse, recycle, repurpose, or refocus? What can we tithe, save, or invest before we spend?

7. **Humility + Learning = Exponential Growth.** Only when members or customers feel their own transformations will they come full circle to further *immersion* in your value-add. When they do, they'll look for fresh ideas, fresh perspective, new learning, and new heights previously unimaginable. If you provide it, they'll continue the journey; otherwise, they'll move on and explore other opportunities. The individual, his or her team, and the organization at large must always be in the learning mode—from every touch point. Replace dumb touch points with smart ones. Keep in mind that in the formula above, both ingredients are equally important. Humility alone leads to complacency; learning in isolation leads to self-doubt. The solution is in embracing these paradoxical interdependencies, using organizational humility as an antidote to fear and as a cushion in the face of organizational or industry setbacks. Social interaction powers the exponential.

8. **Purpose is created and reinforced by your discoveries.** *Members* or customers return, expand their involvement, and refer others to

an organization's breakthrough products and services, thus fueling the organization's growth. Bringing innovation to the market more quickly, while preserving quality and commitment, serves as a guiding light. Purpose is the foundation that the organization builds upon, and in the process of building, finds ways to express the unique skills of its people and their passions, focusing on outcomes larger than the institution. The successful organization is constantly searching for ways to reinvent R&D with early feedback on in-flight projects or prototypes via file sharing, forums, blogs, tweets, and wikis. Ideas are challenged, reborn, refined, and deployed in advance of committing costly resources to production.

9. **If you don't respond, you'll signal that you're incompetent or just don't care.** Social interaction is viral, immediate, engaged, responsive, resolute, and unforgiving. If the organization is engaged by others who choose to *participate* and it doesn't respond, particularly to requests for clarification of information, dissemination of misinformation, and inaccurate or blatant mistruths, the brand and all of its constituents risk alienating those most crucial to the organization's social ecosystem. We all have an infinite capacity for self-deception. To avoid pain, we rationalize, minimize, deny, and go numb. The antidote is a willingness to look at the organization with unsparing honesty and to *consistently* hold individuals and teams accountable for the brand the organization aspires to become.

10. **Be the starfish and not the spider.** My friend Rod Beckstrom, co-author of the bestselling book *The Starfish and the Spider: The Unstoppable Power of Leaderless Organizations,* believes that at the extreme, all organizations behave either like centralized, top-down spiders, or like decentralized, collaborative starfish. Understanding the difference can be the key to success. Beckstrom sees a rise in the power of starfish and hybrid organizations like YouTube, eBay, Toyota, LinkedIn, Tesla Motors, AA, al Qaeda, and Facebook, among others. These organizations are highly disruptive to traditional markets, business, and society, but their techniques can be understood and leveraged. The pendulum of power is swinging toward a new model of organizations and leadership that others want to align themselves with—hence, one of the values of *accreditation.* To be effective, leaders must understand why the catalysts that start or guide starfish-like networks can be very different from traditional CEOs.

High Adoption Leads to Organizational Anticipation

Empowering your organization's ability to execute on its strategy using social media is based on the premise that collaboration can, in fact, improve decision cycle times and organizational effectiveness. But a social solution produces these results only to the extent it is adopted by the organization and the users in its ecosystem. An ecosystem includes not just the marketing staff, but everyone from the CEO down to the receptionist, from the national organization serving global members and customers, to the local chapters or remote offices serving members and customers down the street. Social media, by definition, is a group productivity function versus a personal productivity tool, making large-scale adoption critical to success. Social strategy benefits the organization if it is used throughout the organization as a function of its operations and a renewed foundation of its existence.

Here is the challenge: Adoption can seldom be mandated. Adoption occurs when the consumers, who need information, knowledge, and actionable insights, choose to believe that social channels provide them with a net benefit. When the organization appeals to their logical self-interest and they want to use social channels to enable their individual function, that's when they take action. Users across the organization and the industry quickly ascertain "How will I be better off?" and counterbalance any perceived investments of time, effort, resources, and the pain of giving up the old way of performing their functions.

As such, here are five critical success factors for adoption:

1. **Integrate old-fashioned social networking.** We're social creatures, so leverage a rich picture of the people doing the work today; help them *really* get to know and appreciate each other, discover others in and outside the organization who could provide expertise, learn from interactions with diverse people, and automate their ability to keep key pieces of information updated.

2. **Lead with what's in it for me?** If you're going to get any adoption off the ground, much less thriving, your target audiences must be shown that what you're proposing is intuitive and will improve their lives, that they will be in control, and that it won't depend on other functions such as IT, legal, or HR. And they must be socially incentivized to get involved, (Think of the peer pressure power of "Are you on Facebook, LinkedIn, or Twitter?" Who's going to risk their social lives and say no?)

3. **You can't round a square.** Make sure you're integrating the way people work today, such as email, calendars, documents, support of mobile devices, offline access, and working with people outside the organization.

4. **Add value with information arbitrage and aggregation.** Employees can spend up to 30 percent of their day—note: your staff costs—looking for information. Build a hub for that information and attract people who need access to it, want to contribute to or enhance it, and must use it to perform. Aim to aggregate information from multiple data sources, normalize them, and make disparate types usable by non-techie people.

5. **Don't create $2 solutions for $1 problems.** Assess the total cost of ownership in not just getting a social collaboration project off the ground but also allowing for maintenance, training, adoption, support, upgrades, administration, hidden costs, and time.

Only when the approach to your execution efforts becomes "highly adoptable," can you begin to implement your specific business strategies not with, but rather *through* social.

As a process consultant, I often find myself in search of cause and effect, framing what the current circumstance is and isn't and figuring a systematic, disciplined process to execute consistently to create predictability, reliability, and repeatability. In helping clients understand their current and desired status in integrating social into their strategic thinking and operational execution, I've identified a continuum of digital relationship maturity. (See Figure 7.3.)

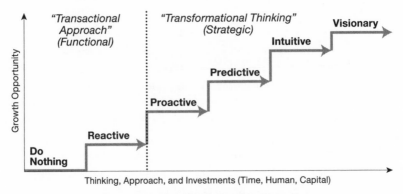

Figure 7.3—Digital Relationship Maturity

Some organizations still choose to *do nothing*. They don't believe social is relevant to their industry or target audiences. They're classic laggards in many technological innovations and will require a significant market pull to abandon their current mindset. They're often operating in very mature industries, where they believe that their ecosystem isn't interested in, can't get access to, or wouldn't see value in social media interactions.

A preponderance of member-based organizations and small businesses today are *reactive*. Although they may have a blog, use a Twitter account around their annual meeting or to rebroadcast their press releases, a Facebook fan page that a summer intern created, or some amateur videos on YouTube, none of it is strategically positioned to provide thought leadership or a clear differentiation. They have yet to understand that content leads to credibility and connections to collaboration. They don't see the value of integrating business processes into the more agile operation that social demands and are struggling to gain traction with additional mindshare or wallet share from existing members/customers or any new markets or audiences.

Unfortunately, much of the social presence of organizations that are doing nothing or are reactive is purely functional and highly transactional in nature.

When an organization expands its thinking; approach; and investment of time, human resources, and capital in really integrating social as part of its day-to-day operations, that's when it can begin to realize both relational and financial growth opportunities. The clear line of demarcation for most clients I work with is the formulation and implementation of a social strategy, not as a disconnected part but rather a highly integrated enabler of their business goals and objectives. They become proactive in expanding their definition of "a market." They begin to use different social channels for distinct purposes, moving beyond rudimentary and often free analysis to more robust analytical capabilities and institutionalizing social to become *proactive* in their markets or industry. Charity: water—described extensively later in Chapter 8—is one such example. Another one is Ashoka, which many believe is leading a profound transformation in society. Since its founding in 1980 by Bill Drayton, this network of 2,000 social entrepreneurs (Fellows), policy makers, investors, academics, and journalists, in more than 60 countries has grown exponentially, creating innovative solutions to improve the lives of millions of people. Their network of highly connected social interactions has identified 20 key challenges in today's world that require entrepreneurial thinking. Beyond their support of thousands of social innovators over the last three decades, Ashoka is now looking for 20 entrepreneurs to "engineer the big systems change by taking the key patterns to scale, adding what's missing, and cracking new strategies."

Elevating that proactive presence to one of organizational learning from social interactions allows the organization to become more *predictive*. Leaders and front-line contributors alike begin to integrate the voice of members or customers into unique products and services, abandoning underutilized assets—in essence, stopping what hasn't worked for some time—and anticipating the next stage of member or customer lifecycle stages. Key business goals and objectives are clearly affected by social strategies, and strong analytics throughout the organization allow for operational benchmarking and key insights from every interaction.

The final two stages, where the organization becomes *intuitive* and *visionary*, are rare. Organizations integrating mobile and social, location-based insights, and digital payments tend to fit into these categories. Beyond applications or tools, the way they do business points to a unique perspective on the evolution of their market or industry. They challenge the status quo every day by providing far superior real-time experiences to a broad base of constituents. Many refer to themselves as operating on the "bleeding edge," yet a closer look at their engagement models illustrates true innovation in every facet of their planning and execution efforts across the organization. They don't have challenges in attracting world-class talent, because their reputation for forward-looking development—of the organization and its people—are well known.

Organizations that are laying the groundwork to be proactive, predictive, intuitive, and visionary in their views and applications of social are learning to be strategic in their institutionalization of social (from pockets of best practices, such as using Twitter for events, to a broader application of microblogging for knowledge management) and, in the process, are transforming their people, markets, and industry.

Getting to the Future State

So, if you're not thinking it already, let me ask: Which type of organization do you work for or lead? Where are you on the continuum outlined above (in Figure 7.3) and how can you elevate the mindset and the toolset in your organization to implement and integrate social differently?

Here are eight steps to successful organization-wide integration of social in your strategy execution efforts:

Step 1—Enable open thinking in social applications.

Get a small group of staff, and volunteers/members you respect—highly intelligent, creative, energetic, tenured, and fairly new—around a conference table for a day and think of the top several aspects of the organization that make it difficult to deal with, frustrating for people to work for, challenging for outsiders to partner with, and a bear for members or customers to engage. Eliminate traditional obstacles such as resources (financial, time, or people) and think broadly in terms of organization-wide, as well as smaller, more group-centric approaches. Where and how is value conceived, created, communicated, and connected with those who need and want it most? Where are the most influential wells of information, how do they get filtered or fueled to become organizational insights, and how do people learn those insights to attempt implementation or applications of them? Who inside and outside the organization has village knowledge and how is that knowledge discerned and captured? If you begin by asking the right questions, you have a much stronger chance of framing the best operational challenges or opportunities to focus the social collaboration lens. It doesn't matter that you may not have answers about how to address them at this point. You're simply formulating possible use cases.

Step 2—Recruit unwavering champions.

Successful implementation of social collaboration is often conceived and driven to execution by a core group of highly engaged and energetic champions. They're undeterred from traditional organizational bureaucracy or perceived limitations such as funding or "not invented here" mentality. They are committed to the cause or the mission of the organization and are determined to make it more open, engaging, and effective. Executives are ideal champions, because they more easily can achieve buy-in for new ideas up the ladder and gently nudge other functions to support the use cases identified in step number one. Here are some of the more common traits of champions I've observed within a multitude of client organizations:

- They have a strong and highly diverse portfolio of relationships, within and external to the organization, online and offline; personally and professionally, they're well known and trusted.

- They conduct their own due diligence on the viability of an idea and enthusiastically take a stand; they believe in efficient, effective outcome and the investment necessary to get the organization to its goals.

- They are constantly exploring innovative uses of technology; although they may not be highly technical themselves, their insatiable appetite to reduce labor intensity and do things differently drives them toward undiscovered territories.

- They are highly influential and respected in their particular area of focus; they have a proven track record of having developed a business case for taking prudent risk and delivered extraordinary results from past investments.

Step 3—Engage new users with hands-on activities.

Any social collaboration strategy isn't worth the paper it's created on if the organization's key constituents don't try it. Make the foray into integrating social interesting, intriguing, and really easy to use and see immediate benefit or value from. Champions should lead the broader audience with highly interactive and engaging sessions—think brown-bag-lunches—to dip their toes in the water. Take the functionality on the road to where they are, where they work, where they need to access and benefit from it the most. Ask new users to bring their laptops and get online with you to experience the journey for themselves. Have people complete their profiles in five easy steps; bring in a photographer to help with new headshots; provide them with templates, simple best practices from their colleagues, links, stories that will help them get to know and engage each other easier and more effectively. Create short video tips and techniques and make the learning fun. One of my clients does "information scavenger hunts," asking a group to work together to find a certain number of individuals or pieces of information throughout the organization or across industry partners. It's consistently ranked as one of the best ways for the users to learn a new social collaboration tool.

Step 4—Integrate social as an enabler of their everyday functions.

Social collaboration really shines when it streamlines daily functions and makes it easier to get to what you need without having to jump through hoops. Recall step one, identifying what frustrates the daylights out of people to try to accomplish—and integrate social collaboration into eliminating those frustrations. Route repetitive activities through your social environment and capture how much more efficiently or effectively the same redundancies get accomplished. Wiki pages make great destinations for meeting agendas, pre-work, and notes from the off-site meeting. Question-and-answer forums help address FAQs about products, processes, customers, partners, and employee benefits. Project plans, where multiple people and dependencies must work in concert, are ideal because social collaboration tools make the individual activities more efficient. Notes, documentations, case studies, and great examples all can become enduring and searchable assets of the organization. If you help individuals stop reinventing the wheel, the value is felt across the entire organization.

Step 5—Integrate with other systems to empower their value.

Take the organization's daily workflow, infuse social collaboration, and integrate other systems the users already have to access vital information. Make sure solutions you narrow in on can easily integrate with other systems the organization uses for its core business activities. Automate as much as possible to save users keystrokes, import/export functions, or existing redundancies—information in eight different formats, in four different locations, none of which match! Again, think of what people access most often in a "day-in-the-life-of" a typical staff member: company directories, intranets, document storage and retrieval, customer relationship management (CRM) systems, accounting, payroll, time or expense tracking, inventory, or asset management. Don't try to boil the ocean. Start with boiling a cup of water and develop a path to grow the functionality. If you overwhelm the users early on, they'll disengage faster than you can imagine.

Step 6—Leverage the medium.

At the advent of the web, many websites were simply online brochures. Don't do that with social collaboration. Don't just put the text of the company directory online. Help create 30-second videos about staff roles and responsibilities. Stream live events and create digital libraries of self-directed training sessions. Animate, add voiceovers to presentations, and use a sequence of still images to tell a story. Integrate QR codes throughout your printed material that takes them back online. Make it interesting and fun—social media is all about multimodality.

Step 7—Empower the community.

Fuel the fire by empowering the community to constantly reach beyond its comfort zone and get to know new people within and outside of the organization. Give partners access to key sections so that they can interact with the staff in the same community. Create digital media rooms for members to see key organization or industry events live. Invite them to share what's working and what's not. Help them continue to learn and to assess their own progress. Encourage them to share best practices with their colleagues down the hall or across the globe. And make certain that there is local support when and where they need it. One of my clients has integrated click-to-chat for internal support of the organization's social community, for example.

Step 8—Celebrate and build on the results.

Social collaboration is about helping the organization become more efficient and effective. Capture and celebrate results when staff across all functions spend 20 percent less time searching for information, compress project cycles by 30 percent, or reduce email volume by 40 percent or more. Demonstrate not just what but how and why the organization is becoming leaner, accomplishing more with fewer resources, and serving a broader base of constituents. And when other organizations have to lay off employees, show how yours has been able to retain and grow its base of knowledge workers.

Social media is about progress, not perfection; social collaboration implementation success comes in incremental stages. Nor is it the time to be humble. Use early positive momentum to build on your success, up, down, and across the organization, and tackle the next use case you created in step number one!

Social Manufacturing?

According to Business.com, even though 81 percent of B2B companies use social networks, the manufacturing industry is one sector that has been slow to adopt social media. "Many manufacturers aren't even online, let alone using social media," said Jeffrey Cohen, social media marketing manager at marketing agency Howard, Merrell & Partners and managing editor at SocialMediaB2B.com, in a recent interview for *The Network, Cisco's Technology News Site.* "But the few manufacturers using social media are getting value out of it to connect with prospects, customers, and partners."

In 2011, 30 percent of global manufacturing companies had planned to increase spending on social media and community marketing, according to a March report from Forrester Research titled *Bigger B2B Marketing Budgets Come with Great Expectations.* That compares with 53 percent of pharmaceutical companies and 50 percent of business and professional services companies.

Most manufacturers know social media holds the promise to serve as a powerful marketing channel. So why have so few taken the plunge? The problem may lie in the way

continues on next page

continued from previous page
manufacturers traditionally approach marketing. Accustomed to focusing on RFP processes and lead-generation tactics, most manufacturers "don't think like brand marketers," says Jeff Reinke, editorial director of Advantage Business Media's Manufacturing Group. "For decades, manufacturers have focused on internal initiatives to make their companies more competitive," he adds. "But with ever more competition from India and China, some manufacturers are starting to look at social media as a way to gain global recognition for their businesses."

The other challenge manufacturers face in adopting social media is the very distributed, complex nature of manufacturing itself. If a manufacturer has 500,000 parts that end up in thousands of products, how does it craft global messages to encompass all of those products? To overcome this challenge, manufacturers can use social media to tell stories that indirectly promote their businesses, without getting into the details of individual parts or products.

"Early adopters are using social media to create educational or inspirational content, and that drives discussion within their industries that may eventually turn into sales leads,"

says Cohen, who pointed to Corning's *A Day in the Life of Glass* video as a B2B social marketing success. The YouTube video didn't promote any one product, but by obtaining nearly 15 million views, it helped build awareness of Corning's core business. Cohen also pointed to Boeing and GE (@ecomagination) as leaders in social media.

B2B marketers use social media to "showcase their expertise and build trusted relationships with prospects when they first start looking for information," according to the Forrester report. Some manufacturers have found creating their own social network, to which they invite employees, prospects, and partners, to be an effective communications tool. Baker Hughes, a manufacturing and services company in the oil industry, created an in-house social network using Cisco Pulse to connect collaborators worldwide, and others have expanded these networks externally.

"The manufacturing industry has adapted to so many changes, and they will eventually adopt social media marketing," Reinke says. "But they will do so at their own pace, and many will probably create their own social networks instead of just jumping into the public fray on Facebook and Twitter."

The complex natures of associations or similar organizations also create a headwind for both the adoption and stronger integration of social into their operations. The sheer number of strategic priorities, expansive demands by various members and partners, limited resources (human, capital, time), conflicting priorities, and most visibly, the entrenchment of the status quo keep many associations from being able to use social to engage a broader audience and tell a more compelling story.

Henry H. Chamberlain, APR, FASAE, CAE, is the President and Chief Operating Officer of the Building Owners and Managers Association (BOMA) International, a 104-year-old trade association for commercial real estate headquartered in Washington, D.C. BOMA concentrates on advocacy, education, networking, and benchmarking building performance as a best practice. BOMA's value proposition is to be the early warning system for members, informing them of tax or building code issues on the horizon. BOMA uses data, standards, and its business network to help members improve property management, drive value to the bottom line and enhance their assets. BOMA is a business partner for the member in terms of creating value by helping to attract and retain tenants or new business, and putting a top product out into a competitive marketplace.

BOMA members aren't just working in offices anymore. They are working on smartphones or iPads. "As members manage bigger and bigger portfolios, they are really looking for how people are getting it done. They have kids, their jobs are 10–12 hours a day, plus they are on call. When groups like BOMA ask for volunteer time they are scratching their heads because they are doing it after hours or on weekends. They want some family time too."

It's becoming harder over time to engage members in between meetings. BOMA publishes a magazine and a bi-weekly eNewsletter that leads with the issues and advocacy. To engage local boards, BOMA uploads a 3–4½ minute video to YouTube every month that sets out two issues to explore at the upcoming meeting. Henry Chamberlain: "Three years ago I would have put that in a memo, but people aren't reading those anymore." Board members are teeing the videos up, however, and having much better

Meet the Building Owners and Managers Association International (BOMA)

Founded in 1907, BOMA is a federation with 93 local associations across the United States, 11 in Canada as part of BOMA Canada, and 15 international affiliates. Its 16,500 members are companies and individuals who own or manage commercial real estate, a $118B marketplace. Major players such as Grubb and Ellis are represented by BOMA, as well as the individual and smaller companies such as Washington Property Company, Akridge, and Carr Properties. Some 3–15 percent of BOMA members crossover with dual memberships in the Institute of Real Estate Management (IREM), International Facility Management Association (IFMA), National Association of Industrial and Office Properties (NAIOP), International Council of Shopping Centers (ICSC), and CoreNet Global based in Atlanta. The breakdown is 50 percent of revenue is dues, 25 percent conferences, 15 percent education and programming, and 10 percent publications and advertising. A vendor partnership program brings in $575K.

discussions as a result. In terms of using social media, BOMA has some distance to go. "We have to be thinking about mobile access to our website and materials. We do that for our conference but people need access to data and tools while they are working."

BOMA is making the shift to allow committees to work virtually. Instead of the traditional website, team sites have been created using a SharePoint platform. "Our committees can go in any time they want to, check out the materials, email people, etc. I don't know if anyone has standing committees anymore, but what we are finding is that people will give you five to ten hours a month or get involved in a project if you wire it up for them so they can do it after hours."

KIOLs as Social Tour Guides

A lesson that I learned from my dad and that I'm trying to instill in my children is that "life is too short to make all the mistakes yourself; learn from other people's mistakes." Socially enabling your execution is far less painful if you learn from the insights of *key influencers and opinion leaders* (KIOLs). Social represents cultural change, and if the organization is aiming to raise its performance, influence and opinions become greatly valued currencies. Many organizational leaders approach social strategies with confidence in the purity of their goals and perhaps with a touch of charisma, as the organization's opportunity to shine among industry peers. People fear what they don't understand and a comment such as, "We don't want people wasting time on Facebook all day," calls into question a leader's motives and ability to effect change.

So how do you help people overcome fear? Unfortunately in many organizations, there is a formidable information and education barrier when it comes to social collaboration and marketing. The enormous amount of hype, the irrelevant examples (most B2B organizations don't care what Skittles is doing on Facebook), and general unfamiliarity with what the social universe really is capable of makes the topic a yawn for most observers. Celebrating successes makes the subject more palatable, believable, and relevant. Success stories that match the organization's strategic aspirations have a tendency to convince specific subgroups and individuals in key areas of the organization where change is most needed. If the organization is aiming to drive cost performance, social strategies could focus on eliminating unnecessary meetings and oversight reviews. By selecting individuals whose active participation in a social collaboration campaign is most needed (and those who are likely expected to push back), you can demonstrate that adopting new behaviors can deliver higher performance and illustrate metrics that result from this change. The next chapter will elaborate on this topic.

In my experience, there is often a direct correlation between how much time a change agent spends in the field at the edge of where the organization creates its greatest market impact and the successful integration of social collaboration into the organization's execution efforts. Essential to embracing the value of social mechanisms is the change leader's cultivation of allies across the entire organization. Who are the most influential functional pillars, those who already have the respect and trust of their functional silos? Once they can see that social strategies will increase quality sales leads or streamline accounting reports, social becomes a genuine motivator. Gradually these individuals become advocates and when they experience the social impact, they become evangelists for evolving and thinking differently. The change leader's respectful but persistent approach eventually earns the confidence of key influencers and when the influenced begin to internalize the value of change, social is no longer the "change flavor of the week" but is good for the organization and the industry.

Three types of influencers are particularly important to any organizational cultural change fueled by social:

1. **Culture conductors.** Similar to objects that can conduct electricity, these are highly visible figures who are the positive and negative conductors of the organization's beliefs and values. They aren't exclusively in hierarchical roles such as senior executives or board members; they're also the highly popular front-line contributors, project managers, or organizational communication teams who write and distribute an internal newsletter or a blog or are fairly active on various social networks in their personal dealings. It is important to identify these highly visible figures and understand what they can do to influence cultural change inside and outside the organization. How can the change leader marshal this army of "ambassadors of change" to carry the social flag?

2. **Culture pillars.** These people are officially responsible for the conceptual agreement about the desired outcomes of social strategies and the specific behavior modifications that will help the organization meet its goals. Considering the unique functional nuances within an organization or specific parts of the value workflow, these

are typically very different leaders. A sufficient number of them must be seen as having a vested interest in the change they're advocating.

3. **Culture change early adopters.** These respected peers are involved in the groups where organizational culture change through social collaboration is targeted. When they embrace new behaviors, they tend to influence others with their actions. They are role models for their colleagues, and gaining the cooperation and support of these individuals will broadcast a "voice of the employee" into every new approach and guideline introduced because of social strategies. Equally valuable are the lessons the change leader can learn from early adopters in refining the specific changes that are needed and how to most effectively integrate social to implement them.

If the change leader is seeking to accelerate the pace of change, coordinating these three types of influencers to work in sync will help each of them to notice the impact created by the behaviors of others. The sudden sharing of information, open collaboration, and social support of accelerating key project milestones all become the norm and not the exception. In member or customer service environments, culture conductors can lead with inspirational messages of first touch resolution and exceptional experiences, thus fueling social users outside the organization to rave about the brand and help attract other members or customers. The culture pillars can demand a closer "expectation-to-experience gap" from the entire team that includes incentives, rewards, and metrics necessary to demonstrate progress. The culture change early adopters are willing to embrace solving members' or customers' problems differently; they can demonstrate how to translate the idea of "members or customers first" into new types of social behaviors, such as using CoTweet to solve service issues via Twitter or Yammer to internally raise awareness of the effect of exceptional service. For every infusion of social collaboration that is an enabler of organizational change, all three influencers are critically important to integration.

There are four traditional methods for identifying opinion leaders (the second half of KIOLs), each with its unique set of advantages and disadvantages:

1. *Observation Method.* An outside observer familiar with the community identifies its most influential members. This is the most objective approach, but the process relies heavily on the outside observer's bias toward the more visible and higher-profile individuals

in an organization or industry. This method also can't identify and prioritize the impact that hundreds of individuals have on a network of connected relationships.

2. ***Self-Identification Method.*** Using individuals' impressions of themselves as opinion leaders can be faulty because most people in an organization or industry view their own work and contributions as important, so the process may exaggerate reality.

3. ***Informant Method.*** Individuals are solicited to name someone they believe to be influential. This works out reasonably well, but community samples are often not sufficient and it is possible to get skewed results that underrepresent minority groups/perspectives.

4. ***Sociometric Method.*** Surveying is the most common. Community members are asked to rank individuals in their network on criteria ranging from quality of education and expertise to the impact of their ideas and perspectives on the organization or the industry. The challenge is that bias that may creep in during the survey design process, making the choice of questions and the interpretation of the results highly subjective.

Here is where social collaboration can help identify and prioritize opinion leaders within and external to the organization. Social is powered by social network analysis, the study of patterns in human interaction. It is unbiased, empirical, and analytical and is holistic enough to include a wide variety of candidates in the selection pool. Connected relationship maps (Figures 7.4 and 7.5) can illustrate rich contextual information about the centrality or number of connections, hidden connections among clusters

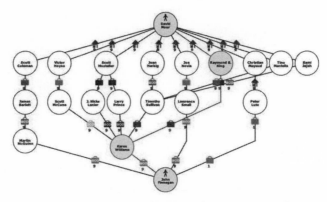

Figure 7.4—Sample Relationship Map of Key Industry Influencers

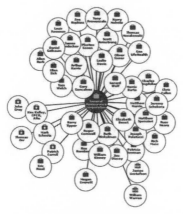

Figure 7.5—Sample Connected Relationship Map of Influencers within an Organization

of people, and the social gravity of the influencers who benefit from strong followings.

Social collaboration is a cultural intervention, and it is often difficult for organizations and change leaders to introduce this idea into the organization's strategy execution efforts. Countless failed attempts point to the critical need for clearly defined goals and a plan for how to achieve them. The organization and change leaders need to shed preconceived notions and adjust the implementation plan when reality creeps in. Resistance is to be expected and may crush the initiative if social integration is approached in a heavy-handed, top-down manner. By approaching social's impact on the culture more thoughtfully and taking a panoramic snapshot of how the entire organization or the value chain in the industry could be streamlined, the real impact on an organization's efficiency and effectiveness becomes evident, even if it starts with a small part of the culture that previously seemed intractable.

## CHAPTER 8

Deploy Social Analytics to Listen Louder and Tell a Compelling Story

IF A BRAND can be defined as a vision delivered, social analytics is the barometer of how well that vision is, in fact, being delivered, implemented, and applied to solving business challenges or taking advantage of market opportunities. Metrics should measure against agreed-upon objectives and values and help to create course correction along the way—more like a *dial* you turn up or down than a *switch* you turn on or off. Here is the problem: The overemphasis on social media tools, propagated by a cottage industry of vendors and platforms, once-a-week conferences, and fly-by-night consultants and their glorified blogs, is the tail wagging the dog. Too often organizations allow the tools to dictate rather than define what to measure. Social analytics should be about aligning objectives with the strategy, the implementation process, the effectiveness of each smart touch point, success metrics that move

the member or customer to their next logical decision point, rich data sets and finally, the tools. Social analytics should help to measure these stages and modify the original objectives or the strategy. (See Figure 8.1.)

Figure 8.1—Seven Steps of Social Analytics

Organizational objectives, as defined by business outcomes outlined in earlier chapters, must be a driving force in implementing a social campaign for desired change in an organization. Understanding organizational objectives will facilitate the design of broad social parameters for analyzing and selecting the right tools. For example, a review of organizational objectives may indicate that the strongest priorities are member/customer reach or geographic coverage requirements, content within and external to the organization and the context for its use, and the organization's current and future engagement capability. The *implementation process* should be focused entirely on the business function that the social campaign will address. If the desired business outcome is strengthening a brand, ideally, the organization is focused on measuring the impact of the social campaign on the brand pyramid—establishing a market presence, performing through credible content, creating distinct advantage from the customer's point of view, and converting interest to engagement. (See Figure 8.2.)

If member or customer acquisition is the organizational objective, a funnel process (creating awareness, supporting consideration, developing organizational or brand preference, getting people engaged to join, and sustaining loyalty) may be most appropriate to measure. Other

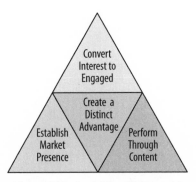

Figure 8.2—Social Brand Pyramid

implementation processes often encompass member or customer support, customer relationship management, organizational reputation, and advocacy generation.

Success metrics depend on the preceding implementation process, as each social process requires unique metrics. Member or customer acquisition objectives drive metrics such as percentage of unaided awareness, percentage of the total target market audience who would consider the organization/its products and services, percentage who prefer the organization/its products and services, incremental revenue, percentage of member renewals, or repeat purchases from key customers. Understanding how social engagement drives a specific implementation process is also important to the organization's ability to describe the impact and the return on that impact that social presence, in fact, creates. Other metrics such as exposure, engagement, reach, opportunities, shared positive discussions, comments-to-post ratios, number of mentions, and retweets per followers are all examples of typical metrics of interest to many who implement social media campaigns.

Rich social data sets that are actionable are derived from ratios—a numerator and a denominator—that when independently modified will create both "what if" scenarios to explore alternative paths as well as the necessary course correction in the implementation process, engagement through the touch points, or recalibration of the success metrics. It's important to clearly identify what specific pieces of data the organization will need to compute meaningful ratios that highlight its social impact.

Only when the organization understands what data is needed to calculate meaningful social metrics can it assess the right class of tools to best deliver the insights it seeks. In many instances, no one tool may be able to deliver the insights you need about not just *what's* happening but much more importantly, *why* and what to do about it. By understanding the preceding steps, the organization or its change leader can make more informed tool decisions focused on what the organization *should* measure instead of what metrics a tool *can* measure.

For example, according to the *July 2011 comScore U.S. Smartphone survey,* why in-store purchases are abandoned among U.S. Smartphone users has more to do with their ability to uncover pricing transparency in real time ("found it online for a better price" or "found it at another store for a better price") than the fact that mobile internet and social campaigns are driving foot traffic to the local stores. "Saw a negative review about the item," which points to real-time negative sentiment from a social interaction, was also mentioned as a key driver.

Listen More Intently

To understand why key current processes are or aren't working and to ensure that social campaigns deliver the desired impact, organizations must learn to *listen more intently.* If you want to tell a better story—about your brand, unique value add, and impact on individuals, organizations, or industries—you must begin by understanding and planning for the notion that one size does not fit all in the social environment. Different audiences have distinctly different requirements from the organization's social presence, platforms, and purpose. You must begin by segmenting your members by their unique requirements, profiling key stakeholders within this group of members or customers, and examining the scope of your listening capabilities.

Ten discussion points about segmentation will make the fundamental difference in the organization's ability to develop a strong listening platform from its social media efforts:

1. *Who needs it?* When it comes to key individuals within the organization who would benefit from segmenting target audiences you're trying to engage, how well do you understand these internal staff member's requirements? Who and why are they trying to engage and influence, how are they getting information from the organization today and what are they getting from social channels? What are the "must-have" versus the "nice-to-have" functionalities in their ability to listen to the voices of the members or customers? Ask each group of stakeholders key questions to really narrow down whom the organization will listen to, what unique conversations are of particular

interest to various individuals, and what the organization will learn from listening more intently.

2. **Where do they need it?** The language and countries you are particularly interested in segmenting will influence your choice of social listening and engaging platforms. China may not be a target market for the organization's social campaigns today, but if it becomes one in a couple of years, double-byte language support and translation capabilities in your implementation process and analytical effectiveness will be essential.

3. **How do we support it?** In earlier chapters, I discussed the "iTunification" of the organization's capabilities. If you think about how iTunes functions today, it's primarily "self-service." Beyond initial setup, very few people are calling Apple for help walking through the sync process. How will your organization monitor and analyze a self-service process and workflow of products and services? Social analytics isn't about watching what individuals do in a silo. It's their interaction across your broad array of products and services that will give you a more holistic view of their unique requirements.

4. **Where are they?** Many tool vendors typically look at content from major social networking sites, such as LinkedIn, Facebook, Twitter, YouTube, blogs, and forums. Is that where the organization's listening beneficiaries think their target audiences are? The types of channels the listening platform scans must be consistent with both the current member/customer social spheres and future ones. The aggregation and frequency of the social content that is being crawled is also critical, given the real-time nature of social interactions.

5. **What do we really need to measure?** Social analytics platforms often group a set of predetermined analytics or offer customizable "widgets" or application programming interface (API) to hook into unique communities. Out of the box, these metrics are designed to amplify listening capabilities such as share of dialogue, volume of discussions around a specific topic, or trends in tone. The organization must set the analytical requirement beyond what the tool vendors think it should understand from its social presence. One self-preservation strategy has become a broad array of tools measuring very different important attributes; here is the best part—*differently!* One measures reputation based on one set of metrics,

while another proclaims that reputation is composed of an entirely different set of characteristics.

6. ***What conversations matter?*** As you recall from previous discussion, taxonomies are a compilation of key words or topics of particular interest to the organization. Beyond mentions of name, brand, products, executives, or competitors, social analytics should provide a deeper level of sophistication in their search and present capabilities. Boolean logic and proximity searches help filter as much out as they include in.

7. ***How do we collect it?*** For a social analytics listening platform to be effective, it must integrate with and across a broad range of data types—search, web, social, ads, member or customer opinions—today and in the future. Multiple data streams, connections into web analytics applications, and even some enterprise applications such as supply chain, member or customer management, accounting, or marketing automation may be particularly useful.

8. ***What do we report?*** Social market leadership campaigns are often an array of searchable fields. Each profile, chat, blog, link, response—in essence, all dialogue—can be searched and reported on. But just because you can, doesn't mean you should. The organization should invest the necessary time, effort, and resources in advance to ensure the right report generation capabilities are present within the social analytics/listening platform.

   It would be ideal if three types of reports are offered to users: pull, where they can pull their own data aggregation and reporting; push, where, based on a consistent routine, specific reports are generated and sent to key beneficiaries; and event-driven, where, based on a set of business rules, key reports are triggered, data is gathered and organized, and reports are created and pushed to specific individuals. (Think of fire alarms for social analytics.) Keep in mind that during a time of crisis, content latency and reporting frequency may cause real problems if the crisis is a fast-paced event or series of crisis events.

9. ***Who else needs access?*** A double-edged sword of social analytics is that some people in the organization may be surprised by the raw nature of many discussions, the candor with which point and counterpoints are argued in blogs and forums, and the volume of the information. The organization must discern who needs access

to what information, and what can and will be done with information once it is in the system. Do different departments, functions, business units, locations, brands, and even individuals want or need customized views of the aggregated data? It is a good idea to establish administrative hierarchies for training and support purposes as well as to raise the bar on a broader team's abilities to transfer listening to action.

10. *How do we scale it?* Social analytics and listening platforms should be elegant and intuitive, allowing various beneficiaries to tag content, assign content, manage assignments, track workflow, and learn from every interaction.

Once an organization has this dialogue regarding its segmentation requirements, it can begin to explore platforms to fuel social analytics. With a strong emphasis on the nonprofit sector, J.D. Lasica and the team at Socialbright.org have compiled a number of useful lists for smaller organizations, including:

- Ten paid social media monitoring services for nonprofits;
- Twenty free social media monitoring tools; and
- How to create and manage a monitoring dashboard.

One of the stronger association dashboards I came across in my interviews was from Holly Ross, executive director of the Nonprofit Technology Network (NTEN). Ross has spent more than seven years at NTEN, working with community members to identify the technology trends that will reshape the nonprofit sector. From ubiquitous access to

---

Meet The NonProfit Technology Network (NTEN)

The Nonprofit Technology Network (NTEN) is a membership organization whose mission is to help nonprofits use technology, using a three-fold strategy: connect, learn, and change. In that framework, the organization provides community building, an annual conference, more than 100 online events annually, research, and advocacy. Membership is individual or organizational; its 2,800 members represent 12,000 individuals. Total market capacity is 500,000, so percentage of market capture is small. The underlying philosophy of NTEN is that technology is more than printing and email; it can play a role in changing the world. NTEN members are using technology tools to raise money online, collect data in the field, and connect people to the program work in new and exciting ways. The annual budget of $11.2M is 15 percent membership fees, 40 percent meetings and webinars, 20 percent sponsor and exhibitor fees, and 25 percent foundation support.

technology leadership to social media, Ross brings the wisdom of the NTEN crowd to the nonprofit sector. Ross has been recognized as one of the *Nonprofit Times* Power and Influence Top 50 for the past three consecutive years. In our conversation, she epitomized someone who not only *gets the impact of social* but is constantly trying to learn and lead differently from it.

"We have a few goals for social," says Ross. "To build a reputation as a thought leader in the space, create connections between members, and create engagement with NTEN offerings." For NTEN reputation, they measure what percentage of the nonprofit technology conversation happening on social media concerns NTEN, versus their perceived co-opetition. They track total raw numbers for NTEN mentions across social media spaces, mentions of staff versus their conference, guest posts on their blog, retweets, how influential their tweets are, and some sentiment analysis, such as how many of their mentions are positive versus neutral. NTEN also tracks lead referral sites and referral sites with the longest online time because that web traffic is particularly important to their engagement strategy. To measure how they are building connections between people, Ross and her team look at the number of comments on the NTEN blog, Facebook wall posts, and LinkedIn posts by the community and not by the staff. In time they'll track the number of posts to the communities of practice that were answered by those community practice members. To help measure engagement, which isn't exclusively calculated via social channels, the NTEN team looks at metrics such as how many webinar registrations they captured this week through a social source code or that came from social media.

Below are lists of the key community metrics—categorized by reputation, connection, and engagement—that Ross and her team track on a consistent basis:

NTEN Reputation

Percentage of Conversation
TechSoup % of Convo
NTEN Mentions for Week
NTEN Mentions for YTD
Total Mentions NTC
Total Mentions Staff
Total Mentions Sector
Staff Guest Posts
Staff Speaking Engagements
of Retweets (NTENorg)
Member Inquiries (Membership
  Team)
Total Positive Mentions
Positive NTC Mentions
Positive Staff Mentions
Leading Guest Blogger
Leading External Referral Site
Leading Social Media Referral Site
Referral Site w/Longest on-site time
  (top 10)

Build Connection

of Staff Comments on Member
  Blogs
Blog comments—NTEN.org
Outbound Tweets per Week
Outbound Tweets YTD
% of Outbound Tweets w/link
Twitter followers
Facebook Fans
Outbound FB Posts per Week
Outbound FB Posts YTD
Facebook Active Users
Facebook Community Posts
Interactions on FB Community Posts
Interactions on NTEN Posts
LinkedIn group members
LinkedIn Discussions/Questions
LinkedIn Discussions/Links

Increase Engagement

Tech Clubs	Participation	NTC
# attending 501Tech Club events	# of Memberships w/ 1+ Event	# of Social Events Attendance at CoP Events
# of Tech Club Events	% of Memberships w/ 1+ Events	% engaged in online commu- nity (myNTC)
# of source codes used	# of Memberships w/ 3+ Events	Ignite
# of Tech Club online group members	% of Memberships w/ 3+ Events	number of com- munity + staff meetings
	Attendance on New Member Calls	
Local Events	# of CoPs	
# attending Local Events	# of CoP calls/webinars	
# of Local Events	Avg Attendance on CoP calls	
# of speakers and sponsors	# on Discuss List	
	# of Members Guest Posts	
	# of Members Presenting	
	Facebook Post Views	
	Facebook Feedback	

"The number I consistently think about is that renew rate, which, I think for organizations like us, should be around 80 percent," says Ross. "Ours hovers right around 62 percent; people renew because they want to be part of the NTEN community," she adds. Her assumption is that NTEN isn't doing enough with new members to make sure they are engaged with the community. She believes that her members see the initial value of all the programs, but not the repeat value. The impact she ascertains from her social analytics directly affects NTEN's monthly membership metrics below—the first tab in the Google Doc (of course, what else?) that she shared with me:

Month:		
Memberships	**Total Memberships**	**Membership Benefits**
Joins for MONTH	Goal YTD	Individuals Receiving
Goal for MONTH	% of Goal	Benefits
% of Goal		Goal YTD
Renewals for MONTH	**Membership Revenue**	% of Goal
Goal for MONTH	Revenue for MONTH	
% of Goal	Goal for MONTH	**Events/Membership**
Joins YTD (Jan-Dec)	% of Goal	% Mem w 1+ Reg
Goal YTD	Revenue YTD	Goal YTD
% of Goal	Goal YTD	% of Goal
Renewals YTD	% of Goal	% of Mem w/ 3+ Reg
(Oct-Sep)		Goal YTD
Renewal % YTD		
(Oct-Sep)		
Goal YTD (Oct-Sep)		
Goal % YTD (Oct-Sep)		
% of Goal		

How Do You Measure That?

When an organization reaches a certain size—often with hundreds of daily social mentions—the popular search engines and many of the online free monitoring tools such as Google Analytics or SocialOomph, no longer suffice. More robust platforms are capable of turning disparate mentions into actionable insights, such as key centers and topics of influence, the authoritative influencers, more engaging sentiments, and the breadth and depth of an organization's social reach. At the 2011 Enterprise 2.0 Conference in Boston, two IBM analysts, Rawn Shah and Hardik Dave, who focus on social business metrics and analytics, presented interesting perspectives on the types of social metrics an organization needs. (See Figure 8.3.)

To effectively measure both qualitative and quantitative metrics, more socially mature organizations require a platform that can retain thousands of daily posts and activities from numerous social networking sites, social

3. What types of social metrics do you need?

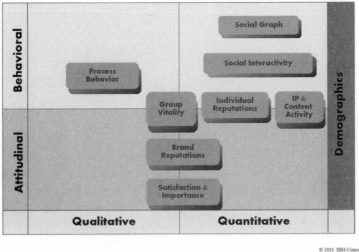

Figure 8.3—Various Categories of Social Metrics

media platforms, and present the insights in support of the organization's social market leadership. Radian6 offers a tool for organizations to listen better to its members and customers, the competitive landscape, and key market influencers, by providing detailed, real-time insights in a concise monitoring dashboard (Figure 8.4). It can track social media mentions on

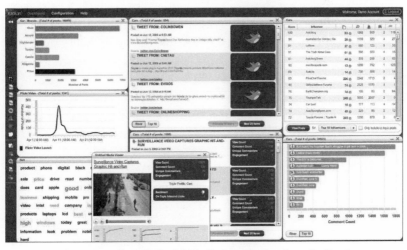

Figure 8.4—Sample Social Media Monitoring from Radian6

more than 100 million sites and provides an engagement console for the organization to coordinate its internal responses to external activity by immediately updating multiple sites from a centralized location.

There are some social sentiments that, unfortunately, even the most powerful social analytical tools may find difficult to measure. One example of an internal social campaign may be Boeing's Workplace Innovation Lab, a pilot campaign to pair "Gen Y" employees with their managers and provide 90 days' support to accelerate business priorities, focusing on leveraging personal networks, powerful conversations, and new technologies. Although the organization learned that there is real power in bringing together broad generational perspectives and in using the energy and questions of early-career employees to stimulate change, many pilot campaign participants found it hard to see the connection between learning and immediate work performance.

The underlying lessons are often difficult to quantify—the improved relationships between participants and managers, the improved understanding of each others' perspective, the impact of the manager's demonstrating the importance of the project. Although all these may be crucial elements to employee engagement and retention, they are rarely measurable in the short term. But their combined impact on projects and outcomes is tangible, and stories can be used to capture these. (See Figure 8.5.)

The Impact of Social Benchmarking

So how does an organization realize the comparative effectiveness, or impact, of its social efforts? That's where social benchmarking, *comparing* common processes or metrics across different initiatives, becomes particularly insightful. Similar to traditional operational, human resource, or revenue benchmarking, which compares the results with the process used to achieve those results, an organization can also benchmark its social analytics. If you achieve 43 percent increase in positive sentiment, is that great, average, or poor? As I'll discuss in Chapter 10 on reinventing ROI, you must start with a baseline with a succinct definition of what great, average, and poor means.

According to the 2011 eNonprofit Benchmark Study conducted by M+R Strategy and NTEN, online fundraising revenue grew overall by 14 percent between 2009 and 2010. This rebound was led by an enormous 163 percent increase in the international sector spurred by emergencies like the earthquake in Haiti and flooding in Pakistan. However, all sectors

Knowledge transfer and improving virtual collaboration	• Trial installation of webcams to improve communications within a dispersed team • Improved use of internal social networking system (Insite)—90 percent of team now has a profile, set up "how to's" to teach basic InSite skills to ease the transition for new InSite users and encourage group members to input "skills I have" and "skills I want" into their InSite profiles *"(By using InSite) each person will know how to make better use of their network and the resources in it, which will save time, reduce OT, reduce overhead costs, and increase overall revenue."*

Cost reduction	Opportunities for cost/resource savings identified, e.g.,
	
	• Change to process
	
	   "At minimum we anticipate the following: Improved employee morale, potential cost reduction, and an increased opportunity for folks to raise environmental concerns."
	
	• Change to team structure
	
	   "We've restructured the team to address resource issues, moving from a geographic work structure to one that is programmatic."

Improved communications between managers and employees	Several teams reported a positive impact from direct manager-employee interaction:
	
	• Results in positive two-way mentoring—both benefit
	
	• Using manager-employee teams to problem solve is extremely effective
	
	Evaluation: Average score 4.1 (max 5) for increased awareness of other's perspective (manager/employee)
	
	   "Opened communications between the management level and the technical workforce on our project… (manager) will increase the amount of one-on-one interaction with team members."
	
	   "Having the manager-employee team was extremely effective… (combining) people who have the power to get things done with individuals who are seeing the problems differently…"
	
	   "We will also seek to have more continual, engaging conversations so that 'change' doesn't necessarily need to appear overwhelming."

Increased motivation/ engagement amongst participants	Feedback from participants:
	
	   "A paradigm shift in how we viewed our problem—instead of asking why they leave, ask why they stay."
	
	   "It was motivational to see Boeing willing to experiment with innovative new ways to work and involving employees in their development."

Figure 8.5—Sample Benefits from Boeing REACH Members

saw an increase of some size in overall revenue from 2009, driven by an increase in the number of online gifts. Below are some of their other key findings:

- The 2010 advocacy response rate was 3.3 percent.
- Annual email list churn was 18 percent, while the average study participant sent 3.6 emails per subscriber per month and sent six emails per subscriber in December.

- Facebook users for nonprofit fan pages grew an average of 14 percent per month in 2010, with nonprofit Facebook fan pages attracting 15,053 users, defined as people who "like" a fan page. Users were much more engaged with nonprofits in the wildlife/animal welfare category.

- On average, an organization's text messaging list size was 1.9 percent of its email list size, with an annual mobile list churn of 14 percent in 2010.

An organization can begin social benchmarking efforts with how it segments and engages its target audience, its proactive presence and participation on a variety of social channels, key financial and nonfinancial impact factors, and the business outcomes these key social metrics are affecting. These will be discussed in more detail in Chapter 10. NTEN, tracks a number of key metrics in its community, correlates those directly to membership key performance indicators and scorecards its operations on a consistent basis. (See Figure 8.6.)

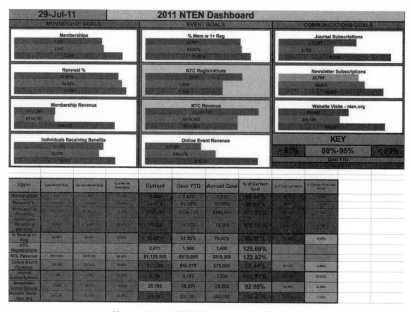

Figure 8.6—NTEN Program Dashboard

It's critical to highlight that the results of individual comparisons may not represent a dramatic difference but rather the collective comparisons of efficiency and effectiveness. While individual metrics can contribute to a benchmarking effort, they are not in and of themselves benchmarking because they do not compare results to anything. One of the more challenging aspects of social benchmarking is ensuring that there are common and comparable criteria in place, which requires a consistency of approach between multiple social initiatives and the diverse base of organizations. While the analysis of each single initiative is more time consuming, ensuring the consistency of analysis is critical for insightful benchmarking.

In social campaign benchmarking, timeliness provides its "freshness date," while consistency preserves its integrity and insightfulness toward continuous improvements. Particularly with the accelerated traction of mobile applications, social campaign benchmarking will also keep the organization from becoming stagnant in its channel utilization efforts. For social campaigning, such as creating awareness for a specific events or nonprofit fundraising, it often means:

- Having a faster and greater impact,

- Recruiting more members and maintaining current engaged members and customers who become supporters, and/or

- Cutting ineffective activities and the associated investments.

There are generally three different styles of social benchmarking:

1. **Internal Benchmarking**—Social analytics are compared internally over multiple activities, timeframes, geographical reach, or other factors.

2. **Peer Benchmarking**—Social analytics are compared between organizations in the same sector.

3. **Collaborative Benchmarking**—Multiple organizations across multiple sectors contribute data for the benchmark exercise.

Social benchmarking within an organization is relatively straightforward because information and actionable insights, if measured, are readily available. Unfortunately, many organizations provide insufficient internal social benchmarking, largely because of limited bandwidth, lack of integrating social benchmarking in performance discussions, or lack of the learning ecosystem/technology infrastructure to capture key insights and apply lessons learned from multiple social campaigns. Peer benchmarking is more difficult because it involves the use of publicly available data—often incomplete or over-aggregated—or is restrained same-sector organizations' hesitancy to compare insights due to competitive, disclosure, or intellectual property concerns. What they fail to realize is that social analytics help organizations with current and aspirational campaigns.

Furthermore, social benchmarking can be *quantitatively oriented*, where social metrics are calculated and compared, for instance, a strong performance level and close or farthest proximity to it. This type of quantitative social benchmarking is often data-strong, as it tends to analyze across multiple social initiatives, but often context-weak, with considerably less information and fewer actionable insights about each unique social initiative. The quantitative social analysis requires key steps, such as identifying the measures that are important and measurable; collecting uniform input data in terms of what the data represents and how it is formatted; analyzing the input data with consistent formulas; and comparing the results between emails, social presence, and decision actions, internally across the organization or among various organizations, social themes, member or customer segments, unique geographies, or other factors.

The other social benchmarking approach is *qualitatively oriented*, where social processes and market perception is critiqued and compared. For example, what a "most engaged donor campaign" looks like and who was closest/farthest to that performance profile. Conversely, qualitative social benchmarking is often data-weak, as fewer social initiatives tend to be compared, but context-strong, as more actionable insights regarding each social initiative are compared. Qualitative social benchmarking is more of an iterative cycle to determine a baseline of defining what social "success" looks like and how to recognize it, design a way to record and report the key social analytics findings, apply the current social campaign methodology to a few parallel initiatives, review whether the campaign methodology is creating the right level of awareness and engagement, and continue the refinements as necessary.

Shortcomings of Net Promoter Score

A deceptively simple tool used by many organizations to gauge their favorable impressions in the market, is the Net Promoter Score (NPS) developed by Fred Reichheld. NPS is based on the fundamental perspective that every organization's members or customers can be divided into three categories: promoters, passives, and detractors. By asking one simple question—How likely is it that you would recommend [organization X] to a friend or colleague?—you can track these groups and get a clear measure of the organization's performance through its members' or customers' eyes. Participants respond on a 0-to-10 point rating scale and are categorized as follows:

- Promoters (score 9–10) are loyal enthusiasts who will keep buying and refer others, fueling growth.

- Passives (score 7–8) are satisfied but unenthusiastic customers who are vulnerable to competitive offerings.

- Detractors (score 0–6) are unhappy customers who can damage your brand and impede growth through negative word-of-mouth.

To calculate an organization's Net Promoter Score (NPS), you simply take the percentage of members or customers who are promoters and subtract the percentage who are detractors.

There are, however, some fundamental shortcomings with NPS when it comes to social analytics and listening platforms, including:

- *Not strategic enough when it comes to social*—NPS offers an ultimate question designed to change the way organizations think. Beyond loyalty, NPS is a single metric to which all facets of the organization could be held accountable. The challenge with social initiatives in many organizations today is that they are functionally or departmentally focused. This makes NPS lacking in capacity to truly drive organizational change, losing the power of the NPS ultimate question about likelihood of recommending an organization and making it not much stronger than any other satisfaction metric.

- *Ignoring the member or customer lifecycles*—Not all social interaction responses can or should be aggregated. Where the customer or the member is in the lifecycle outlined in the IMPACT model dramatically affects what the data means to the organization. Are long-term members or customers passive and, thus, collectively have a lower NPS than new members or customers? Are members or customers who recently benefited from a product or service more loyal than those who have renewed, upgraded, enhanced, or are on the second or third generation of the product? Lifecycles provide the context necessary to interpret and analyze social feedback much more thoughtfully.

- *Social is dramatically more responsive*—To uncover an issue requires not only consistent collection of regular feedback but timely feedback as well. NPS is a way to check up on members or customers once or twice a year. That's a huge disconnect with the real-time nature of social engagement channels, where trends can be identified much more rapidly. An organization's reaction to its original action several months ago is ineffective when it comes to social—after the members or customers have left, it's too little, too late.

- **Too much of a good thing is still too much**—Entirely too many organizations suffer from paralysis by analysis, slicing and dicing the NPS data in too many different ways, creating further confusion. Social analytics aim to get timely information in the hands of the right stakeholders so they can make insightful decisions about course correction. More research will only influence what the organization needs to do to enact change, not in making the decision *to change.* Knowing exactly what you want to do with the data in advance of launching social analytics helps make the listening initiative more meaningful.

- **Discard other feedback engines at your peril**—A single-question NPS survey can't possibly uncover all the cause and effect insights. No one question can fill in all the parts of the puzzle. Social interaction analytics transform the engagement puzzle, addressed by NPS from 2D, into 3D, and using an analog device to measure digital impact will be myopic at best.

Analyze Social Interactions So You Can Tell a More Compelling Story

As mentioned at the beginning of this chapter, social analytics should help organizations begin to humanize business operations and tear down silos between internal teams. By designing and implementing listening platforms, the organization can uncover insights and create more meaningful and influential relationships. The narrative from online interactions fuels connected relationships. Great storytelling by organizations about the benefits they've been able to create for a broad range of stakeholders—from highly empowered employees to engaged members and loyal customers, to supportive investors and media advocates—consistently sets them apart.

Word of mouth is the gift that keeps on giving and when it comes to connected relationships; advocates attract and influence other advocates. Beyond promoting products or services, conversations between individuals about an organization can be incredibly insightful—*if* the organization is savvy enough to listen, not interrupt, interject, defend, position, or posture, but simply listen, learn, and translate experiences into compelling narratives. Connected people who become advocates talk about the organization, even when the organization isn't listening. Connected relationships are trusted amongst their peers and within their microcommunities, as they aid and influence others down their individual decision journeys. Although the reach of one connected relationship may be minimal, as an aggregate, the total reach can have a strong business impact on any organization.

According to Forrester Research, every year more than 500 billion consumer opinions are shared online. The secret of monetizing these highly connected relationships for any organization is finding the right individuals and engaging them to talk about the right things in the right places. Those opinions, often internalized through stories, are affecting talent acquisition, revenue growth, and emotional loyalty and making the advocates who write them highly influential, since they have the ability to shape thoughts, perceptions, and behaviors.

So how does an organization tell more compelling and interesting stories from its social analytics capabilities?

In *The Dragonfly Effect*, authors Jennifer Aaker and Andy Smith share the story of Scott Harrison, who at 31 left the New York City nightclub and fashion promotions business to launch charity: water, the water-focused nonprofit that has raised $43 million dollars to date for clean water projects around the world. His organization has helped 2.06 million people in 19 countries via more than 250,000 donations in the past five years. However, that only accounts for around 1/500th of the global problem, according to Harrison. His new goal is to reach 100 million people in the next decade with clean water projects. To do so, charity: water will need to raise $2 billion. This, said Harrison, is a goal that many people think is impossible in a shrinking nonprofit sector. Charity: water, though, has been experiencing significant annual growth in the past few years—revenue was up 85 percent in 2010 and 65 percent in 2011.

One recent example of an impossible goal is the organization's Dollars to Projects campaign at the Social Good Summit in September 2011. (See Figure 8.7.)

Dollars to Projects is a charity: water feature that tracks online where every dollar raised is being used in the world. The new initiative allows donors to track their donations to specific projects and receive reports of where that money goes and how it has been used. The reports, which include Google maps and photo galleries, detail exactly how the money

KISFA ELEMENTARY SCHOOL
Completed: 2011

COUNTRY [?]	PEOPLE SERVED [?]	PROJECT TYPE [?]
ETHIOPIA	503	DRILLED WELL

- **Region:** Tigray [?]
- **GPS:** 13.6113891601562, 39.2041664123535 [?]
- **Project Cost:** $7,326.00 [?]
- **Local Partner:** A Glimmer of Hope and REST [?]
- **Project ID:** ET.GOH.Q4.09.048.214 [?]
- **Field Notes:**

  charity: water projects at schools like this one use clean water as a catalyst to improve the overall health of kids and the surrounding community. That means each school project includes a water source, but also hygiene training, a handwashing station and toilets for the students.

  Girls in developing countries miss up to a week of class each month, or even drop out of school, when they hit puberty because they don't have a private place to use the bathroom or wash at school. charity: water invests in separate latrines for girls and boys to ensure privacy and maintain dignity for students. Improved sanitation (toilets) alone can reduce the likelihood of waterborne diseases by 32%. And private latrines built at schools not only improve health; they have been shown to increase attendance, especially among girls (World Health Organization). Read why latrines are so important to Khadija from Bangladesh here.

Google Maps
See This Project on a Map »

Figure 8.7—charity: water Launch of Dollars to Projects

is used, who the project affects, and who else donated. The reports can be shared with friends via social media channels.

Charity: water exemplifies social analytics empowering a compelling story. It evokes themes of redemption, change, and real hope—a story that engages and compels others to act, support, advocate, and evangelize. By candidly discussing in online videos why and how he started charity: water, Harrison—thoughtful, engaging, accessible, yet youthful—helps viewers emotionally connect with him and his cause.

Charity: water lets individuals (Relationships are between individuals, remember?) engage online with his brand and connect the dots between what's important to them and how it relates to his social campaign. Use of amazing photos and videos, Google maps, and blogs from the edge of where the impact is created articulate a sense of urgency for this cause and allow the audience to *empathize with the brand.* Beyond relying just on stats, they promote compelling stories that force people to think about what it would be like to live without access to clean water.

Social analytics can help an organization emphasize authenticity. In our current low-trust environment, true passion is contagious and genuine connections create influential cause and effect. Because of charity: water's transparent, reports and updates on the organization's website, donors know exactly where their philanthropy goes. Results of generosity are not just communicated; with social analytics, they're amplified. (See Figure 8.8.)

ETHIOPIA 2006 - 2008

Figure 8.8—charity: water Google Map of Impact in Ethiopia

Social analytics also help organizations match the media with the message. Charity: water has a dedicated staff member focused on updating the organization's distinct messages for Twitter and Facebook fan pages. Video vignettes that are tagged and distributed broadly, reach millions of highly segmented audiences who act upon the emotionally engaging content and decide to raise funds or donate.

Social analytics allow astute organizations to listen more intently to capture and share amazing stories about the organization's impact. Skillfully employing real-time analytics to the implementation progress of a social strategy is another example of *thinking and leading differently.*

Fail Intentionally and Learn From It

D URING A RECENT visit to a client's headquarters, I wandered about looking for a restroom. In an obscure corner, I found the following whiteboard:

Figure 9.1—Experience Quote

It reminded me that success from social innovation ultimately comes from experiencing many lessons. Few would disagree that technological innovation is a major enabler of long-term economic prosperity or that it is beset by a high degree of uncertainty. Understanding the nature of social media's uncertainty and the obstacles to surmounting it, inside and outside the organization, is not a trivial matter. It goes to the essence of how new social campaigns and collaborative applications are designed and deployed, how rapidly and virally they can spread, and how they influence an organization's economic performance.

The deep uncertainty associated with social innovation makes it hardly surprising that many organizations and change leaders have historically experienced high failure rates in translating seemingly good ideas at the time into social awareness, adoption, traction, engagement, positive sentiments, brand mention, and conversion. Indeed, the vast majority of attempts at effective social engagements fail. Fortunately, failure is not the end of the story, because when it comes to social theory, application, and implementation, nothing is a better teacher than failure. For many visionary leaders, failure is a badge of honor or a rite of passage for those who have stumbled—some more spectacularly than others—to the summit of success.

The organization must understand and focus on the art and science of *success in social failure.* If it can deploy stronger signal scouts to anticipate when it's headed for a fall, it can turn things around or put them back together for round two, three, or four. The overarching message is simple: It's never as bad as it seems or as great as it seems. Celebrate every success and failure, learn from it, apply it to the next iteration, and enjoy the journey, because the destination is a constantly moving target. Here's an apt example.

Leigh Wintz came in as CEO and executive director in 1991 for Soroptimist International of the Americas, Inc. (SIA), an international organization headquartered in Philadelphia, PA. Its 40,000 members are business and professional women who improve the lives of women and girls through economic empowerment programs. SIA is a cause-related organization based in local communities, where members meet to work as a group to help local women. The community dynamic of chapters provides professional women more clout to be able to have an impact and networking opportunities. Members are in a variety of occupations and professions, but typically they are the movers and shakers in the community.

Five years ago SIA launched a soft media campaign called Live Your Dream (LYD), where a separate website was used to attach to a market instead of hitting them up directly with the mission and a request for donation. The campaign morphed into several different public awareness initiatives over the next few years and was eventually integrated into the company website. SIA launched a new program around Live your Dream this fall, which Leigh believes will strengthen the brand. Leigh: "Part of the shift that's had to happen internally with LYD was because the members would say, 'why aren't you doing something directly for us?' Increasing public awareness doesn't necessarily drive membership. So here we are, a dues organization, our headquarters exists to serve members, and members are asking for public awareness but we can't always turn that into a direct donation or membership in a local chapter. So you are out on a limb. A lot of inquiries come in offering help, people who want to get involved, but there may be no club in their area, and/or that club may or may not be doing one of those programs. Most clubs do the signature project (Soroptimist Women's Opportunity Awards). But if a potential member is interested in our disaster recovery program or trafficking, the local club may not be working in that area; they've got limited resources too. Or they may not meet at a time and day that's convenient for her or suitable to her demographic. The new program for LYD, Soroptimist Affiliates (working title), will allow women to contribute in other ways outside the local geography.

After 20 years at Soroptimist, Leigh left to become a full time principal consultant with Tecker International, LLC. Elizabeth Lucas now serves as the executive director.

> **Meet Soroptimist International of the Americas, Inc. (SIA)**
>
> SIA has 40,000 members in 1,500 chapters in 19 countries, 40 percent of whom are in Asia (Korea, Japan, Taiwan, and the Philippines). The chapters are part of a federation of clubs. SIA is one of four federations, which are part of Soroptimist International, an umbrella organization headquartered in Cambridge, England, which coordinates the activities of the four federations. The annual budget of SIA is $5.5M, and there are 27 staff in the HQ in Philadelphia. Revenues are approximately 50 percent from dues, 30 percent from contributed income, and 10 percent investment income. The remaining 10 percent comes from other sources such as profits from sales items and meetings.

The Honeymoon is Over

If 2010 and 2011 were the explosive years of this shiny new thing called social networking, then social media in 2012 and beyond has to be about making business sense of it and seeing effective return from it. (See Chapter 10.) An organization's thinking must evolve from social *media to business, market leadership, and impact.*

According to a Gartner release:

> Through 2012, more than 70 percent of IT-dominated social media initiatives will fail. When it comes to collaboration, IT organizations are accustomed to providing a technology platform (such as email, IM, Web conferencing) rather than delivering a social solution that targets specific business value. Through 2013, IT organizations will struggle with shifting from providing a platform to delivering a solution, resulting in a 70-plus percent failure rate in IT-driven social media initiatives. Fifty percent of business-led social media initiatives will succeed, versus 20 percent of IT-driven initiatives.

This past year, more organizations hit the social restart button because the preconceived notion was that if they didn't jump on to the great "engagement manifesto," they'd be left behind by the entire universe. After all, *Time* magazine did name YOU Person of the Year in 2004 and gave Mark Zuckerberg the coveted title in 2010. In the past several years, marketers invested haphazardly and came up empty when leaders asked for outcomes of their Facebook "likes" or Twitter followers. By the way, if that's the organization's return on investment, it's in trouble!

So, why do organizational social efforts fail? Here are the top 10 culprits:

1. ***Lack of a prioritized social ecosystem.*** The IMPACT model presented in earlier chapters is an ecosystem. Social media is equally an ecosystem of interdependencies; it isn't a megaphone or a billboard to push a message and expect change. Nor is it about the tools or technology—they are enablers. Very similar to relationships where there is an art and a science, an organization's realm of responsibilities within the landscape of social media also requires artful discipline. Only when the organization immerses itself into the community, learns from it, builds subgroups of likeminded individuals, and develops genuine and value-based relationships will the organization gain awareness, earn authentic respect, and be able to monetize the trust.

2. *Lack of organizational agility.* Some equate a lack of planning with a failure to have goals; I believe they are distinct challenges. Many organizations try to apply their traditional planning and forecasting tools to social. "We need a thorough workplan before we can start a blog," exclaimed one departmental participant at a client's roundtable discussion. Instead, we spent the next 45 minutes and, subsequently, weeks designing, developing, modifying, presenting, redesigning, and repackaging the workplan, when a blog could have been started to begin engaging the organization's target audience. Many organizations simply aren't able or willing to embrace the agility and responsiveness required of the entire organization by social. The idea that social media shift, perhaps altering their distribution channels, is an uncomfortable one. In my experience with senior leadership teams, not many organizations are willing to devote a percentage of their budgets to a category labeled, "We're just not sure yet!" Social is agile, and opportunities don't telegraph an appearance in the organization's plan; they are disguised as dialogue looking to alleviate a pain. The organizational gap of appropriate roles and responsibilities relating to social is another recipe for disaster. Leaders must iron out the internal battles or insecurities within an organization; clearly define roles for internal employees, partners, and interns; and hire a consultant or agency if appropriate. Agility is most impactful when the windshield is clean and all the critical components—from the engine and transmission to the steering wheel and the brakes—understand their roles and realm of responsibilities. The authority to act in and around social must also be pushed to the edge of the business, where accountability and responsibility for performance, execution, and results often reside.

3. *Lack of credible and expansive metrics.* PR experts turned social strategists have been quoted as saying, "Accountability, metrics, and outcomes serve as the foundation for social media success." And yes, the *Titanic* should have turned before it hit the iceberg. As mentioned in the previous chapter, quantitative results alone will not paint a holistic picture of the organization's progress; qualitative measures are equally critical. Organizations that haphazardly roll out a random social initiative without a plan to see it through, learn from it, grow it, scale it, or kill it when it has outlived its purpose dilute their credibility with members and customers as well as the industry's leadership. Business drivers must be the goals

and performance metrics. Don't "throw together" Facebook fan pages, don't tweet randomly, don't create a Flip video and post it on YouTube because someone thought it would be "cool." Instead, integrate social into the fabric of the business and watch how it will g row, mature, and reinvent itself.

4. *Lack of an executive champion with a professional net worth.* Because of the highly disruptive nature of social integration across the entire organization and the potential to create a ripple effect in the industry when executed flawlessly, I've yet to see a successful social initiative that wasn't a top-five business priority for a senior executive. An executive champion has enough relationship currency, reputation capital, and professional net worth—all described extensively in my book *Relationship Economics*—to marshal the resources and shepherd key initiatives up, down, and across the organization. Selling a product or service via social channels is useless if the service infrastructure isn't omnipresent in parallel to support it before, during, and after the purchase.

5. *Lack of organizational vision beyond marketing.* Social opportunities continue to be underutilized within many organizations, across multiple distribution channels, and across global markets because of localization and customization challenges. Unfortunately, integrating social strategies continues to be typecast as a "marketing function." Social collaboration, knowledge management, and innovation—all processes and not technological systems—can connect experts in far corners of the organization or the globe.

6. *Lack of organizational commitment to invest in social.* Commitment to social involves investing the time, effort, and resources to learn, explore, try pilots, and yes, fail, but grow in the process. An organization that isn't failing isn't trying, and without investment—beyond the summer interns or those who have a large number of personal Facebook friends leading the charge—social engagement will remain largely transactional versus transformational in many organizations. Social is too vast for anyone to know it all. Some very competent consultancies and agencies have unique expertise that can help accelerate an organization's thinking, development, and time-to-results. Unfortunately, there are far more hacks espousing really bad advice. Organizations must conduct a deep due-diligence process to evaluate the expertise they need the most, realizing that

more firms are becoming specialists and that the one-size-fits-all model is often dangerous and expensive. Social market leadership, unfortunately, isn't free. Strong firms that are tough and smart, focus on the outcome versus their input, and bring competent thought leadership to your efforts are worth the investment. *Do not abdicate social to third parties*; it must become an internal core competency. Leverage specialists to get you started and use their expertise as needed to continue to elevate your knowledge and best practices.

7. ***Lack of creative engagement.*** In an effort not to offend anyone, many organizations are engaging no one when it comes to their social presence. Engagement is dialogue, disagreements, and different perspectives. Think about it—if everyone agrees with the organization's most recent blog post, why would they take the time to comment? (Many useless sites still do only "nice post.") Unless there is something, ideally of value, for them to obtain, why would they "like" the organization's Facebook page? Unless the organization is engaging and offering something that they can't get anywhere else, why would they follow it on Twitter? The organization must learn to tweet with its audience, not just at them like a billboard. If the organization aims to inform, inspire, interact, intrigue, interrupt, and introduce the target audience to interesting ideas, that's when social becomes creative and engaging.

8. ***Lack of social guidelines.*** Although I dislike the term "policy," largely because of its overcomplicated legalese, I do recommend a strong set of social guidelines for every client. An internal understanding of expectations, book-ended by acceptable interactions, protects the organization and establishes a set of standards for individuals as ambassadors and stewards of the organization's brand, repute, and market presence. Beware: Many discussions regarding social guidelines are uncomfortable. Tough love, past experiences, and facts—more than opinions—will carry the day.

9. ***Lack of realistic expectations or assumptions.*** Some leaders believe social will fix their broken organizations. If the people are damaged, the processes are broken, member/customer acquisition is not supported by marketing, the value-add doesn't resonate, the target audience doesn't like or respect the organization or its people, sorry, but these problems can and will not be solved by implementing social initiatives. Unfortunately, in many instances, social's raw

candor and vast reach will worsen organizational problems. In my consulting experience, many unrealistic expectations come from top leaders who read about exaggerated miracles of big brands achieving *their version* of success, and automatically assume "we can do that too." What they don't realize is the army of people and millions of dollars as well as the painful lessons from past failures that contributed to that success. Social success comes from diligent research, thoughtful planning, and obsessive execution. It's patient and humble as a lifelong learning engine for the organization and its people.

10. *Lack of swinging for the fence.* Years ago, a speech coach repeatedly drummed into me that the first 10 seconds of a speech aren't to thank the academy or your parents for having you. It's a chance to come out swinging, to grab your audience's attention as a messenger with a message important enough to listen to! Social initiatives are very similar. Dipping your toe in the water is the digital version of thanking the academy—it's boring! Rambling endlessly on a platform, whether it's at a conference or in the social sphere, is also boring—so please stop. Come out swinging on a blog, Facebook page, Twitter account, or video channel. Make it count with a great first impression. People don't want to know everything you know. Focus on success in incremental stages, with the first rung of the ladder being immediate engagement. If the organization makes a terrible first impression, it has to work that much harder to dig itself out. Leverage social to meet business goals and objectives. Plan the organization's social initiatives so they don't scream "amateur hour" when coming out of the gate.

Poor Social Judgment

The recent political unrest in the Middle East heightened the use of social media as an enabler of democratic ideals. The world sympathized with Egypt's public protests of oppression and the protestors' will to install a different political system. The social media buzz surrounding the uprisings, unfortunately and inexplicably, motivated fashion retailer Kenneth Cole (@KennethCole) to take advantage of a country's misery by hijacking their hashtag (#Cairo) and posting a silly remark about its spring collection. It was short-sighted, inappropriate, opportunistic and the perfect example of poor social judgement.

Although they subsequently launched a PR campaign to overcome the public outcry, it highlighted an important organizational social lesson: *think twice, tweet once!*

Social Learning Strategies From Failure

If an organization and its prominent change leaders candidly internalize why and how they've failed in any past endeavor, they'll soon realize that:

- Failure is not always bad, wrong, detrimental, debilitating, or catastrophic; and
- Learnings from organizational failures are hidden gems, with insights about how to uncover, analyze, and institutionalize them.

Just think about how many times, on average, employees of a global organization—or a local association, for that matter—fail daily? One of the best ideas I've ever heard was to designate a "failure wall" for staff to record scenarios where they failed, lessons they learned from failure, and sign their name. Granted, it's not a Facebook wall or a Twitter hashtag—neither were in existence 10 years ago when the idea was shared with me—but because it was in a prominent location and visible to all employees, partners, customers, guests, family, and friends who visited, it communicated a sincere and honest need for the culture to share growing pains and recognize how the organization was better off because of them. Another client has launched Yammer internally and is asking employees every day, "What problem are you trying to solve?" This one simple idea has spun off a socially enabled knowledge management system, highlighting pockets of amazing discoveries across the organization.

Social adds an additional layer of complexity to organizational failures. It provides context-specific scenarios where multiple dependencies affect the less-than-stellar results. Beyond the obvious excuses, such as "the right process wasn't followed" or "we were ahead of our market," it's time to think differently about the organization's belief system. Step number one is for the organization and key leaders of a social evolution of the business or the industry to get beyond what Harvard Business School professor of leadership and management Amy Edmondson refers to as the blame game. During an HBS Idea Cast video interview, she described it as a deeply ingrained unpleasant feeling in our psychology from early childhood. We bring those emotions into the workplace as adults and connect them to dismissals and promotions. The dilemma becomes that beyond learning from failures, people withhold sharing those incredibly valuable insights for fear of lowering the performance standards or expectations across the organization.

Social modifies much of the reality that we face at work: greater uncertainties and the need to be more creative, to respond in near real time, and to engage and influence more sophisticated audiences. Professor Edmonson has created a spectrum of reasons for failure (Figure 9.2), citing specific causes ranging from deliberate deviation to thoughtful experimentation. Whereas the top of the scale is "blameworthy," the bottom is "praiseworthy."

A Spectrum of Reasons for Failure

BLAMEWORTHY

DEVIANCE
An individual chooses to violate a prescribed process or practice.

INATTENTION
An individual inadvertently deviates from specifications.

LACK OF ABILITY
An individual doesn't have the skills, conditions, or training to do execute a job.

PROCESS INADEQUACY
A competent individual adheres to a prescribed but faulty or incomplete process.

TASK CHALLENGE
An individual faces a task too difficult to be executed reliably every time.

PROCESS COMPLEXITY
A process composed of many elements breaks down when it encounters novel interactions.

UNCERTAINTY
A lack of clarity about future events causes people to take seemingly reasonable actions that produce undesired results.

PRAISEWORTHY

HYPOTHESIS TESTING
An experiment conducted to prove that an idea or a design will succeed fails.

EXPLORATORY TESTING
An experiment conducted to expand knowledge and investigate a possibility leads to an undesired result.

Figure 9.2—Edmonson Spectrum of Reasons for Failure

Careful correlation of this spectrum, with key attributes required for strategizing and implementing successful social engagement, points to a low percentage of most social failures as blameworthy. If experience from social engagements is to be derived via lessons from failures, leaders must uncover and capture these lessons by encouraging experimentation, trials, pilots, process reinventions, or eliminations across the entire organization.

The uncertainties created by social initiatives in many organizations are derived from a unique combination of real-time needs (buyer behavior and decision process) of people (segmentation—internal and external) and problems (access to specific information, processes, or insights) unfamiliar to the organization. Unpredictable situations, technology failures, process missteps, or previously unrecognized patterns are all perpetual risks of social engagement. To think of failure in these environments as bad is to misunderstand the complexity facing the organization and to ignore that unproductive avoidance of smaller mistakes often leads to bigger failures.

Edmonson tells the story of a team of leading physicists, engineers, aviation experts, naval leaders, and astronauts who devoted months to analyzing the space shuttle *Columbia* disaster. Their findings reinforce the two levels of analysis that can equally help avert many social initiative failures:

1. If the organization responds to small failures along the way versus ignoring them, "we have too many other things to worry about" is a very real and omnipresent syndrome. If key trends in member or customer engagement deficiencies by the organization are not highlighted early in the process, member or customer churn becomes a much larger failure for the organization later.

2. Attempts by key individuals to get senior leaders to further analyze early problems are unfruitful, or individuals are unable to get attention to potential failures up, down, and across the organization. If the failures get attention earlier, course corrections can be not only feasible but worthy of an effort. This attention is a factor of an individual's propensity for polished persistence as well as the leadership's fiduciary responsibility to remove the earplugs, listen, and respond to weak links in the organization.

Designing Social Failures—*Intentionally*

Beyond *preventable* failures, such as when the organization hires the wrong person to lead its social campaign, and the *unavoidable* failures due to the complexity of the environment, such as an attempt to integrate disparate relationship, accounting, and supply chain systems for a more holistic view of customers or members, certain types of failures can be considered extremely productive. According to Duke University professor of management Sim Sitkin these *intelligent* failures dramatically affect an organization's ability to learn when:

- They provide valuable new knowledge that can help the organization create a dramatically unique market position against its competitive peers;
- Experimentation is essential or uncertainties from an exact scenario mask the possible answers; and
- The organization or the industry is investing in new drug R&D, new business or revenue models, innovative product or process design, or testing member or customer reactions in a new market.

Organizations aim to learn through proof of concepts, or pilot projects. Unsurprisingly, when it comes to social engagements, many of these campaigns are designed to succeed rather than to uncover intelligent failures that generate incredibly valuable insights regarding the organization's preparedness for *social business*. Figure 9.3 highlights some of the top pilot or test campaign differences between aiming to succeed versus pushing the envelope to intelligently fail and learn from the process.

Pilot Attributes	Aimed to Succeed	Intelligently Fail
Circumstances	Optimal and highly controlled conditions	Typical and ad hoc conditions
Operating Environment	Limited scope of users and a sliver of the organization's access to resources	Real employees, members or customers, and resources
Goal of the Pilot	Demonstrate value of the offering/campaign from those involved	Learn as much as possible from the people, processes, and capabilities required
Learning Objectives	Performance objectives set, but learning opportunites are unknown or unclear	Clearly understood by all staff and management
Metrics and Rewards	Successful outcome directly impacts performance reviews or compensation	Learning outcomes impact performance metrics for the team
Preparation	Carefully selected and highly protected bubble	Raw circumstances of daily situations, relationships, and interactions representative of the organization's real business challenges or opportunities
Postmortem	Massive launch of a bigger, more complex engagement	Explicit changes implemented as a direct result of the pilot performance

Figure 9.3—Pilots Aimed to Succeed Versus Intelligently Fail

The single most important outcome from intelligent failures is the learning opportunity in the postmortem. Unfortunately, these learning opportunities are often diminished because of the organization's emotional instability or the painful nature of examining why or how something failed. Most people are uncomfortable discussing their shortcomings, as it tends to chip away at self-esteem or confidence. We view failure analysis to be as pleasant as getting a root canal, and although we may realize we need one, we'd rather get numbed to it and hurry along the process. That's the wrong attitude for dissecting social initiative failures if you want to really understand how the organization will need to function differently. Social initiative failure analysis requires a childlike wonder, a natural curiosity about why the organization or industry functions as it does, how it has arrived at its current status quo, and what it will take to challenge it rather than defend it. The required ingredients for an effective social failure analysis include openness, candor, and patience in times of chaos and ambiguity.

No one has the answer for where social innovation will go next. What we do know is that it dramatically shifts the way organizations engage and influence individuals. This really is the digital version of the wild West and it will require *digital EQ*—emotional intelligence—thoughtful reflection, and introspection, not mere decisiveness, efficiency, and action, to learn from social engagement.

But learning from intelligent failures takes more than emotional stability; it takes cognitive reasoning to see the evidence. If the target audience in this social channel simply isn't engaging in a dialogue or call to action, can we accept an alternative explanation instead of support of our existing beliefs about why it is happening? We attribute failure to factors other than the discipline we control.

Similar to how scientists understand that although a breakthrough is possible, failure is more probable in a large percentage of experiments, so must social change leaders understand the role of failure in growth. Only by accepting social media as a learning and adapting engine for the organization and its key functional drivers in its business model can its leaders understand the information that will keep it ahead of the competition.

Learning to fail intentionally won't be perceived as natural by many people. To be successful with social integration initiatives, organizations and the key change agents within them must have the *courage and the support infrastructure to fail.* It's a confrontation of our own imperfections as well as those of others around us, supported by leadership that doesn't discourage reporting of or express strong disapproval of bad news about the performance requirements. If lessons from social failures are gold, those from intentional failures are the equivalent of building an organizational Fort Knox.

Equally Important: Learn from Social Success

During a recent keynote on Adaptive Innovation™, a CEO asked me, "How do you innovate when you're focused on execution, your people are already at full capacity, and business is good?" Beyond learning from failures as outlined above, there are also learning opportunities from an organization's social success. Three highly interrelated factors come to mind:

- **Wrong Answer**—It's natural to gloat when a social campaign works and produces the expected results. But were the leader's brilliant strategy and flawless execution (as a popular talk show host likes to say, "with talent on loan from GOD") or the environmental factors and random events responsible for the success?

- **10 Gallon Hat**—It's a Texas thing, but it implies overconfidence. Getting a dozen ecommerce sites up in the last few years for several organizations doesn't make someone a social expert. Success fuels self-assurance in all of us, reinforcing faith in our knowledge, skills, and the ability to muster the right insights to apply at just the right time. Too much of that self-assurance, though, is still too much.

- **It's Not Broken**—This is a particularly dangerous attitude; one that actually believes ignorance is bliss. The organization is succeeding, but it has no idea why! Executives and their teams who suffer from this shortcoming are not questioning their assumptions, expanding their informal learning opportunities, or identifying their market or industry anomalies until it's too little, too late.

Social performance, execution, and results are currently perceived to be unambiguous, measured by followers, fans, connections, impressions, and the like. The social environment is also unforgiving. It won't wait if you're unresponsive. The competition for mindshare is a click away and vies for ideas, information, insights, and unique perspectives. Social presence strongly impacts top-of-mind brand equity and conversion of interested to engaged. As highlighted in the IMPACT model, it's an iterative process; subsequent moves to the next stage depend on smart touch points and success in guiding, not leading, members or customers to their next decision points.

Herein lies the danger. An organization explores social engagement, puts a plan in place, identifies the right team and creative assets, and launches its plan with the goals of learning from experience and "warming up" the organization to social tactics. It gains immediate traction with employees and, voilà, huge success! Kudos come in from every direction, media outlets want to know the secret, and pictures of the CEO appear on industry "most influential" lists. Now the organization is trapped, focused more on maintaining its stature and less on learning from *why it succeeded*. Few of the social analytics that were the pillars of the learning experience at the outset are reviewed, much less analyzed. After all, who looks at the car's instrument panel when everything is going great? It happens only when the car stops running or bright red lights begin to flash, alarming the driver of a less than optimal condition.

So, with this amazing success, the organization decides to "go big or go home," and bets the farm on social strategies. It hires the biggest consultancy or the most prominent agency it can find and develops grandiose visions of intergalactic peace and integrated disparate information all rolled into a customer community and presented in real time for a holistic view of the member or customer's lifecycle. Why not, right? The rookie organization knocked the cover off the ball with the internal rollout, and the leader of the initiative is a rock star. Why not go for gusto now that the organization has such dramatic success under its belt?

As you can imagine, the externally focused social initiative doesn't quite deliver on the planning hype. It's late, over budget, and bloated with features few customers actually value, and the endless internal bureaucracy becomes maddening. The organization can't tie legitimate business results to the millions spent on developing and promoting it. Although metrics are in place to highlight traction, the conversion isn't there and the social initiative is seen as a failure at delivering on expectations. The organization and change leader quickly understand that social success comes incrementally, and when they abandoned the drivers to learn and grow from each experiment, they lost their edge.

C4

No, not the kind you use to create massive explosions. Since we've covered a lot of ground in identifying predominant culprits of social failures, how to learn from them, and how to fail fast, cheap, and even intentionally, it's time to shift the lens to recovery and progress. C4 is about *cultivating a culture of connected confidence.* Failure has a way of bringing out the hypocrite in most individuals and organizations. Search online to find euphoric celebrations of inevitable failures and the importance of learning from them. But in real life—in organizations, industries, boardrooms, and mailrooms—failure is abhorred. Many people are afraid of it, avoid it at all costs, and witness how it is penalized. We are programmed at an early age to think *and feel* failure is something bad. That single belief holds many individuals and organizations back from learning and growing—personally and professionally.

A visionary leader must recognize that it's time to deprogram years of cultural baggage and must help the organization understand that the difference between a successful social engagement, campaign, enablement, strategy, or rollout and an unsuccessful one is how you handle the rejection, the perceived missed opportunities, the cost, the slips, slides, and the need for turnarounds. It's OK to fumble, because you'll get the ball back. It's OK to make a mistake, because you'll get another chance. It's OK to fall behind, because you'll make it up. The organization's ability to recover and get back on course quickly is critical for social initiatives to succeed as long-term strategic enablers.

People both inside and outside the organization must feel free to express their ideas, concerns, and perspectives without fear of retribution. Furthermore, the organization's knowledge workers must be encouraged to help identify small failures that, when left unaddressed, can cause larger and more detrimental negative effects. Leaders must make it safe for the voice of a broad base of stakeholders—from employees, to members, customers, and partners—to be heard and listened to and for learning from failures to be captured, shared, and cascaded down and across the organization.

How? By making it a psychologically safe and productive environment to speak up. If a tweet expresses a negative sentiment, the new staff member hired to support members and customers must be able to discern why the recipient's experience is breaking down and what the organization can and should do immediately to resolve it. Social challenges are opportunities in disguise, and when front-line social talent is empowered to respond, engage, and resolve with the utmost level of professionalism, it's the equivalent of bringing the Nordstrom or Ritz-Carlton experience to that social interaction.

According to Edmondson, five unique steps help an organization reduce its failure rate when its leaders develop a psychologically safe environment; I've added the social context to each:

1. *Frame the social confidence accurately.* Preempt the types of failures likely to occur, probably will occur, or have a high chance of occurrence, so the organization and key stakeholders are on the same page when it comes to the value of openness and collaboration. As I often reference in my Adaptive Innovation™ keynotes, the manner in which we frame a challenge or an opportunity often focuses us on how we attempt to solve or address it. Start by accurately framing potential failures and the lessons from them to minimize the shock to the culture. "We have no idea what kind of response we'll get from this social campaign," is one of the best opening lines I've heard from a client executive when launching a new initiative. "But we've done our homework, and although optimistic, think that our strategy and execution plan can become a great learning opportunity in how we engage our customers." The kickoff meeting for that particular engagement set an unequivocal tone from the top that the organization wanted to learn from smaller failures along the way to avoid potentially consequential ones ahead. Key training sessions were scheduled to get both local and remote employees educated and functional in the new community during a soft launch period.

2. *Reward, don't shoot, social detractors.* We often admonish naysayers and "devil's advocates." Certain levels of pushback are healthy and productive, as long as they shine light on aspects of the social engagement the organization may have not previously considered. Reward dissent, both those who offer bad news or pushback and those who question or express concerns. Accept as much feedback as feasible and then decide how to mitigate the risks of failure. Figure out how to take the anonymous "suggestion boxes" we all had around the office back in the 80s and 90s to social "blameless reporting." Beyond the facts, try to seek out opinions, perspectives, and causes of why something is happening, not just what has happened. Assign teams to analyze every concern, comment, question, or suggestion. Quickly escalate the most relevant to the top and use transparency to illustrate action on shared failures or concerns.

3. *Give them bookends.* I've never been a huge fan of "policy" because it sounds like we're trying to transfer the legalese of our organizations

to social channels. I prefer guidelines or bookends as a framework for open dialogue about what we don't know but will seek to learn, what mistakes we've made and the lessons we've learned from each, and what is and, candidly, isn't doable within an organization, and the reasons why. That level of humility, vulnerability, and candor from a transformational leader is refreshing for most organizations where the rest of the team often follows suit. This is a big reason why *Bloomberg Businessweek* recently reported more than 50 CEOs—from Virgin Group's Richard Branson to Zappos.com's Tony Hsieh—have embraced blogging and Twitter to clue customers in on new services, help them with questions about their products, and generally get a little bit personal with customers, business associates, and the public.

4. ***Beam from inside out.*** If you encourage internal adoption, participation, dialogue, feedback, ideas, and general observations, any social engagement is dramatically more effective out of the gate. There is a reason restaurants do soft launches with friends and family. Think of social initiatives as the organization's restaurant launch to create opportunities for the chefs (social architects) to the wait staff (customer service), host (community concierge), bartenders (purveyors of all things knowledge), sommelier (subject matter experts) and shift managers (community managers) to identify and work out the kinks. By encouraging them to try intelligent experiments, the organization can reduce resistance, minimize defensiveness, and may surprise the leader with those who will volunteer to help enhance the experience.

5. ***Live the commitments.*** If the organization becomes crystal clear on the "rules of engagement"—what clearly is and isn't acceptable behavior—most people will feel emotionally more secure. I simply do not believe that many people show up every day, intentionally or maliciously choosing to deviate from expectations. Unfortunately, the expectations aren't as clear, succinct, or articulated as they could or should be in many organizations. One of my favorite lines from a client's social media guidelines is, "If you trash this organization or any of your colleagues online, it is grounds for termination!" I'm not sure how much clearer plain English can become. That statement contains a clearly expressed expectation as well as the corresponding consequence. If the commitment isn't met and the organization

must displace an employee, dismiss a social community member, ban a blogger, or fire a customer or a partner, tell those directly affected what happened and why specific actions were necessary. When facing a crisis or a difficult situation, in lieu of available, credible, and timely information, most of those affected will create their own perceptions of what really happened—seldom positive for the organization.

Much of social looks and feels like a *failure on the move*, when any individual parts or timelines of it are viewed out of context. An organization is constantly competing for mindshare, if not wallet share or market share, from its online constituents, where ideas, information, and actionable insights are table stakes and the currency of the realm is repute, trust, credibility, connections, and influence. Inevitably, even the best ideas get rusty and the most streamlined process will falter. The challenge is not the failing; the challenge is when a team or an organization becomes complacent and feels entitled to those members, customers, and market presence and has lost the hunger to compete for them. It's the 13–0 team that dismisses the next opponent and gets beaten in the first round of the playoffs and sent home by the 7–6 wildcard team playing on the road!

In her book, *Confidence: How Winning Streaks & Losing Streaks Begin & End*, Rosabeth Kanter compares organizations to sports teams with extended winning records as well as those with long losing streaks and explains how their leaders attempted to create turnarounds. Kanter found that as an organization begins to fumble, unless course corrections are made immediately, the very nature of failure may produce behaviors which make it more difficult to recover. There is a reason organizations should develop a social media strategy and then work diligently to execute it. One negative tweet based on a relatively minor incident becomes a flurry of internal meetings and discussions as "crisis management" and responses makes the situation dramatically worse. Compare a team's panicking and throwing its playbook out the window to the many organizations in the midst of a change in control (think mergers and acquisitions or reductions in force). Self-protection, vulturism, and abandoning one's colleagues reign supreme.

These behaviors seldom happen in pockets; they're consistent and pervasive throughout the organization, making for cultural challenge. According to Kantor, "To transform this culture of failure to one of confidence, leaders must surround high performers with a support system to avoid these temptations." If they've anticipated customer or member requirements through social engagement, they'll be ready for the unique products, services, or support they'll require for an exceptional experience. Add social engagement to the mix, and these high performers are now connected, running set plays as outlined in previous chapters, rehearsing through practice and preparation. They leverage applications such as CoTweet to distribute the Twitter stream and engage a broader audience to respond from unique corners of the organization or the industry. They are as disciplined and focused on execution as they are professional in learning while they perform.

Transformational leaders in high-performing organizations leverage social analytics strategies mentioned in the last chapter to provide the organization with facts, not just opinions, of key business drivers on target and those in need of improvement. They aim to move beyond who did it to how it happened and how we can prevent it from happening again in the future. They encourage personal responsibility for actions, exemplify collaboration in the achievement of their own goals, inspire commitment to the organization's vision, and build respect and trust around them. When others drop the ball—and they will—a team member is there to pick it up and run with it.

The lesson for leaders is clear: Build the cornerstones of confidence— accountability, collaboration, and initiative—when times are good, and achievement comes easily. Maintain a culture of confidence as insurance against the inevitable downturn. And while no one should deliberately seek failure, remember that performance under pressure—the ability to stay calm, learn, adapt, and keep on going—separates winners from losers.

## CHAPTER 10

Reinvent ROI

T HE VALUE OF having fans or followers is minimal if an organization can't bridge its earned credibility and connections—social *creation*—to social *capitalization*. This idea is equally applicable within the organization when using social to empower knowledge management, reduce operational redundancies, and drive awareness and revenue growth. The effort of many organizations to justify their social initiative budgets is impeded by an absence of *perceived* value. Leaders are genuinely concerned when the only business value articulated by consultants, agencies, and internal champions is "engagement" measured in "number of likes or followers." Volume does not equal revenue, business value, or even relevance.

As discussed previously, numeric representation of popularity isn't social analytics. The trial period for social strategy is over. It's time to

demonstrate the business value of this channel. Organizations must find ways to move beyond engagement metrics and offer insights that trace the path from social engagement to cost performance or incremental revenue conversion, such as quantifiable metrics for "cost per fan," or "revenue per follower." Associating fans and followers with conversion data will begin to move social engagement to social actionability and impact.

Monetizing Social Marketing

Let's take one of the most obvious applications of social media and marketing that creates awareness and gravity. According to the *MarketingSherpa 2011 Social Marketing Benchmark Report,* chief marketing officers' (CMOs) priorities have changed dramatically. Not long ago, few marketers believed that social media was a channel that could be quantified in terms of a financial return on investment (ROI). The value of social media was qualitative and defined in terms of "awareness," "engagement," and other soft metrics difficult to attribute to ROI. This is no longer the case. Senior marketing executives are adamant about quantifiable ROI or enablers of logical conversion steps that lead directly to ROI.

The financial value of improving the cost efficiency of customer support programs is often overlooked when calculating ROI. Using social channels to enable customer "self-service" after the initial transaction can significantly reduce associated post-acquisition costs as well as enhance retention and renewal metrics. Yet only about one in 10 organizations considers implementing social customer service a priority.

I'm a Cub master of my son's local Cub Scouts pack. We recently decided to order Activity or Class-B uniforms—t-shirts the kids can wear with scout shorts for weekend hikes or service projects. One of the more prominent players in this space is, appropriately, Class-B. Shortly after placing an order for our pack t-shirts, I received an email from Class-B with a user ID and a password to its client community. There I can not only see and approve the art work but, equally valuable, track the status of my order through every stage from production to shipping (Figure 10.1).

Monetization drives an organization's growing investment and confidence in social marketing. Beyond the "hype" surrounding the business value of social media in the last several years, with few proven practices or success stories, marketers are turning the promise of social media into the ROI of social marketing. In the same *MarketingSherpa 2011* report, 20 percent of CMOs said that social marketing is producing a measurable ROI for their organization, and that they would continue to invest in it as

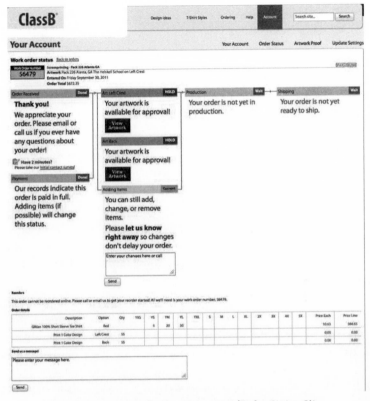

Figure 10.1—Sample ClassB Account/Order Status Site

a viable channel, nearly tripling 7 percent who said that a year ago, so the perception of social marketing's value continues to improve.

What's interesting about the Cub Scout community is now I can invite others, such as members of the pack committee, my den leaders, or other volunteer parents, to share the same experience. Although electronic order processing has been around for some time, I can't help but appreciate how much time, effort, and resources this organization saves by not making me call customer service to check on the status of my order, exchange multiple emails to see and approve artwork, track the shipment, or forward received information to others. Social effectiveness is as much about the post-sale experience as it is about creating awareness and traffic and converting individuals to customers.

What's Your Focus?

One of the most direct ways to capture and articulate ROI from social efforts is to conceptually agree on business objectives, measures, and value in advance of crafting the social strategy or an implementation plan. Succinctly understanding the business outcomes the organization seeks makes it easier to not only focus the efforts on that desired outcome but also craft the most relevant strategies and use the most effective tools in the market. With a clear set of objectives, measures are correlated (or not) to actions the organization applies to engage its target segments.

Whether it's producing content, presenting coupons, offering collaborative consumption opportunities, or soliciting feedback from an audience, if the organization is not getting interaction, downloads, comments, or transactions, then it's time to recognize that the efforts have become vibration and part of the mass social noise. They may not necessarily be wrong actions; they simply are not amplified, effective, or perceived as compelling enough to engage the target audience. Organizations that are making progress in their social execution are seeing comments, interactions, responses and the like; but they are also seeing business metrics move along a continuum that consists of downloads, registrations, questions asked and answered—often by peers in the same community versus just the organization—issues resolved, and purchases made.

What specific aspect of your organization's business operations could dramatically benefit from social initiatives? If your Facebook fan page or Twitter account isn't producing business results, why keep investing in it? At the 2011 Corporate Social Media Summit in New York City, the following case studies illustrated how organizations generate real business value in multiple manners:

- **American Express' focus on its customer's customer**—In November 2010, a time of economic turmoil for many small to medium-sized businesses, American Express launched a hugely successful "Small Business Saturday" campaign, a day consumers could be rewarded with a $25 statement credit for shopping at a small business. According to Open Forum VP of Social Media Laura Fink, the campaign engaged more than 1.2 million small businesses around the country and helped those businesses see a 28 percent sales increase on the day of the promotion. Perhaps more importantly, it demonstrated that an altruistic motivation for social engagement can generate real business impact for customers as well as for the big brand, thinking *through its downstream* value chain.

- **Union Pacific's focus on the passion and pride of local communities**—One of the largest railway companies in the United States, Union Pacific leveraged 150-year heritage to launch a crowd-sourced competition. For its "Union Pacific Great Excursion Adventure," people voted which route would be ideal for one of the company's old steam engines. The voting was split into several rounds, and the competition became fierce, as unexpected locations produced consistently surprising results: smaller markets, where residents had enormous passion and pride for their communities and for whom winning may be the headline in the local paper, routinely outpaced big metro markets. Senior Manager of Media Technology Tim McMahan noted that nearly 200,000 votes were recorded and more than 100,000 email addresses captured.

- **Coca-Cola's focus on happiness, globally**—Expedition 206 became a mission to send three lucky travelers on a journey to all 206 countries around the world where Coke is sold in search of what makes people happy. What started as an ambitious PR idea that would build on the company's existing brand platform and marketing campaign, "open happiness" became the largest social media campaign the brand had ever attempted. The winning trio embarked on their journey January 1, 2010, and anyone could follow their travels and adventures on the Expedition 206 website. The answers the trio collected in response to what made people happy ranged from family to music to dancing to soccer. Coke Director of Digital Communications Ashley Brown said that, through the lens of this social experiment disguised as marketing, the team reached what may be the most profound conclusion of all—that happiness is always simple.

- **Best Buy's focus on creating meaningful communications in the virtual world**—Commonly known as "Twelp Force," Best Buy's inner circle of 26 team members dedicated to social media, and an extended 3,000 employees who are actively encouraged to use social media, are consistently trained on best practices in making meaningful communications the definitive guide to all of their efforts. Gina Debogovich, a former customer care person herself, has spent the last three to four years building up Best Buy's customer service and social care center. Her team is a resource that individual stores can use for advice about tasks such as how to effectively use Facebook specifically for their store as well as leverage an in-house production studio to create content such as their Best Buy Unboxing feature. You want proof of impact? Gina and her team have reduced the volume of one "call driver" (the top reason that people call a contact center) by 50 percent simply by producing a video to answer that question.

- **Samsung's focus on social experiences, one problem customer at a time**—Samsung has made great strides in integrating social media into its customer service by creating online conversations about the brand. Jessica Kalbarczyk, a former marketing/PR practitioner turned social media analyst, shared how her team of only four colleagues manages to engage people online and help solve their very real problems. Instead of sitting through painful marketing meetings discussing social media, Jessica and her team are on the front lines, turning negative experiences into great opportunities. She shared a point of view that is common among customer service pros: They would much rather spend their time finding negativity and fixing problems, ultimately changing consumers' perceptions.

- **Dell's focus on integrating social into their broad operations**—As one of the most progressive brands to use social engagement to run its business differently, Dell didn't disappoint. Richard Binhammer, Strategic Corporate Communications, Social Media and Corporate Reputation Manager at Dell, shared how six business areas have fully embraced social strategies for different business outcomes: marketing, product development, sales, online presence, customer service, and communications. He made a compelling case for how perceptions of social ROI must expand to describe the real value behind the social engagement.

- **New York Life's focus on trust in employees as ambassadors of its brand**—Gregory Weiss, the assistant vice president of Social Media for New York Life, began his session with an entertaining look at the hypocritical nature of businesses who are afraid of questionable employee behaviors with social media, yet give the same employees access to phones, fax machines, and people outside the company. He reiterated that if organizations can't trust their employees to do the right things and make the right choices, then maybe they needed to modify their hiring practices. He offered case studies illustrating how New York Life is using social channels to support its sales force, train new hires with the company's social presence, and encourage employees to add their social media properties to the end of their email signatures. He also described an internal vetting process used before any social media property can link to an outside website.

- **Pepsi's focus on digital research and development**—Josh Karpf's group runs a number of really interesting experiments about how to use social and geo location to engage consumers. When partnering with Foursquare, a location-based social application, to offer couponing to check in with Hess convenience stores, they found that using a promotion in a particular location offered a 47 percent boost in volume of purchase over previous weeks when the campaign was not running. They also learned that coupon redemptions were much higher when offered to people as a reward for some behavior. This reinforced the logical conclusion that people are more likely to follow through to claim the discount or product from a coupon if they feel they had to "earn" that coupon in some way, such as by checking into the gym for 10 days in a month.

Focused Social Fueled by Small Business Agility

Although the preceding examples illustrate how large brands are spending millions on developing and launching social campaigns, there is enormous value for small, perhaps less-endowed, organizations that have the agility to focus on creating concrete financial returns from virtual relationships. Following are several examples, from vastly different industries, that demonstrate how others are singularly engaging a targeted audience in real time. What's particularly interesting is that I couldn't find any mention of such social success stories on respective industry associations' websites, newsletters, or blogs (if they exist), touting the creativity and entrepreneurial impact of these individuals.

- **Marination Mobile** (Seattle)—In early 2009, partners Kamala Saxton and Roz Edison hatched the idea for a truck-based dining experience gone gangbusters. They included social web strategies in their marketing efforts

four months before Marination Mobile served its first taco. Today, Marination Mobile isn't just mobile. Contrary to the traditional practice of brick-and-mortar restaurants launching food trucks, they've taken the reverse path in the value-chain and now have opened a storefront location. "We sell $2.25 tacos. That's not unique," Saxton says. "What's unique is the audience we've built. We have well over 10,000 eyeballs on us between Facebook and Twitter. That means we have 10,000 supervisors and managers waiting to tell us when we do something great—or when we don't."

- **Crème Brûlée Cart** (San Francisco)—Curtis Kimball, who operates a mobile crème brûlée cart in San Francisco, often posts his location and flavors of the day on Twitter. Kimball currently has more than 20,000 Twitter

continues on next page

continued from previous page

followers. Twitter "has been pretty essential to my success," Kimball told the *New York Times,* adding that he quit his job as a carpenter to keep up with his burgeoning dessert business.

I'm not sure whether the National Restaurant Association caters to these mobile businesses, but as our society becomes more mobile and social, wouldn't this be a logical special interest group (SIG) in that association? Also, why not highlight these success stories to broaden the horizon of members' mindsets in evolving their business models through social?

- **Animal General Hospital** (Port St. Lucie, Florida)—When Dr. Enrique Borrego opened his veterinary practice in 1990, location and word-of-mouth were all a vet needed to bring in clients and their furry friends. Borrego opened his current location in 2000 to better serve his neighbors in quiet Port St. Lucie, Florida. But in 2004, the town became one of the fastest-growing communities in Florida,

and soon there were multiple vet practices within walking distance of his office. It was clear he had to find a way to differentiate Animal General Hospital. Over 18 months, ads in the local magazines and the Yellow Pages netted no new clients. Using YouTube, Facebook and email marketing, a client-care strategy that spanned from the moment of first interaction to long after clients had gone home from their latest appointment has produced some astounding results. Borrego estimates he spent $27,000 over 18 months for Yellow Pages ads. In a single 18-month online campaign combining Google advertising with Facebook ads, $3,600 in spending brought in a remarkable 250 new clients and $75,000 in revenue. "Yellow Pages ads are static. Facebook and Google are interactive. We've built ourselves to be an online resource for our clients," Borrego says. "Great information coupled with great care; that's why people keep coming back. That's the *social* part of social marketing."

Beyond Media to Impact

What many best practices continue to reinforce is the expansive nature of social's impact—beyond media and marketing to create awareness, deal with real business challenges, and address upside opportunities. In review of the IMPACT Model introduced back in Chapter 2, here are the key business drivers social can deliver in a quantifiable ROI (Figure 10.2).

The challenge extends beyond simply understanding these statements. The toughest kind of work when reviewing a model like IMPACT is to search for the real meaning of its core concepts. Those insights are highly unique to each organization. But if visionary leaders can empower their organizations to think differently, for example, they'll create dialogue with respected colleagues and peers alike that asks: Why should associations think of their *members more as customers* and, conversely, why should

Figure 10.2 — IMPACT Model

businesses think of their *customers as members?* If you own an iPhone or an iPad, are you Apple's customer or a member of the iTunes community, where you derive most of your end value from the decision to buy and engage Apple and its partners AT&T and Verizon?

Social, *beyond media to business and impact,* should force an organization and its leadership to think differently about their business. Here are the seven core business outcomes that organizations can accomplish through social using the IMPACT model. These core strengths are a starting point for framing questions for the leadership team:

1. *Place the members at the center of your organization's operations.* How can you reach a broader audience beyond the current membership—others in and around your industry with a particular interest in their own personal and professional growth—who would benefit from your unique and highly differentiated value? Beyond what you do, how will you set yourself apart and why would they benefit from aligning their brand with yours?

2. *Maximize the insight generated through member interactions.* How are you facilitating and adding unique insights in member-to-member interactions in a community of engaged, informed, and interested individuals? What lessons are you learning from those interactions, and beyond simple facilitation (often a commodity), how do you continue to infuse unique intellectual property/capital into the member community?

3. *Capitalize on social and mobile information exchanges.* How are you helping members/users access insightful and actionable information, evaluate options, and interact with others in the communities

at the time of their choosing, on the devices of their preference, and at the point of their need?

4. *Synchronize your entire value chain to deliver consistent and predictable outcomes.* How are you reaching your customers' customers, partners, employees, and industry influencers to provide unparalleled value, whether perceived, received, or applied? If you don't disrupt your own value chain, who are the most likely others who will and when?

5. *Improve collaboration and visibility for your staff, members, and partners.* Beyond annual surveys, how are you keeping your finger on the pulse of member/customer behaviors and decision points to invest in your brand, join your cause, buy your products and services, and recommend or refer you to their peers? Beyond satisfaction, how are you measuring and monetizing influence and preference via social collaboration?

6. *Increase margins by boosting efficiency at every stage of the member life cycle.* How well do you really understand the unique stages that your members or customers go through in their personal or professional growth? What smart touch points are you creating to make your organization an essential asset at every step of that journey?

7. *Drive growth by enhancing, extending, and redefining the value you provide.* How are people better off because of their association with your organization? Beyond all that you do (*input:* methodology, process, information, education, and networking), how much of what you do is recognized (value awareness), internalized (value perceived), applied (value received), and dramatically altering of their condition (*the output, or their desired outcome*)?

The IMPACT Scorecard

To help the organization ascertain its progress along a continuum of digital relationship maturity, previously presented in Chapter 7, from socially reactive today to proactive, predictive, intuitive, and visionary in the future, below is the IMPACT Scorecard by each of the key member lifecycle stages (Figure 10.3).

By expanding the organization's perspective on a more holistic ROI, it becomes clear that the impact of a social strategy is far reaching when applied to a member or customer lifecycle. Thus, ROI becomes more

Stage	Attribute	Description	Measurement
Immerse	Searchability	Presence in market	Search rankings, social search, brand presence
	Credibility	Market receptiveness to message	Redistribution of messaging
Member	Influence	Importance of market relationships	Influencer mapping
	Relationships	Breadth of market relationships	Percentage of market penetration
Participate	Thought leadership	Depth of information	Perceived value of content
	Responsiveness	To feedback, issues	Member satisfaction
Accredit	Reputation	Market perception	Frequency and sentiment of independent mention
Community	Empowerment	Enablement of control	Member retention
	Evangelism	Contribution to market education	Provide accessibility to market
Transform	Referential	Member perception	Referral rates

Figure 10.3 — The IMPACT Scorecard

complex to define and measure than many understand or have anticipated. Consequently, a *reinvention of ROI* is necessary to align the organization's actions and its target audience's reactions with the appropriate attributes. Only when these attributes are clearly defined and measured can the organization clearly see its return on investment, influence, interactions, ideas, and, most relevant, impact on the outcome of its social audiences.

Let's take a closer look at each stage of the member/customer lifecycle, and the relevant attributes:

- In the *immersion* stage, an organization's consistent and compelling market presence and the market's receptivity to that presence are critical to its *searchability* and perceived *credibility*. Early in this awareness arena, traditional search rankings, social search based on stated pain drivers, brand presence, and the redistribution of the organization's key messages (and key messengers) are critical. Focus your investments on casting as wide of a net as possible on your target audience, so *they may find you wherever they are.*

- Once they are immersed in your unique offerings, the breadth and depth of your market relationships will influence them to seek *membership* in your organization. Beyond existing relationships you have today, it is critical to expand the diversity and quality of and the investment efforts you make in key personal and professional relationships. The more far-reaching your portfolio of relationships, the broader your influence footprint. Pay particular attention to your end-to-end value chain. Key metrics, such as influencer mapping and percentage of total market penetration by your brand, will be critical to your success here. If architects use your products or services, how well do you know and engage them, the general contractors, the building inspectors, the real estate professionals, and the office furniture manufacturers and distributors? Leave no rock unturned where you can build effective market relationships. Focus your investments on building deep and wide relationships, digital connections to and through the hubs and spokes of your industry.

- Once they become members, the depth of the information you manufacture (not just repurpose) cements your thought leadership, as members perceive value in the content they receive from you. Your responsiveness to feedback (a gift) and first-contact resolution of issues reaffirms your commitment to their *participation.* In social collaboration, the community becomes more valuable as more members participate, and more members will choose to participate when

---

Manifestation of Thought Leadership

What are the key attributes of a thought-leading organization or individual? Here are a handful of ideas inspired by Alan Weiss, PhD. Thought leadership:

- Changes other people's perspectives;
- Directs members to you as the authoritative source;
- Guides organizations to seek you out and share your insights;
- Integrates coined phrases, metaphors, concepts and models into everyday vernacular;
- Creates quotes by the originator in the media or by other professionals;
- Translates the complex into the simple and pragmatic;

- Makes the explicit implicit and vice versa;
- Distinguishes the source as well known by key influencers in the market or industry;
- Develops proprietary content and brands highly correlated with the originator;
- Points to a track record of success as evident by clients, members, examples, and war stories;
- Consistently generates new intellectual capital that the originator transforms to intellectual property; and
- Helps the originator become visible in the public eye.

they gain more value from the community. Focus your investment on exceptional experiences at every touch point; constantly monitor feelings and behaviors, likes and dislikes; and proactively solicit real-time feedback loops.

- Proactive participation by the members in your organization's social presence creates stronger visibility for them and your organization in the marketplace. Place touch points in the market that gauge the organization's perception as measured by frequency and sentiment of independent mention. If both are strong and deemed positive, members or consumers will choose to be educated by you and uphold a set of standards worthy of *accreditation* in their chosen field. The accreditation must demonstrate a significant and incremental improvement in their condition, including, but not limited to, business development, personal or staff development, exclusivity, preference, and stature/prominence. Focus your investments on making your accreditation a hallmark of the industry as well as a public force associated with the highest level of quality, craftsmanship, and quality of delivery in the products, services, and experiences for the end recipient of your industry.

- If, after participating in accreditation, members are empowered to share their experiences and expertise with both their peers and the broader market, and those experiences are exemplary, they will join and proactively participate in a *community* of peers, partners, and outside experts. Member retention and renewal, along with their access to key centers of influence in the market, are key metrics in gauging your success at this stage. Make accredited members ambassadors of your brand and evangelists of your unique market position by arming them with insights and identifying early market trends based on their experiences. Focus your investments on developing the community with a holistic view of members, learning from their participation and connecting them with others who would benefit from their expertise.

- Only when you've *transformed* members as individuals and organizations will they proactively refer prospective members. Unsolicited warm introductions to their portfolio of relationships and the velocity and the veracity with which those referrals are made are clear indicators of their perceptions of the organization's longevity and legacy in its industry. Help members make the referral process as simple as possible. Focus on developing exceptional experiences for both the referring and the referred parties. Come out swinging and make the first impression of your organization as polished and impressive as possible.

These impacts can be non-financial (Figure 10.4) and can include the health of the community, or they may be financially driven (Figure 10.5), which would include actual ROI calculations; paid, earned; or owned media values; or purchase funnel metrics.

Non-Financial Impact Metrics	
Community Health—Growth	• Community membership and continuous growth • Content views and downloads • Content or channel RSS subscriptions • Unique visitors and page views
Community Health—Membership	• Customer retention • Customer satisfaction scores (CSAT) • Customer loyalty scores • Overall sentiment within the community
Community Health—Engagement	• Likes, shares, and comments • Twitter @replies and @mentions, Lists • YouTube comments and embeds • Blog comments
Share of Voice and Sentiment	Share of voice is an organization's conversational weight expressed as a percentage of a defined total market. Sentiment is the context of the conversations. It's often categorized as positive, negative, or neutral.

Figure 10.4—Sample Non-Financial Impact Metrics

Financial Impact Metrics	
ROI	These metrics measure the amount of money invested on a program or initiative and the amount of money received from that same program.
Paid, Earned, Owned Media Value	Paid, earned, and owned media value is defined as the monetary value of impressions delivered from different marketing channels and assigning an equivalent cost per thousand impressions (CPM) that a company is willing to pay (or has paid) for those impressions.
Purchase Funnel Metrics	Specific metrics can be defined at each phase of the purchase funnel—Awareness, Consideration, Preference, Purchase, Advocacy. One example is: • Awareness = Total ads served or impressions • Consideration = Total clicks on ad • Preference = Number of users who engaged with branded content, commented on a blog, etc. • Purchase = Number of users who purchased • Advocacy = Number of users who joined a community

Figure 10.5—Sample Financial Impact Metrics

It's Your Turn

One of the challenges in reading any book is to internalize and implement its key takeaways. I'm often reminded in my own readings that *those who only read seldom improve. Those who implement grow and thrive.* Although no one set of advice fits all, here are five immediate steps to implement, now that you've read 10 chapters:

1. When you finish, immediately capture the top three ideas that resonated with you. Don't flip back yet—just jot down what you remember as key takeaways.

2. Next, go through the key section headings in each chapter, and for each of your key takeaways above, capture how you would lead a social campaign *differently.*

3. The best books tend to generate great questions and dialogue. Capture your top questions. What specific topic do you want to know more about? Where do you need additional examples? How can you continue to learn (see the next header Where we go from here?) and grow in this evolutionary space?

4. If you haven't already, start a conversation—remember social is about dialogue. If you have questions, there's a good chance so do many of your colleagues. The challenge isn't to simply address your most perplexing questions; the learning comes from finding others with the same challenge and engaging them in social collaboration to find or create solutions.

5. Take the key concepts in this book to your leadership, your board, your team, and your staff and jointly create a 30-60-90-day plan.

Where to Go From Here

Whether you purchased this book, listened to it in the audio format, or received it as a gift, I want to thank you for your gift of time. Find a reason to continue the conversation, because that's where some of the most insightful ideas surface—not just from me, but also from your peers and others in the community. So if you've found value in these pages, I hope you'll join us at any of the channels you deem appropriate and useful to you. Join as few or as many as you'd like. Participate proactively or simply observe the dialogue.

1. The IMPACT Community at www.ReturnOnImpactBook.com

2. On Twitter @davidnour | #ROIBook | #ASAE

3. Text "ROIBook" to 90210 for a weekly tip on IMPACT best practices

4. Subscribe to the IMPACT Newsletter at www.NourGroup.com

5. ASAE: The Center for Association Leadership author chats and blog posts at www.asaecenter.org

One final idea: I often think about email as one-dimensional, because I can't gauge tonality. Social interaction in some sense is similar to a phone conversation. Because I can gauge tone it seems two-dimensional. In person is three-dimensional, and no amount of great content—static or dynamic—will ever replace the value of an in-person interaction. I'm contemplating an **IMPACT Retreat.** I'm not sure when or where, but am sure it will be a simple format—two or three days of conversations, case studies, best practices and best practitioners who have implemented some or all key aspect of the IMPACT model. I'm curious to learn what worked for you, what didn't, what you tried, and the outcomes you were able to capture. Did you segment your target audience? Did you integrate distributed accountability with your leadership and board? Have you begun to capture psychographic as well as demographic insights about those who find value in your message?

Let me close with one last idea. Alan Weiss, PhD, has trademarked what he refers to as "the 1 percent rule": improve by 1 percent a day and in 70 days, you're twice as good. Many readers of this book won't be able to transform their organizations to a social one overnight. You don't have to. It's about making intentional progress toward a vision in the future, using a robust strategy and uncovering the resources to execute consistently along a development path.

Of all that you've read here, what's your 1 percent for today? What will you choose to do differently because of the ideas contained in this book? Keep in mind, version one is better than version none. Good luck!

Acknowledgements

In my keynote speeches on Relationship Economics, I often talk about how the relationships you choose to focus on and invest in, will determine your direction and ultimately define your destination. If the creation of this book is the destination, I'm grateful to so many friends along the path that has led me here over the past several years. This *social network* introduced, guided, supported, encouraged, reinforced the key insights, provided introductions to their parallel universes, made time for conversations, blessed, cajoled, conceived, perceived, received, edited, rewrote, and, over the past 18 months, has made this journey worth every ounce of the author's energy. I will undoubtedly leave many friends out in this narration, but here is the compass and the roadmap of my gratitude; I hope you will likewise, be able to connect the dots in your personal and professional life to reach your destinations.

Sue Pine, whom I respect as an incredibly decent human being, invited me to speak in New Orleans at the AMCi in 2007. That's where I met Taylor Fernley, one of those all-around great guys you would love to have a beer with anytime you see him. Taylor actually hired me for several speaking engagements in 2008 and I spent some quality time with him and his team on their social strategy in 2009. He eventually introduced me to Dave Gabri at ALHI where I keynoted their 2008 Industry Advisory Council meeting. John Graham sat near the front and we had a great conversation afterwards. At ALHI, I also met several members of the Leading Authorities team: Helena Lehman and Rainey Foster. Several months later, Matt Jones, COO and Mark French, president of LAI, were kind enough to invite me to keynote the U.S. Chamber Committee of 100 in December 2009 where amongst other great leaders, I had a chance to spend time with John Graham again. Our subsequent visits and discussions became the vision for this book. Susan Robertson at the ASAE Foundation and her steadfast leadership, Monica Dignam and her discipline in and passion for empirical research, and probably one of the most impactful people I've met, Keith Skillman, provided the friendship to get us on the same page and the fortitude to support getting this project off the ground and the vision to a reality. Keith and I agreed early on, "if there is a will, there is a way" and he has been true to that mantra every single day.

The research project Monica Dignam and her team at the ASAE Foundation led encapsulated a Delphi model survey of the ASAE membership, narrowed to 400 associations executives who answered a series of social media-specific questions, to 100 who agreed to be interviewed. I created a scorecard prioritizing those who believed social had impacted their organizations, strategically, operationally, and financially. Personal interviews were conducted and excerpts were included with their permission. Separately, I interviewed over 100 corporate executives for their insights and applications of social as an enabler of their strategies.

At ASAE, Reggie Henry, Robb Lee, Amy Hissrich, Amy Ledoux, Anne Blouin, and Mark Athitakis have all been fantastic to work with. I want to personally thank all of the organization executives who were kind with their time and insights in our interviews. I'm grateful to clients who continue to push me to remain a life-long student of business relationships, and the impact of social networks, media, and market leadership on those relationships. To Denise Graziano, Linda C. Chandler, Baron Williams, and Troy Scott Parker, I couldn't have polished this manuscript without your tireless editing, layout, and production support. Ali Kafashzadeh, your research and insights were invaluable.

I want to acknowledge my wife Wendy and children Grayson and Justus for putting up with dad—from writing before sunrise in Positano, Italy, to late nights whiteboarding the IMPACT model at the home office—thank you for your unconditional love. Without you none of this accomplishment would be possible; with you, all of this effort is that much more enjoyable.

Finally, to the dedicated men and women who deeply believe in and work tirelessly in the causes and professional or trade associations they deeply believe in—thank you for your service. Many members, their companies, and your industries are successful because of you and although you may not hear it often enough in what you do, day in and day out, you're amazing assets to the organization you serve.

With my gratitude,
David Nour

About the ASAE Foundation

asaefoundation.org

The ASAE Foundation contributed to this project by identifying executives, through Delphi research, to be interviewed by the author.

The ASAE Foundation maximizes the effectiveness of associations and association professionals through research, leadership, innovation, and research-based knowledge.

Research that Elevates Our Profession
The Foundation collaborates with association professionals, scholars, and leading universities to produce rigorous research that elevates the profession of association management and has practical implications for associations.

Community Events that Connect & Sustain
The Foundation conducts association community events and outreach that build awareness and raise funds through networking and philanthropy.

Environments that Thrive
The Foundation creates environments where people and ideas thrive. Its initiatives help associations keep pace with the global marketplace, explore innovative ways of doing business to ensure we remain valuable, and equip the next generation of leaders with the knowledge and skills to manage into the future.

Programs that Advance Our Leaders
The Foundation provides scholarships and funding for programs that equip leaders of all levels with the mentoring, education, and knowledge they need to succeed.

About the Author

David Nour—CEO, The Nour Group, Inc.
Senior Management Advisor | International Speaker | Best Selling Author

David Nour is *the* thought leader on Relationship Economics®—the quantifiable value of business relationships. In a global economy that is becoming increasingly disconnected, The Nour Group, Inc. has attracted consulting clients such as KPMG, Siemens, Gen Re, HP, and over 100 marquee organizations in driving unprecedented growth through unique return on their strategic relationships. David has pioneered the phenomenon that relationships are the greatest off-balance-sheet asset any organization possesses, large and small, public and private.

He annually delivers 50 global keynotes at leading industry association conferences, corporate meetings, and academic forums. David's unique perspective and independent insights on Relationship Economics® have been featured in a variety of prominent blogs and publications including *The Wall Street Journal, The New York Times, FastCompany, Knowledge@Wharton, Associations Now, Entrepreneur,* and *Success* magazine. He is the author of several books including the best selling *Relationship Economics* (Wiley), *ConnectAbility* (McGraw-Hill), *The Entrepreneur's Guide to Raising Capital* (Praeger), and now, *Return on Impact—Leadership Strategies for the Age of Connected Relationships* (ASAE, 2012).

An Eagle Scout himself, David is passionate about youth with his foundation's support of the Scouting movement, Junior Achievement, One Voice—aiming to create peace in the Middle East—and the High Tech Ministries.

A native of Iran, David came to the U.S. with a suitcase, $100, limited family ties and no fluency in English! He earned an Executive MBA from the Goizueta Business School at Emory University and a BA degree in Management from Georgia State University.

Other Books by the Author

Return on Impact is David Nour's fourth commercial book since 2008. A prolific writer, David has spent the past decade becoming a student of business relationships—how individuals, teams, and organizations can deliver unprecedented growth through a unique return on their strategic relationships. Below are his other books available online or from NourGroup.com.

Return on Impact Audiobook
(The Nour Group, 2012)
The same content in this written book is available in audio CDs, plus a bonus CD of a recent keynote speech by David Nour on Return on Impact—How Will You Lead Differently?

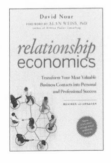

Relationship Economics—Updated and Revised
(Wiley, 2011)
In our current turbulent economy, multi-cultural management teams must execute seamlessly in an environment of increasingly more sophisticated and demanding global relationships. This book is a "how-to" guide. Its applications are beyond just getting and giving business cards, working a room, or getting the most out of a conference. Its focus is how to strategically invest in relationships as your most valuable asset for an extraordinary return.

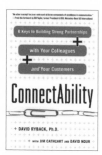

ConnectAbility (McGraw-Hill, 2010)

Drawing from the powerful lessons of emotional awareness and relationship dynamics, this book promotes a sophisticated yet simple method for developing superior partnerships guaranteed to create quality results on a consistent basis. Even the best-intentioned team players too often focus more on communicating their own ideas than hearing and understanding what others have to say. ConnectAbility changes all this using eight steps to foster optimum communication.

The Entrepreneur's Guide to Raising Capital (Praeger, 2009)

Designed to help entrepreneurs navigate the money-raising maze, this book shows how to attract financing to fund the start-up and growth phases any business moves through. David Nour provides real-life, pragmatic advice from entrepreneurs who have successfully raised capital from friends, family, angel investors, banks, and institutional investors such as venture capital and private equity firms.

David Nour Speaking Topics

3500 Lenox Road, Suite 1500
Atlanta, GA 30326
p 404.419.2115 | f 404.419.2116
www.relationshipeconomics.NET

Relationship Economics®—The Art and Science of Relationships

2011 cornerstone keynote delivered to more than 50 corporate, association, and academic forums; based on the bestselling book *Relationship Economics Updated* (Wiley, 2011) focused on the quantifiable value of business relationships and a systematic process to identify, build, nurture, and leverage personal, functional, and strategic relationships.

Return on Impact™—How Will You Lead Differently in The Age of Connected Relationships?

Based on the newly released book, *Return on Impact* (ASAE, 2012) demonstrates how social media has helped swing the power pendulum to members and customers while many industries and organizations continue to get disintermediated. *Return on Impact* isn't about Facebook, Twitter, or YouTube. It's about socially enabling the organization to listen louder and think faster, so it can respond in real time to changing market dynamics. And in the process, the organization can adapt new revenue models, reinvent itself, and grow—its top line, top talent, and top relationships.

Adaptive Innovation™—Adaptable Business Models for Changing Market Demands

How do you create greater market value than your competitors? How do you help your distributors differentiate your products or services? Simple—disrupt your value chain! Adaptive innovation, by definition, is destructive in its character and open to a broad base of business models, and it must be driven by high-performing teams. Teams who are focused on maximizing the current and future capabilities of their respective organizations. In order to create sustainable competitive advantage, companies must develop a relationship-centric culture with the courage to fail and learn from those failures.

ConnectAbility™—8 Keys to Building Strong Partnerships with Your Colleagues *and* Your Customers

Driven by the *ConnectAbility* book (McGraw-Hill), this presentation focuses on a systematic approach for developing superior partnerships (manufacturer/distributor, wholesaler/reseller) by applying powerful lessons learned from emotional awareness, personal authenticity, humor, and servant leadership.

Inner Circle™—Who Are *You* Listening To?

Global CEOs, politicians, professional athletes, and award-winning entertainers all rely on an inner circle of trusted advisors. How about you? Who is in your inner circle, how did they get there, and what makes them so valuable? Who's inner circle do you belong to, how did you get in, and what are the rules for confidentiality and self-interest? If you're not in, what will it take to become the voice others listen to and rely on?

Flight Risk™—Why Most High Potentials Leave!

All of those A-players you've spent time, effort, and resources recruiting are walking out the door. Maybe not physically, but certainly mentally. Learn why they leave and how to keep four generations of diverse workforce wanting to stay.

Delivery Options:

- Keynote—60–90 minutes in duration including copies of David's books for each attendee
- Keynote + Breakout Session(s)—Above option, plus two-to-three-hour mini-workshop, further helping the attendees internalize the key messages
- Keynote, Breakout(s), and Follow-through Webinars—Above option plus a series of webinars